Ancient Mediterranean Philosophy

D1452790

BLOOMSBURY HISTORY OF PHILOSOPHY

The *Bloomsbury History of Philosophy* series offers concise and accessible introductions to the key periods in the history of philosophical thought. Designed specifically to meet the needs of undergraduate students, each book provides a comprehensive historical survey of the period and introduces all the key themes and thinkers. The series builds to give a thorough overview of the whole history of this fascinating subject.

Forthcoming in the series:

Medieval Philosophy, Gyula Klima
Seventeenth Century Philosophy, Pauline Phemister

BLOOMSBURY HISTORY OF PHILOSOPHY

Ancient Mediterranean Philosophy

An Introduction

STEPHEN R. L. CLARK

B L O O M S B U R Y
LONDON • NEW DELHI • NEW YORK • SYDNEY

Bloomsbury Academic

An imprint of Bloomsbury Publishing Plc

50 Bedford Square
London
WC1B 3DP
UK

175 Fifth Avenue
New York
NY 10010
USA

www.bloomsbury.com

First published 2013

British Library Cataloguing-in-Publication Data
A catalogue record for this book is available from the British Library.

ISBN: HB: 978-1-4411-0188-4
PB: 978-1-4411-2359-6

Library of Congress Cataloging-in-Publication Data
Clark, Stephen R. L.
Ancient Mediterranean philosophy: an introduction/Stephen R. L. Clark.
p. cm. – (Bloomsbury history of philosophy)
Includes bibliographical references (p.   ) and index.
ISBN 978-1-4411-0188-4 (hardcover: alk. paper) –
ISBN 978-1-4411-2359-6 (pbk.: alk. paper) –
ISBN 978-1-4411-4886-5 (ebook pdf: alk. paper) –
ISBN 978-1-4411-4754-7 (ebook epub: alk. paper)
1. Philosophy, Ancient. I. Title.

B171.C525 2012
180–dc23
2012016911

Typeset by Deanta Global Publishing Services, Chennai, India
Printed and bound in India

CONTENTS

PREFACE

In composing this study of 'Ancient Mediterranean Philosophy', I have chosen to draw attention to other philosophical traditions than the Classical Greek and Latin, although we know much less about them. My working assumption is that people have engaged in philosophical enquiry and debate from the very earliest times, even if this activity was not always well distinguished from more poetic or free-wheeling speculation. I also assume that even the most parochial or xenophobic peoples have shared stories, arguments and intuitions with foreigners. It follows that any attempt to draw a line around 'Greek' or 'Classical' or even 'Mediterranean' philosophy will fail: in the end, there are only people, of various tribes and cultures, changing and exchanging arguments and ideas about the world, themselves, and whatever lies beyond. It also follows that we cannot draw a line around what is 'Ancient', as distinct from 'Modern'.

So can there really be a study of 'Ancient Mediterranean Philosophy'? Can we even distinguish 'Philosophy' from poetry, history, natural science, theology or proverbial wisdom? The *Instructions of Ptahhotep* (2414–2375 BC) were very much what later, 'philosophical' moralists repeated: not to be greedy; be patient and attentive; do the job you find yourself doing. This may not count as 'philosophy' for the argumentative, but more Mediterranean people agreed with aphorisms like that than any substantive doctrine. There is small reason even to suppose that every native Greek-speaker, or everyone who thought of himself/herself as 'Hellene', from Gadara in Palestine to Gades on the Atlantic coast of Spain, over all the centuries from Hesiod to the final fall of Byzantium (or whenever) shared any concept of the self, or the world, or what to have for breakfast. Kingsley may be wrong to say that 'it was people at Athens who invented the fiction of a united Greece'. But he is right that 'there never was a united Greece, because so many

Greeks [let alone the other peoples of that world] wanted very little
to do with Athens' (Kingsley 1999, p. 197).

Even if we speak only of the Golden Age of Athens, from the defeat
of Persia through its own brief empire to the death of Alexander, we
can only conclude that the Athenians were a disputatious people,
agreeing on almost nothing. Diodorus Siculus (fl. 40 BC) thought
the same was true of 'the Greeks' in general:

> The result of this is that the barbarians, by sticking to the same
> things always, keep a firm hold on every detail, while the Greeks,
> on the other hand, aiming at the profit to be made out of the
> business, keep founding new schools and, wrangling with each
> other over the most important matters of speculation, bring
> it about that their pupils hold conflicting views, and that their
> minds, vacillating throughout their lives and unable to believe at
> all with firm conviction, simply wander in confusion. It is at any
> rate true that, if a man were to examine carefully the most famous
> schools of the philosophers, he would find them differing from one
> another to the uttermost degree and maintaining opposite opinions
> regarding the most fundamental tenets. (Diodorus 2.29.3)

We may doubt that 'the barbarians' were united either. But despite
those caveats, there is still something to be said for trying 'to see
things clearly and to see them whole', as this task was attempted
around the Ancient Mediterranean. According to Chesterton,
'the whole object of history is to make us realize that humanity
can be great and glorious, under conditions quite different and
even contrary to our own' (Chesterton 1923, p. 176). A properly
hermeneutical philosophy may also help us to remember that we
too will one day be considered 'ancient', and such fragments of our
thought as may survive will be acknowledged only as anticipations
of some newly approved idea.

Why pick on 'the Ancient Mediterranean'? The answer is easy:
the people of that Age are at once the immediate ancestors of
Western, Orthodox and Islamic civilization, and yet as alien as the
Hindu or Chinese. They are at once entirely Other and so familiar
as to be forgotten. And though they disagreed with each other,
vehemently and at length, outsiders may still be able to see some
common themes (as our successors will see what assumptions we
unconsciously accept).

The Mediterranean Sea – 'our sea' as the Romans called it – is linked to the outer Ocean only through the straits of Gibraltar and to another inland sea, the Black Sea (also called the Euxine or the Pontus), through the Hellespont. Its two basins, eastern and western, are linked and divided by the Strait of Sicily. The gaps between the northern peninsulas and islands are conventionally distinguished as the Aegean, Adriatic, Ionian and Tyrrhenian Seas. The lands to the north of the Sea are mostly mountainous, bunched up by the northward movement of tectonic plates, which also explains the many volcanoes dotted around the region, and the earthquakes and tsunamis that could eliminate islands and coastal cities. The southern shores are a strip of fertile land north of the Atlas Mountains and the encroaching Sahara. Northern hill-tribes and Southern desert-dwellers were occasional and often unwelcome visitors (and played a part in the eventual end of the 'Ancient' world). 'Civilized' people mostly lived in *poleis*, communities of the more-or-less like-minded with central shrines and market places, cultivating their particular patch of land and trading around the Sea for what they could not grow or make themselves. As Momigliano observes (1975, p. 74), 'ancient travellers did not find it easy to go into the interior'. There were mountain passes, and other river valleys than the Nile, including the Rhone, the Po and the Danube. But most trade and travel passed around the coasts. Civilized peoples could be indigenous, at least – like the Athenians – in their own perception, but were also often colonizers from Greece, Phoenicia or Lydia. Egypt was an exception: its territory reaching south into Africa, along the Nile, and its history into an otherwise forgotten past. The empires of Mesopotamia, especially the Assyrian and Persian, also encroached on the eastern end of the Sea, and there were established trade-routes out towards the East. But those living around the Sea were mostly guarded from too frequent invasions over the mountains or the deserts, and had forgotten enough of their past to be able to invent a novel future. Nor did they much believe the adventures of Hanno of Carthage or of Euthymenes, around the western coast of Africa, or of Pytheas past the Tin Islands: both the latter citizens of Phocaea in Ionia (see Kingsley 2003, pp. 241–51).

The Mediterranean peoples were not entirely isolated. Fashions differ about which other people to praise or blame for changes. Kingsley has emphasized the Northern influence, though not in the same way as the nineteenth-century scholars persuaded of

the superior qualities of 'Northern European' thought; Bernal
the African and Asiatic connection (particularly the Egyptian);
West (1971, 1997) and McEvilley (2006) have demonstrated
connections with the East, and that the influence was not all one
way. Mediterranean languages are descended from languages
spoken across Eurasia and Africa. Nothing in the stories and social
structures of the Mediterranean peoples is entirely new. But for
practical purposes, the philosophy of the Mediterranean peoples
constitutes an almost intelligible subject and a less misleading one
than the common attempt to rationalize 'Greek' thought.

There is one other risk in any such enterprise: the mere fact that
history has led to Us may make it difficult to see or to acknowledge
that things might have happened otherwise, and that We were not
the goal. Indeed, we may yet find that some quite other history will
one day be self-evident, and quite other episodes and authors be
brought back to life. The point is threefold. First, even if it were
true – as some have supposed – that everything that happens is
what must, our own present life and thought is not the culmination
of world history. On the contrary, we are a passing moment in
that story, and probably untypical. History doesn't lead to us, but
through us, and quite other people and philosophies may turn
out to be central when all things come together. Second, on the much
more plausible theory that what happens need not happen, and that
history is shadowed by possible paths not taken, we can expect
that were our history to be repeated it would pass quite differently,
and no mortal mind would notice. Third, what any particular era
remembers of past times may not be what is remembered later:
we know more about the early civilizations than Herodotus and
his contemporaries could and can therefore bring those earlier
worlds back into the stream of history. It follows that our own
successors may know more than we do (and also have forgotten
many things).

The Greeks did not invent philosophy, but Greek texts are bound
to feature most frequently in my account, and Greek-speaking
philosophers will continue to dominate the tradition. Even among
the Greeks, we often have no more than fragments to decipher. Even
when we have complete texts, we may not understand their context,
and especially their absent opponents. There has always been a
temptation for present-day philosophers to make the best we can
of this: to excerpt particular passages, particular arguments, and

examine them in the abstract. Conversely, historians and classical scholars may spend so much of their time in identifying influences that they forget that people at least intended to be speaking truth – and that we should attempt to discern what truths they did discover and judge them for ourselves.

What follows is an introduction only, intended to entertain, inform, exasperate, inspire. It will succeed if my readers turn to reading the ancient texts in the hope of discovering more truths for themselves, about the texts and about the world itself, and in the hope of learning a better way to live. I have my own beliefs about the only truth that matters (and this bias will no doubt be evident), but it is the nature of that truth, as Plato recognized, that it cannot be conveyed by writing. Whatever is conveyed in the following volume is not the truth that matters, but only, at best, a map.

ACKNOWLEDGEMENTS

The present volume takes its beginning from the chapter on Ancient Philosophy I wrote for Anthony Kenny, ed., *Oxford Illustrated History of Philosophy* (Oxford University Press 1994), 1–53. I have also made use of material from other papers, including 'Slaves, Servility and Noble Deeds', *Philosophical Inquiry* 25.2003, 165–76; 'Plotinus – The Enneads' in *Central Works of the Great Philosophers* vol. 1, ed., J. Shand (Acumen: London 2005), 119–39; 'Plotinian Dualisms and the "Greek" Ideas of Self', *Journal of Chinese Philosophy* 36.2009, 554–67 (a paper originally composed for Nicholas Bunnin's Anglo-Chinese Symposium); 'Plotinus: Charms and Counter-Charms' in *Conceptions of Philosophy*: Royal Institute of Philosophy Supplementary Volume 65, ed., Anthony O'Hear (Cambridge: Cambridge University Press, 2010), 215–31; 'Therapy and Theory Reconstructed' in *Philosophy as Therapy*: Royal Institute of Philosophy Supplementary Volume 66, eds, Clare Carlisle and Jonardon Ganeri (Cambridge: Cambridge University Press, 2010), 83–102; 'Animals amongst the Ancients' in *Oxford Handbook of Animal Ethics*, eds, Raymond Frey and Tom. L. Beauchamp (Oxford: Oxford University Press, 2011), 35–60; 'Ancient Theology' in *Oxford Handbook of Natural Theology*, ed., Russell Re Manning (Oxford: Oxford University Press, 2012). Earlier drafts have been read by Gillian Clark, John Dillon, Lloyd Gerson, Michael McGhee, Tessa Rajak and Catherine Rowett (formerly Osborne). I am grateful to all my friends, colleagues, editors and auditors for their patient advice and encouragement over the last few years and also to the many modern scholars and philosophers who have helped form my views.

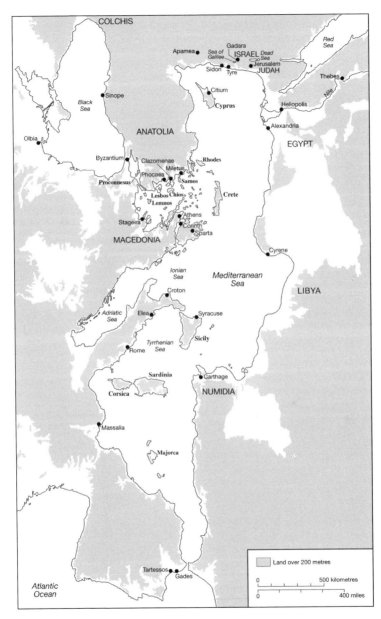

COLCHIS

Red
Sea

Apamea ● Sea of
Galilee Gadara
ISRAEL Dead
Sea
Sidon Tyre Jerusalem **JUDAH** Thebes ●

Black
Sea Sinope ●

Citium
Cyprus Nile

Heliopolis ●

ANATOLIA Alexandria ●

Olbia ● **EGYPT**

Byzantium ●
Clazomenae **Rhodes**
Miletus
Proconnesus Phocaea ●
Samos
Lesbos Chios
Lemnos **Crete**

Stageira ● Athens ●
Corinth
MACEDONIA Sparta

Cyrene ●

Ionian
Sea **Mediterranean
Sea**

LIBYA

Croton ●

Adriatic
Sea Elea ● Syracuse ●

Rome ● Tyrrhenian
Sea **Sicily**

Sardinia

Corsica Carthage ●

NUMIDIA

Massalia ●

Majorca

Tartessos ●
Gades ●

Atlantic
Ocean

Land over 200 metres

0 500 kilometres

0 400 miles

Map of Ancient Mediterranean World.
The map was prepared by Stephen Ramsay of Stephen Ramsay Cartography.

CHAPTER ONE

Beginnings

Pre-historical speculations

The curtain of history rises on a world already ancient, full of ruined cities and ways of thought worn smooth. Mediterranean peoples knew there had been disasters, but remembered little in detail. As an Egyptian priest, according to Plato (c430–347 BC), told Solon of Athens (c638–558 BC),

> [T]here is no opinion or tradition of knowledge among you which is white with age. . . . Like the rest of mankind you have suffered from convulsions of nature, which are chiefly brought about by the two great agencies of fire and water. . . . The memorials which your own and other nations have once had of the famous actions of mankind perish in the waters at certain periods; and the rude survivors in the mountains begin again, knowing nothing of the world before the flood. (Plato *Timaeus* 22B)

Xenophanes of Colophon (570–478 BC) reckoned that there was more evidence of this than anecdote:

> [S]hells are found inland and in the mountains, in the quarries at Syracuse the impression of a fish and seaweeds has been found; . . . on Malta there are slabs of rock made up of all kinds of sea-creatures. He says that these came about a long time ago, when everything was covered with mud, were produced

when everything was long ago covered with mud, and that the impression became dried in the mud. He claims that the human race is wiped out whenever the earth is carried down into the sea and becomes mud, that then there is a fresh creation. (21A33DK: Waterfield 2000, p. 29)

The generations of humankind stretch back indefinitely into the forgotten past, and we are always reinventing ourselves – even the Egyptians. Maybe there was never an absolute beginning, and we have reinvented ourselves infinitely many times. Or maybe there were the Firstborn – but a very long time ago. Opinion was divided.

One group, which takes the position that the universe did not come into being and will not decay, has declared that the race of men also has existed from eternity, there having never been a time when men were first begotten; the other group, however, which hold that the universe came into being and will decay, has declared that, like it, men had their first origin at a definite time. (Diodorus 1.6.3)

We know a little more than Solon did. There were people physically much like ourselves a hundred thousand years ago. Some scholars have suggested that though they were anatomically human, they had not yet developed human languages or culture, since such stone artefacts as we have found, whether from our own or other hominid species, remained unchanged in style for millennia (Wade 2010). The inference is unsound. We do not know what other, transient, artefacts they made: woven baskets, linens, face paints, sand paintings and dramatic art. Even in a later time, one reason why we know so little of how Phoenicians thought is that they wrote, alphabetically, on paper or on parchment, rather than incising ideograms on stone or clay (Van De Mieroop 2004, p. 208): because they were more advanced, their records were evanescent! We have been warned.

A culture as abundantly supplemented with artefacts as any non-metal, non-pottery, Neolithic culture in the world could have existed for two thousand centuries and we would know nothing about it. It is problematic on this time scale whether our own culture will leave anything more permanent. (Greene 1992, p. 19)

Why was it that our own ancestors survived and bred? It may be that they killed the Neanderthals and any other hominid species they encountered. It may be that they simply multiplied a little faster, and so gradually cut surviving Neanderthals off from each other (to the point where all their little tribes drifted slowly into extinction). And maybe our own survival was an accident: genetic evidence suggests that we are all descended from a population of no more than five thousand African humans, and most non-Africans from no more than a few hundred who left Africa around 40,000 BC. Probably the attempt had been made on even earlier occasions and failed each time for no particular reason.

Other hominid populations are half-remembered in our folklore: almost 'human' peoples who seemed to our ancestors to be 'dwarfish', 'elvish', giants, ogres and goblins. But any philosophical insights or arguments attributed to such 'fairies' are probably our own fancies. Fairies, as we remember and reinvent them, are disengaged from ordinary reality, unappreciative of our customs, mischievously deceptive and careless of the time. They are different, that is, from what we think we are. We know little more about our own ancestors. The experience of present-day primitives suggests that even without our tools, in normal times, they easily provided for their daily needs and had plenty of time for play. They chose not to *improve* their tools, maybe, because their tools were adequate, and they preferred not to be too 'efficient' for their own good. Our ancestors' arrival in any region was regularly followed by the extinction of larger mammals – perhaps including hominids – who were their prey or their rivals. There may have been other reasons for the extinctions, but if our ancestors were responsible, some of them perhaps repented. 'Wanting More' (Greek moralists called it *pleonexia*) is the disease of progress: not everyone has succumbed.

The earliest tales seek to explain why non-human animals no longer speak like us, why the sky no longer rests upon the earth, why brothers and sisters must not mate, why we age and die (which was not so, we said, in the beginning) and why there is anything at all. Many of these stories show how courage and quick wits – or even courage and slow wits – can defeat the monsters, whether these are dragons, ogres or ordinarily human. There were warriors then, and gardeners, builders, weavers, nurses, cooks, craftsmen and magicians. Some painted pictures deep in caves, where they would only be seen by torchlight. Some buried their dead with flow, or their favourite tools. Some made up and repeated stories.

The mythologies we find recorded by later, literate thinkers are 'the remnants of philosophy that perished in the great disasters that have befallen mankind, and were recorded for their brevity and wit' (Aristotle, *On Philosophy*, fr.8 Rose: Ross (1952) p. 77 [fr.10]).[1] We wanted – some of us wanted – to make sense of things, to know why things weren't as we thought they should be. We wanted – some of us wanted – to inspire an interest in what happened, even without explaining it. That may indeed have been the more important task: myths are more often inspirations than explanations. That the sun rises every morning is not news: saying that he is a bridegroom coming from his chamber, rejoicing as a strong man to run his race (*Psalm* 19.5), or that he is the king of heaven in a glowing chariot, is a way of seeing more richly.

> 'What,' it will be Question'd, 'When the Sun rises, do you not see a round disk of fire somewhat like a Guinea?' O no, no, I see an Innumerable company of the Heavenly host crying, 'Holy, Holy, Holy is the Lord God Almighty.'[2]

Similarly, when our ancestors divided time into days, months, seasons, years and even astronomical ages, this was not to explain why night and day were different, or why the seasons alter. They were not alien beings landed on an unfamiliar planet. Quite otherwise, they came to life and understanding in the same world as our non-human forebears and found it all familiar: for most of them, as also for most of us, what is familiar needs no explanation, and is hardly even noticed until some shock of change, or an inquisitive stranger, draws our attention to it.

In dividing up their time, they were invoking deity.

> General opinion makes the Hours goddesses and the Month a god, and their worship has been handed on to us: we say also that the Day and the Night are deities, and the gods themselves have taught us how to call upon them. (Proclus, *In Timaeum*, 248d: Cumont 1960, p. 61)

Our ancestors even built the solar year into their architecture, so that the sun's morning light shone on particular spots at different seasons of the year. It may even be that they noticed, after generations, something strange. Because the earth's axis itself rotates, like a gyroscope's, the sun will seem to rise, over the course of a Great Year, against a different stellar background at equivalent moments of the solar year, and gradually trace a circle round the sky until it rises again, most famously at equinox and solstice, within the same zodiacal figures as once upon a time it did. Ptolemy attributed the discovery or the plausible hypothesis (extrapolating from a tiny observable change) to Hipparchus of Rhodes (c140 BC; Ptolemy 1998, 3.1; 7.1–3).[3] Proclus (412–85 AD) reckoned that the Egyptians and Chaldaeans ('who even before their observations were instructed by the gods') had reached the same conclusion – though he himself found it incredible that the stars should ever change (Proclus, *In Timaeum*, 40AB: Kidd 1999, p. 269). Every 2000 years or so, the sun slips back, at its rising at the spring equinox, into a different zodiacal sign, passing from Bull to Ram to the Christian Fish (and so, quite soon, to Aquarius). Another way of putting the same point is to say that the Virgin will have a son: that is, the sun rises in Virgo at the autumn equinox when it rises in the Fishes in the spring.[4] Coincidentally, the Classical period was the Age of the Ram, and its first great adventure was the quest for the Golden Fleece by Jason and his Argonauts, sailing from northern Greece to the eastern edge of the Black Sea. Another Greek story concerned the killing of the Minotaur, the monstrous offspring of a bull and a Cretan queen. Such stories, whether or not they have a zodiacal significance, would have been told to organize and inspire, not to explain. This is the dawning of the Age of Aquarius (or not, as the case may be)!

We are not immune to such fables. Some modern writers suppose that a settled European population served the Earth Mother and her attendant spirits till the displaced hordes of horsemen serving the Sky Father disrupted the ancient harmonies and installed patriarchy and priesthood in the hearts of their successors. Yet others believe that there was a pan-European culture, linked by stone circles, ley-lines and a shamanic metaphysics, somehow derived from Egypt – or Atlantis. But the story that has most affected recent writers is that our ancestors were enmeshed in superstition, that 'the Greeks' invented science to escape, then lost their nerve and succumbed again to 'Oriental' fantasies. Popular works on science refer disparagingly to the 'Dark Ages' and to 'Medieval Superstition'. This story too is a fable.

Mythos and logos

The earliest written stories combine political realism and 'fantasy' in ways we now find strange: though the gods no longer share one world with us, they often visit, and the heroes may cross over into that other world more easily than shamans. 'Surely' their authors 'must have known' they were writing fantasy. Gilgamesh, king of Uruk, didn't 'really' battle past monsters to visit the two immortal survivors of the Flood. The gods did not 'really' manifest themselves at Troy, Odysseus wasn't held captive by a minor goddess, and neither did Pheidippides encounter the god Pan upon the road from Sparta. The gods who engendered royal dynasties must 'obviously' have been artefacts, pretentious ways of saying both that the new king was to be feared and 'who *his* father was, God knows'. We react, in fact, like someone saying that Picasso's *Guernica* distorts the truth, because it's not 'realistic'. We forget what our experience is really like. Our visual field is fractured and delusive, and only our 'reason' – or our ideology – tells us that ghosts, will-o'-the-wisps and monsters don't exist. Our memory is a constant confabulation – and the notion that it was 'the Greeks' who invented Reason is only another delusion, with which most Greeks did not themselves agree. Those who did were consciously controversial.

So Diogenes Laertius, writing his *Lives of the Philosophers* in the early third century AD, recorded the opinion that 'the Persians have had their Magi, the Babylonians or Assyrians their Chaldaeans, and the Indians their Gymnosophists; and among the Celts and Gauls there are the people called Druids or Holy Ones'. He himself responded bluntly (in his Prologue, ch. 1) that 'the achievements which some attribute to the barbarians belong to the Greeks, with whom not merely philosophy but the human race itself began'. By Diogenes' time, the issue was ideological. Christians like Clement of Alexandria (c150–c215 AD), were sure that many of the Greeks' own favourite philosophers were actually 'barbarians'.

> Pythagoras is shown to have been either a Tuscan or a Tyrian. And Antisthenes was a Phrygian. And Orpheus was an Odrysian or a Thracian. The most, too, show Homer to have been an Egyptian. Thales was a Phœnician by birth, and was said to have consorted with the prophets of the Egyptians; as also Pythagoras

did with the same persons, by whom he was circumcised, that he might enter the adytum and learn from the Egyptians the mystic philosophy. He held converse with the chief of the Chaldeans and the Magi. . . . And Plato does not deny that he procured all that is most excellent in philosophy from the barbarians; and he admits that he came into Egypt.[5]

Nowadays, it is routinely claimed that there were two distinctive features of those Greeks who rediscovered writing after the long collapse of Minoan and Mycenaean culture: they preferred impersonal explanations and argued for their theories. Where other peoples thought that trees and cities fell or winter followed summer because the gods were squabbling, or a witch ill-wished them, some Greeks began to appeal to 'Law' instead. At first that Law was simply Destiny: that nothing is allowed to grow too high, that everything has limits, that winter follows spring. Even Zeus, the greatest of the gods, is subject to *Moira*, Destiny. But if Zeus does not, or cannot, subvert that Law, we can do without him. Second, where other peoples defended particular stories by appeal to the authority of chosen texts or prophets, some Greeks began to demand that they be given reasons that did not rely on authority. They invented – or discovered – a world no longer arbitrary, ruled by changing purposes; they insisted that no special gifts – except to follow the argument where it led – were needed to uncover it. That is the world that enlightened people have inherited, although there are archaizers with us still, content to appeal to scriptural authority or charismatic prophecy to defend their moralizing account of how things are. 'The Greeks' triumphantly 'demystified the sacred' – or at any rate some few thinkers did.

Those who insist that 'the Greeks' made all the difference also distinguish *Mythos* and *Logos*. Kirk, Raven and Schofield (hereafter KRS), for example, insist in their account of 'Presocratic Philosophy' that proper rational and philosophical thinking must do away with personification 'before anything resembling logic could appear'. Only so could the Greeks move away from 'the closed traditional society . . . toward an open society in which the values of the past become relatively unimportant and radically fresh opinions can be formed both of the community itself and of its expanding environment' (KRS 1983, pp. 73–4). But we should not demand a particular metaphysical doctrine from all would-be philosophers.

Nor is it obvious that 'the useful and malleable symbols' which KRS wish to see abandoned are any less 'open', 'fresh' or innovative than the myths (of a cosmos ordered by impersonal law, and the 'rational man with a strong sense of what properly counts in human existence') they prefer.

Traditional 'myths' may imagine gods and heroes, with back stories and personal motivations, but these are often allegorical, no more to be taken 'literally' than rhetoric about the 'selfish genes' that control us lumbering robots. Nor are modern 'scientific' explanations necessarily coherent: physicists agree that light and matter alike are simultaneously made of particles and waves, and that the two greatest achievements of twentieth-century physics (namely quantum mechanics and general relativity) have at least not yet been shown to be consistent.[6] We may hope that 'there is no discord of truths which ever sure in union join' (Boethius, *Consolation*, 1969, p. 154: 5.3): it does not follow that we can expect to have that truth entire. The claim that mythic traditions are conservative (and the rational enterprise, by contrast, always changing and prepared for change) can also hardly survive an inspection of mythological or more generally religious history, or any contact with actual living scientists and philosophers. It is also false that myth-makers, even traditional myth-makers, never engage in argument – though the criteria by which one version of a myth is preferred over another may not be as exact or as conclusive as we imagine that 'scientific' criteria are. In brief, the over familiar distinction between *mythos* and *logos* makes it too easy to dismiss the thoughts of those who don't agree with 'us', without rebutting them in detail.

Even the Hippocratic author who denied, around 400 BC, that epilepsy was distinctively a 'sacred disease' does not say what a modern naturalist would expect, but rather that the causes of disease (cold, sun and winds) are divine and that it is impious to imagine that such divinities are controlled by incantations. If the Greeks, or some Greeks, were innovators here, the revolutionary idea is not that they were 'demystifying the sacred', since Nature and the Sacred are at one. The very philosophers who seem to later scholars to be essentially 'Greek' and 'scientific', it should also be noticed, stem not from mainland Greece, but from islands and coastal cities in what is now Turkey, Sicily or southern Italy – where Phoenician influence was strongest. Even in later days, when Greek was the

lingua franca of the Mediterranean world, this did not mean that
Greeks were the chief philosophers: on the contrary, it meant that
people from different tribes and cities did their thinking and writing
in the common tongue but drew on their own traditions too.

The Sidonians, according to tradition, are skilled in many
beautiful arts, and besides this they are philosophers in the
sciences of astronomy and arithmetic, having begun their studies
with practical calculations and with night-sailings; for each of
these branches of knowledge concerns the merchant and the ship-
owner; as, for example, geometry was invented, it is said, from
the measurement of lands which is made necessary by the Nile
when it confounds the boundaries at the time of its overflows.
This science, then, is believed to have come to the Greeks from
the Aegyptians; astronomy and arithmetic from the Phoenicians;
and at present by far the greatest store of knowledge in every
other branch of philosophy is to be had from these cities. And
if one must believe Poseidonius, the ancient dogma about atoms
originated with Mochus, a Sidonian, born before the Trojan times.
However, let us dismiss things ancient. In my time there have been
famous philosophers from Sidon; Boethus, with whom I studied
the Aristotelian philosophy, and his brother Diodotus; and from
Tyre, Antipater, and, a little before my time, Apollonius, who
published a tabulated account of the philosophers of the school
of Zeno and of their books. (Strabo [c64BC–24AD] 16.2.24:
1929, vol. 7, p. 71; see Kidd 1999, pp. 366–7)

But the tale persists. Maybe the Ionian Greeks invented science,
even if the distinction between *mythos* and *logos* is poorly drawn.
Unlike other speculative thinkers, it is said, they believed in seeking
evidence for the truth of their theories, and such theoretical entities
as they posited for their explanations were obedient to the laws of
their own natures. Of course, their theories were mistaken (as we
now suppose), but they were on the right lines: they did not appeal
to arbitrary acts of God either to explain things or to evade the
natural consequences of their own acts. But the story is misleading.
It is not clear what *evidence* the Ionian philosophers had for their
speculations, nor even that they sought it. The elements of which
they said the world was made (whether these were earth, air, fire and
water, or more abstract somewhats, as the Limit and the Unlimited)

were not entirely other than the abstract powers that Hesiod – as we shall see – imagined. We should not label one speculative thinker 'a philosopher' and another only 'a poet' or 'mystic' merely because they speak of 'elements' instead of 'spirits', especially when neither offers any abstract reasons to accept their story. Saying that 'water', or 'air', or 'fire' or all of them together make the world is no less 'mythological' than saying that Oceanus and Tethys did. The supposedly rational cosmologists had no better reason for identifying the four elements than the supposedly rational doctors had for postulating that there were four 'humours' in the human body, blood, phlegm, yellow bile and black bile: their 'vaunted evidence and proof [in *On the Nature of Man*] depend chiefly on the observation that all four are found in the excreta' (Lloyd 1990, p. 49). Writing on 'the sacred disease', the devoted Hippocratic

> directs some well-aimed blows at the purifiers who 'diagnosed' one type of epilepsy as the work of the Mother of the Gods, a second that of Poseidon, a third that of Enodia and so on. . . . Yet his own talk of bile and phlegm coursing round the body, and his own account of the vascular system by which they are conveyed, while different in *style*, to be sure, are also very largely a product of his imagination. (Lloyd 1990, p. 52; see also Buxton 1999)

His charges, in brief, are no more scientific, or even rational, than the standard accusations brought by any charlatan against competitors with an opposing theory![7] Hippocrates did not 'establish medicine as a science', as popular histories say, and neither did the Ionians establish a 'scientific' or even a 'rational' cosmology. Which is not to say that they are not worth noticing, but only that we should not exaggerate their novelty nor misrepresent their theories.

Whereas later theorists have assumed an explanatory and axiological gap between the 'human' and the 'natural' worlds, the Greeks, in common with other Mediterranean thinkers, took it for granted that the human and the natural were the same – and for that very reason such human disturbances as war and pestilence were of a piece with earthquakes and eclipses. So far from easily imagining an ethically neutral world, they took it for granted that there were limits on all endeavour, that no one part of the world (including us) could hope to live or grow forever, that the gods strike down the arrogant. Maybe this thought was obvious especially to peoples who lived on islands or in narrow valleys, at the mercy of earthquake and tsunami (see Kidd 1999, pp. 299–306).

Perhaps we are looking in the wrong place to find traces of experimental science. Herodotus of Halicarnassus (c484–c425 BC), the first 'historian' whose work we still possess, records an experimental, controlled enquiry: Croesus, ruler of the Anatolian kingdom of Lydia (595–c547 BC) investigated the claims of assorted oracles by arranging for them to be asked what he was doing on a particular day, and was satisfied only by the oracles of Apollo, in Delphi, and of Amphiaraus, in Thebes. His relationship with those oracles, notoriously, did not end happily. Cyrus of Persia (c600–530 BC) in turn attempted a sort of theological experiment: if Croesus was, as it was said, a holy man, might his god intervene to prevent his being burnt alive (reputedly, he did). The story is no less significant for probably being false! Herodotus also records (*History* 2.2) the legend that Psammetichus of Egypt (fl.656 BC) attempted to discover the 'original language' of humanity by having orphans reared wordlessly (he was persuaded by the results that it was Phrygian).

Herodotus is also a good witness to the practical and political good sense of Thales of Miletus (c624–c546 BC): he used his wits to corner the olive market, predicted a solar eclipse, got Croesus's army past an unbridgeable river to attack the Persians and advised the Ionian cities that their best hope was federation. His prediction of a bumper olive crop is of a piece with other stories about philosophers and their predictive powers: Anaxagoras of Clazomenae (c500–438 BC) predicted the fall of a meteor (Diogenes *Lives* 2.10), and Pherecydes of Syros (fl.540 BC) an earthquake, by inspecting water freshly drawn from a well (*Lives* 1.116). Cicero (106–43 BC) did not believe that story: 'it would be presumptuous enough, I think, for natural philosophers to attempt to explain the cause of an earthquake after it had happened; but can they actually tell, from looking at fresh water, that an earthquake is going to happen? Such nonsense is often heard in the schools, but one does not have to believe everything one hears' (*De Divinatione* 2.13).[8] That Thales predicted an eclipse looks more probable than once it did. He had access to Babylonian records and the lessons to be learnt from them. The pattern of eclipses is roughly repeated every 54 years, and that pattern is employed in the Antikythera Mechanism (see Marchant 2009 for a readable account of the object's discovery and interpretation). The Mechanism, admittedly, itself dates from around 100 BC, but it is so elegant, so sophisticated, as to demand a long back history of trial and error development.

Thales' other achievements did not all end well. His management of the river to allow Croesus to march his army against Cyrus also made use of Mesopotamian technology: a ruler of Babylon had previously diverted the Euphrates for her own ends (Herodotus 1.136: the ruler was Queen Nitocris), and Cyrus repeated the diversion – down the constructed channel – so as to capture Babylon. Cyrus also, it was said, attempted to 'punish' a river for drowning a favourite stallion by dividing it into 360 streams (he may have had a better reason). There is, at least, no doubt that both Mesopotamian and Egyptian engineers were familiar with water management, and that Thales, who had Phoenician connections – may even have been Phoenician – and had allegedly visited Babylon, had learnt from them. What neither Herodotus nor any other witness tells us is that Thales used any similar practical test to determine that the underlying stuff of everything was water (whatever quite that means) or tested the hypothesis. It was not the Ionian *theories* that marked them as experimentalists but the engineering skills that they had learnt from older societies.

Gods of the Greeks and others

Taking a step backwards from the Ionians, consider instead the account that Hesiod of Boeotia gave of the world's beginning in the late eighth century BC:

> Verily at the first Chaos came to be, but next wide-bosomed Earth, the ever-sure foundations of all the deathless ones who hold the peaks of snowy Olympus, and dim Tartarus in the depth of the wide-pathed Earth, and Eros (Love), fairest among the deathless gods, who unnerves the limbs and overcomes the mind and wise counsels of all gods and all men within them. From Chaos came forth Erebus and black Night; but of Night were born Aether and Day, whom she conceived and bare from union in love with Erebus. And Earth first bare starry Heaven, equal to herself, to cover her on every side, and to be an ever-sure abiding-place for the blessed gods. And she brought forth long Hills, graceful

haunts of the goddess-Nymphs who dwell amongst the glens of the hills. She bare also the fruitless deep with his raging swell, Pontus, without sweet union of love. But afterwards she lay with Heaven and bare deep-swirling Oceanus, Coeus and Crius and Hyperion and Iapetus, Theia and Rhea, Themis and Mnemosyne and gold-crowned Phoebe and lovely Tethys. After them was born Cronos the wily, youngest and most terrible of her children, and he hated his lusty sire. (Hesiod, *Theogony*, 116–38)

So begins the first 'Classical' account of the deathless ones, the gods, as told to Hesiod by the daughters of Mnemosyne (which is Memory). The genealogy continues with increasing complexity, and darker implications, occasionally dipping into narratives about selected gods, especially the line from Ouranos (Heaven) to Kronos to Zeus, whose children include both mortals and immortals. The defining character of 'gods' is that they are glorious and undying. But their glory is not kindly, and their kin are terrible.

In a hollow cave, Ceto [daughter of the Sea] bare another monster, irresistible, in no wise like either to mortal men or to the undying gods, even the goddess fierce Echidna who is half a nymph with glancing eyes and fair cheeks, and half again a huge snake, great and awful, with speckled skin, eating raw flesh beneath the secret parts of the holy earth. And there she has a cave deep down under a hollow rock far from the deathless gods and mortal men. There, then, did the gods appoint her a glorious house to dwell in: and she keeps guard in Arima beneath the earth, grim Echidna, a nymph who dies not nor grows old all her days. (Hesiod, *Theogony*, 295–305)

Echidna, in turn, bears many monsters, including the Hydra, the Chimaera and the Sphinx. As also does Earth herself, including Typhoeus, in whose contest with Zeus for the kingship 'the whole earth seethed, and sky and sea: and the long waves raged along the beaches round and about, at the rush of the deathless gods: and there arose an endless shaking'.

The message of Hesiod's *Theogony* is that there are deathless powers, both glorious and terrible, and that mortals must be content with the peace – such as it is – imposed by Zeus. Heroes may struggle with the smaller monsters: only Zeus himself can defeat Typhoeus and his siblings. 'It is not possible to deceive or go beyond the will of Zeus' (*Theogony*, 613). Far more successfully than his father or grandfather, Zeus has made sure (so far) that he will not be deposed by a more powerful son – a reflection, it is easy to imagine, of the fears and hopes of a fervently patriarchal, woman-fearing culture, and also of the fears and hopes of people who have survived disaster, and know that disasters always occur again. The volcanic eruption that demolished the island of Thera has left its mark in folklore, in the battle between Olympians and Titans. That battle, that eruption, was followed by another monstrous revolt, the eruption of Mount Etna (see Greene 1992, pp. 46–72).

> Strength was with his hands in all that [Typhoeus] did and the feet of the strong god were untiring. From his shoulders grew an hundred heads of a snake, a fearful dragon, with dark, flickering tongues, and from under the brows of his eyes in his marvellous heads flashed fire, and fire burned from his heads as he glared. And there were voices in all his dreadful heads which uttered every kind of sound unspeakable; for at one time they made sounds such that the gods understood, but at another, the noise of a bull bellowing aloud in proud ungovernable fury; and at another, the sound of a lion, relentless of heart; and at another, sounds like whelps, wonderful to hear; and again, at another, he would hiss, so that the high mountains re-echoed. (Hesiod, *Theogony*, 821–5)[9]

There was intolerable noise, and fire, and earthquake: 'a great part of huge earth was scorched by the terrible vapour and melted as tin melts'. As the priest told Solon, we have suffered many catastrophes, and the hill-folk, hidden in mountain caves, have always had to begin again. 'As far as the cities and centres of civilization down in the plains and close to the sea, they were totally annihilated. . . . So this is what is left of human experience at the time of the devastation – terrifying, infinite desolation; enormous wastes of land without limit; almost all living creatures made utterly extinct' (Plato *Laws* 3.677e; see Kingsley 2010, p. 172).

Hesiod's story is both like and unlike those of other Mediterranean nations. Archaeologists have uncovered Hittite myths about the god Kumarbi which look to be Hesiod's originals, despite the many years between Hesiod and the Hittite Empire.

Philo of Byblos, a Hellenized Phoenician (c70–c160 AD), preserved a Phoenician version, by Sanchuniathon, of the Kronos legend that may have been the route through which the story was transmitted (Gruen 2011, p. 342; see Baumgarten 1981, pp. 3–6; López-Ruiz 2010, pp. 94–101).

> The first principle of the universe [Sanchuniathon] supposes to have been air dark with cloud and wind, or rather a blast of cloudy air, and a turbid chaos dark as Erebus; and these were boundless and for long ages had no limit. But when the wind, says he, became enamoured of its own parents, and a mixture took place, that connexion was called Desire. This was the beginning of the creation of all things: but the wind itself had no knowledge of its own creation. From its connexion Mot was produced, which some say is mud, and others a putrescence of watery compound; and out of this came every germ of creation, and the generation of the universe. So there were certain animals which had no sensation, and out of them grew intelligent animals, and were called 'Zophasemin', that is 'observers of heaven'; and they were formed like the shape of an egg. Also Mot burst forth into light, and sun, and moon, and stars, and the great constellations. (Eusebius, *Praeparatio*, 1.10: 1903, p. 15)[10]

There are also similarities with other myths. In Egyptian thought, Atum emerges from Nothing (which is called Nun), and generates Shu and Tefnut, from whom in turn come Geb and Nut, and from them Isis, Osiris, Nephthys and Set, their enemy (these gods constituting the primeval Ennead). In Babylon, Apsu plots against the younger gods and is destroyed by Ea, who in turn gives way to Marduk who fights with his grandmother Tiamat and her new monstrous offspring. According to the Hittite text, Kumarbi castrates Anu, swallows the phallus and so bears Weather and the Euphrates (Burkert 2004, p. 92). In each case, complexity and personality gradually emerge from Chaos (which is not confusion, but – like the Egyptian Nun – a void), younger gods seize their power from the older, and peace is somehow established. Or rather, Law is established: 'Peace' is projected back into the rule of Kronos, or of Osiris before his murder. Ethiopians (Homer, *Iliad*, 1.421–22) and Hyperboreans may somehow retain their innocence, but we here-now can only rely on Law. And Law won't last:

The father will not agree with his children, nor the children with their father, nor guest with his host, nor comrade with comrade; nor will brother be dear to brother as aforetime. Men will dishonour their parents as they grow quickly old, and will carp at them, chiding them with bitter words, hard-hearted they, not knowing the fear of the gods. They will not repay their aged parents the cost of their nurture, for might shall be their right: and one man will sack another's city. There will be no favour for the man who keeps his oath or for the just or for the good; but rather men will praise the evil-doer and his violent dealing. Strength will be right and reverence will cease to be; and the wicked will hurt the worthy man, speaking false words against him, and will swear an oath upon them. Envy, foul-mouthed, delighting in evil, with scowling face, will go along with wretched men one and all. And then *Aidos* and *Nemesis* [that is, Shame and Indignation], with their sweet forms wrapped in white robes, will go from the wide-pathed earth and forsake mankind to join the company of the deathless gods: and bitter sorrows will be left for mortal men, and there will be no help against evil. (Hesiod, *Works and Days*, 175–201)

The prophecy is also a memory, of how life was when the world was turned upside down, and is echoed in later accounts, for example by Thucydides of Athens (c460–c395 BC) in his history of the great war:

The Peloponnesian War [chiefly between Athens and Sparta, in the late fifth century BC] was prolonged to an immense length, and was without parallel for the misfortunes that it brought upon Hellas. Never had so many cities been taken and laid desolate, here by the barbarians, here by the parties contending (the old inhabitants being sometimes removed to make room for others); never was there so much banishing and blood-shedding, now on the field of battle, now in the strife of faction. Old stories of occurrences handed down by tradition, but scantily confirmed by experience, suddenly ceased to be incredible; there were earthquakes of unparalleled extent and violence; eclipses of the sun occurred with a frequency unrecorded in previous history; there were great droughts in sundry places and consequent famines, and that most calamitous and awfully fatal visitation, the plague. (Thucydides, *History of the Peloponnesian War*, 1.23 (2004, pp. 10–11; see also 2.53)

We live both before and after this event, since time is cyclical, and faint memories of what went before may prepare us for the future. Later philosophers made this a metaphysical thesis, 'the eternal return' whereby the very same story is played out again and again 'forever'. In its origins, the notion was simply an observation.

The thing that hath been, it is that which shall be; and that which is done is that which shall be done: and there is no new thing under the sun. Is there anything whereof it may be said, See, this is new? It hath been already of old time, which was before us. There is no remembrance of former things; neither shall there be any remembrance of things that are to come with those that shall come after. (*Ecclesiastes* 1.9–11)

But perhaps there is remembrance after all. Hesiod's *Theogony* is revealed to him personally by the Muses, daughters of Memory, and conveyed in verse, alongside his other, moralizing poem, *Works and Days*. There seems to have been no priestly caste in Greece, though some priestly duties were handed down in families. Nor was there any grand revelation – except in the poems of a much greater poet, Homer. In *Iliad* and *Odyssey* and the *Homeric Hymns*, the major – mostly Olympian – gods are on display, all with mature personalities and family histories. Satirists usually portray these gods as merely more powerful humans. But the gods were more than this: first, as for Hesiod, they were deathless, and never to be evaded. They were more than personalities: they were whole worlds of meaning.

Aphrodite, for example, is the mind-beguiling, limb-loosening charm of lust, a real presence not to be denied, born – mythologically – from Heaven's severed phallus (and so the youngest Titan), but also conceived as the child of Zeus and the goddess Dione. Similarly Athena, daughter of Zeus and Metis, is born from Zeus's head (Zeus having swallowed her mother, on being warned that any male child born to her was bound to surpass his father), and Dionysus, son of Zeus and Semele, is reborn from Zeus's thigh after his mother was burnt up by Zeus's self-revelation. According to the Derveni papyrus, one of our oldest surviving documents, dating from about 400 BC, Zeus – like the Hittite Kumarbi – swallowed 'the phallus [of the king] who had first ejaculated the brilliance of heaven (*aither*)' (Burkert 2004, p. 90), and so carries 'all springs and rivers, together with all the other gods in himself' (Burkert 2004, p. 92). What might have been independent powers are given a place in the order maintained by Zeus, who is himself the overarching sky from which lightning strikes down the mighty. Zeus also holds men to their oaths, defends the laws of hospitality and forbids the eating of people. It is this last offence which brings down the Flood (and will one day bring down worse). Though the gods aren't kind, and owe us nothing, they demand some minimal morality from mortals. Sometimes some gods have favourites: Athena, for instance, favours the much-tried Odysseus. But she can't (won't) always save him from the malice of another god, and even Zeus's favourites can't escape from Fate. Indeed, being Zeus's favourite guarantees his wife's hostility! 'Zeus loves Hector and Sarpedon, Patroclus and Achilles; but by the end of the Iliad three of the four are dead, and the fourth is to be slain very soon' (Griffin 1980, p. 86). Our best hope is to remember we're all mortal and find what dignity we can in knowing it.

> The deathless gods are near among men and mark all those who oppress their fellows with crooked judgements, and reck not the anger of the gods. For upon the bounteous earth Zeus has thrice ten thousand spirits, watchers of mortal men, and these keep watch on judgements and deeds of wrong as they roam, clothed in mist, all over the earth. And there is virgin Justice, the daughter of Zeus, who is honoured and reverenced among the gods who dwell on Olympus, and whenever anyone hurts her with lying slander, she sits beside her father, Zeus the son of Cronos, and tells him of men's wicked heart, until the people pay for the mad folly of their princes who, evilly minded, pervert judgement and give sentence crookedly. Keep watch against this, you princes, and make straight your judgements, you who devour bribes; put crooked judgements altogether from your thoughts. (Hesiod, *Works and Days*, 248–64)

The tales of Greek mythology were told in many variants, constantly being rewritten to serve some dramatic or political purpose. They incorporate echoes of barbarian myth, and inquisitive travellers, like Herodotus, were eager to identify the gods of other nations with the Olympians. Some of those Olympians indeed – most obviously Aphrodite and Dionysus – always felt 'foreign' to their Greek worshippers: that was, after all, their nature – to be invading powers, of sexual obsession or drunkenness. Even Athena, so Herodotus suggested, was 'originally' brought from Libya, despite being – as it now seems – the Athenian goddess of good sense. '[Athena] represents a world of action, not, however, unconsidered and brute, but reasonable action which her clear awareness will most surely lead to victory' (Otto 1954, p. 59). The world has many faces, and our task as mortals can only be to keep our balance among competing powers. The world of ancient Mediterranean experience is full of omens, oracles and disappointed hopes – and Hope itself is one of the evils loosed from Pandora's Box rather than our comforter. We should know our place.

> Lay up these things within your heart and listen now to right, ceasing altogether to think of violence. For the son of Cronos has ordained this law for men, that fishes and beasts and winged fowls should devour one another, for right is not in them; but to mankind he gave right which proves far the best. (Hesiod, *Works and Days*, 274–6)

The Olympians aren't kind, though they are bound to keep their promises (or else, so Hesiod tells us, lie frozen by the Styx for a span of years). But they are also glorious and offer occasional brightness to their devotees. 'A shadow's dream is man, but when a god sheds a brightness, shining light is on earth and life is as sweet as honey' (Pindar, Pythian 8.95f [522–443 BC]). That brightness *is* the god (see also Hornung 1982, p. 134). Indeed, the very term '*theos*' in origin means 'amazing' (see Burkert 1997).

Nature and spirit confounded

On this account, the very realism of much Greek thought was not friendly to the growth of anything we could call 'science'. It was better not to disturb things, not to imagine that we could control the world, or always evade disaster. Even if we succeeded in the short term, the effects might not be good. Consider again the technical skills of Thales, who enabled Croesus of Lydia to bypass the river that was in his army's way. Notoriously, Croesus's assault ended badly. Thales employed the skills he had learnt in Egypt or Mesopotamia. Perhaps he should have employed instead the moral lessons that the Greeks preferred (especially 'don't go too far')!

The other story – that the Greeks reasoned their way to a modern sensibility, without appeal to inspiration or to worlds of meaning, and without conservative fears of failure – appeals to all Whiggish historians. Those most convinced by it are compelled to admit that the Greeks quickly sinned and fell away. Plato remoralized the world, suggesting that things happened because they should. Even Aristotle – conventionally depicted as Plato's opponent – thought that there were 'final causes' for what happened 'naturally', and that whatever helped us to see God was best. Even the Stoics, though they cultivated logic and 'the natural sciences', are now best remembered for their 'stoicism', their moral commitment to the divine presence, and their objection to merely 'naturalistic' explanation. According to Plutarch,

> Cleanthes [of Assos, and an early Stoic] (c330–c230 BC) thought that the Greeks ought to lay an action for impiety against Aristarchus the Samian (c310–c230 BC) on the ground that he was disturbing the hearth of the universe because he sought to save the phenomena by assuming that the heaven is at rest while the earth is revolving along the ecliptic and at the same time is rotating about its own axis.[11]

Few philosophers rejected ordinary religious practice or wholly abandoned the authority of traditional story. Some of them (Epimenides the Cretan, for example, who said, epigrammatically, that all Cretans were liars, about 600 BC, or Iamblichus of Syrian Chalcis in the early fourth century AD) behaved like witch-doctors. Solon of Athens, who is now chiefly remembered for his radical response to the Athenian economic crisis, brought Epimenides in to exorcise and purify the city by prayers and sacrifice. The whole Greek experiment, so modernists suppose, succumbed to mystifying Platonism and occult practice, and even unbelievers, because they had lost confidence in the power of 'reason' to uncover truth, reverted to their ancestral pieties. But there had never been any such confidence. The bits of past philosophizing that such moderns choose to praise are only might-have-beens, momentary anticipations of 'the true philosophy'.

So why should we discuss the ancient texts at all? It may be historically important to recognize that the Mediterranean peoples were aware that the earth was round, but no-one expects to find new details of the earth's circumference by reading Eratosthenes (c284–192 BC), who calculated it by comparing the noon-shadows at Aswan and Alexandria. Even if Hippocrates of Cos (c450–c375 BC) or his disciples helped to define the healer's art, we had better not use their medicines:

> [Their] main areas of innovation were in surgical practice and in dietetics, including drug therapy. But in both cases some of the new techniques introduced were drastic and may well have done more harm than good. Thus one new-fangled dietetic fad was a reducing diet, but according to critics of the treatment among the Hippocratics themselves that sometimes amounted to seriously weakening the patients or even starving them. . . . Again some of the surgical procedures described appear to be little more than adaptations of standard Greek instruments of torture: forcible straightening on the so-called Hippocratic bench . . . bears an uncanny resemblance to the rack. (Lloyd 1990, pp. 49–50)[12]

Nor do we expect Empedocles of Agrigentum (484–424 BC) to offer us a rival to Darwinian evolutionary theory, even though we detect a resemblance.

The practice of interpreting the writings of our predecessors as lisping attempts to speak a truth we understand more clearly than did they is not without merit. Aristotle himself described the earlier philosophers as ones who were groping for the distinctions he expounded – notably, the distinction between four sorts of explanation (material, efficient, formal and final). He may have misrepresented them, but we cannot be sure that we will do much better: our knowledge of that past is fragmentary and distorted, and he at least had access to an *oral* record. Where are the 232,808 lines of Theophrastus, Aristotle's first successor, or the seven hundred and five works of the great Stoic Chrysippus? (c280–207 BC). They would have been many fewer if he had quoted less, so his detractors said. Where are the four hundred books of Cleitomachus (187–110 BC), a Carthaginian philosopher at first called Hasdrubal? Where are the writings of the people we don't know at all? As West (1971, p. 219) remarks, we should certainly reject the hidden assumption 'that nobody contributed to the development of thought except the few whose writings survived them'.

Not every serious thinker wrote a book – we have but one book by a slave, and none by any woman[13]; we have hardly anything from the craftsmen (weavers, potters, smiths, metal-workers, builders, bakers, cooks, musicians) on whom all civilized life depended; not every book was copied often enough to have much chance of lasting; many books were destroyed, deliberately or not, by fire (but very few by Christians); many that survive have strayed so far beyond their context as to be unintelligible; even those we think we understand have lost whole realms of context, commentary and implication. In the end, each age, each individual sees in the texts what they can understand, for good or ill. But we can occasionally be quiet enough to listen. Reading the past philosophers, even (or especially) when they are, we think, mistaken, may be a helpful exercise in at least two ways: it may induce us to identify our own beliefs more clearly, and it may remind us that the very beliefs that we think obvious may also turn out, someday, to be entirely wrong. But there is a third possibility: past philosophers may really have been correct.

CHAPTER TWO

Influence from outside

Tales from the East

The Mediterranean is an almost intelligible subject – but this is not to say that the Outside is irrelevant. To the east of the Mediterranean, on the far side of mountains and deserts but still within the reach of travellers and traders, lay the land 'between the rivers', Mesopotamia. Those rivers, the Tigris and the Euphrates, arise in the Taurus and Zagros mountains and empty into the Persian Gulf. The first cities seem to have been built here, founded around shrines and markets, each with their tutelary deities, and each permitting the growth of specialized professions: augurs, doctors, potters, smiths, weavers and accountants.[1] The first, Sumerian, cities and the culture they engendered from Syria to the Indus were conquered by the Akkadians in the late third millennium, by the efforts of Sargon of Kish (reigning from 2334 BC). He compelled tribute from what had been independent cities, and sought to control their cults. His grandson, Naram-Sin, declared *himself* a god after defeating rebellious cities. Akkad's empire did not last for long, but the precedent – of central control through priestly as well as military means – was set. The region at first reverted to a mosaic of independent cities, but over many centuries one imperial city after another grew to power: Ur of the Chaldees, Babylon, Assur and Nineveh. The Hittite Empire of Central Anatolia, speaking an Indo-European tongue, may also have had an effect both in Mesopotamia and around the Mediterranean coast, but we know too little to gauge its contribution. There were also cities in the Indus Valley, but we know even less of them.

In both Mesopotamian and Greek myth there are elements which suggest that the most powerful gods – even those of our own particular city – are at least not our friends. In the Mesopotamian version, notably the Epic of Atrahasis (sixteenth century BC), human beings were created as slave labour for the gods (by killing a minor god and mixing him with clay). The supreme god, Enlil, finding them too noisy, then attempted their destruction by plague, drought, famine and flood. We had an ally of sorts in Enki, who managed, like Prometheus in the Greek story, to secure a future for humanity by tricking Enlil. In both traditions, the gods demand sacrifice. In both, they are sometimes malevolent – and silly. At least in Greece they offer us sex, harvests, crafts and a code of justice, but also withhold or corrupt those gifts at their pleasure. We cannot admire such deities, but we must put up with them, and may sometimes even love them – a paradox surprising only to those who have forgotten their own emotions at the sight or thought of tyrannosaurs or tigers, tornadoes or live volcanoes. There is a natural and acknowledged impulse there – to run and hide – but we may also be exalted in the sight. War too is a god, though Homer testifies that Ares is the most hated of the Olympians (*Iliad* 5.699). Even Aphrodite, the cause of so much evil to Trojans, Greeks and all humanity, is still tremendous, 'terrible and numinous' (Griffin 1980, p. 156). Plague is harder to conceive as numinous, though Homer made the attempt, describing Apollo's response to the prayer of his priest, humiliated by Agamemnon (*Iliad* 1.43–52).

In another Mesopotamian epic, that of Gilgamesh of Uruk, we are shown the folly of attempting any rebellion: Gilgamesh is a great king, early in the third millennium BC, and bold enough to insult Inanna (as later Greek heroes also insulted gods, to no good end). The gods respond at first by raising up a rival to defeat him, the wild man Enkidu. Gilgamesh manages to have that rival domesticated, or civilized, by the attentions of a courtesan, and the two swear friendship. But Enkidu dies and Gilgamesh, confronted by the sudden reality of death, goes in pursuit of immortality. He locates and talks with Utnapishtim, survivor of the Flood (in the earlier epic, this was Atrahasis), who has been made immortal by the gods' mere whim. He is told of a plant that would grant him immortality, discovers it – and loses it to a snake. Snakes, so we are told, can cast their skins and renew their youth – but not so Gilgamesh, nor any other human.[2] We are mortal, and that is what we must acknowledge in striving 'to know ourselves'. Even the heroes, born of the mingling of gods and humans, perish, unless a god intervenes. Giants may pile mountain on mountain to climb up to heaven; the king of Babel may seek to build a tower for the same purpose (*Genesis* 11.1–9). None of them will succeed.

> Who, my friend, can go up to heaven?
> The gods dwell with Shamash for ever,
> But as for man, his days are numbered;
> All his activity is just wind.[3]

We may have been meant as slaves – but slaves are often rebels. 'The Greeks' were not the first to think of themselves as other than the gods, or than the gods' obedient servants. Nor were they the first to try to manage their lives in the presence of mightier powers. The Mesopotamian stories may have been known to the Mediterranean peoples. There may at least have been a 'common religious language' available to Homer, in the sense of a celestial pantheon of more or less anthropomorphic deities, 'mutually related as husbands and wives, parents and children' (Griffin 1980, p. 186, after Burkert), though this is, Griffin adds, a conception 'alien to later Greek religion'.

Individual Olympians were later identified with many foreign gods, but such motifs as are encountered in both traditions are put to different purposes. Inanna's self-aggrandizing descent into the Underworld, shedding her clothes of power as she goes, and her eventual rescue (ransomed at the expense of her mortal husband, Dumuzi) is not much like Orpheus's descent to retrieve his wife (he fails), nor Persephone's abduction by the lord of the Underworld, Hades. The most that can be said is that there is a common tradition – of an Underworld below, a Heaven above and travels between these and our earth. And the gods, though personally often unfair, require that we obey the laws of hospitality and fair dealing, and that we keep our oaths. Hammurabi of Babylon (1792–49 BC) received his office directly – so he said – from Shamash, as Moses did from Yahweh on Mount Sinai, or Minos of Crete from Zeus[4]. Strictly, the stele that records this claim is not a code of laws, but only a declaration that Hammurabi is a king dispensing justice: the cases mentioned are what he proposed to do, not principles he promised to obey (Van De Mieroop 2004, pp. 106–8). But it indicates that there was a sense that his god demanded justice, even of him. And it was a seed, at least, of the idea that the laws should rule, and not a particular man, however just or powerful. Since Babylon fell (yet again) soon after Hammurabi, his ideals were not consolidated there, and later peoples, in the Mediterranean cities, thought that these were *their* ideas – to be contrasted with the rule of the eastern emperors (who reckoned their subjects to be slaves, to be dealt with as they willed).

What Mediterranean peoples themselves admitted that they learnt from Mesopotamians were Divination, Astronomy and Mathematics. The Babylonians had calculated the square root of two, and knew 'Pythagoras's Theorem' (as we call it). They used these calculations both for practical ends (e.g. to estimate the size of a grain pile) and in time-keeping. We still employ their sexagesimal system, counting 60 seconds to a minute, 60 minutes to the hour, 12 hours to both day and night, and 12 months in the year (though the Egyptians claimed to have originated that), as well as 360 degrees to a circle. It was also in Mesopotamia that records were kept of the stars and their annual alterations – though we cannot now trace the invention of the zodiac much before the sixth century BC. Divination, whether from the flight of birds, the condition of sacrificed animals or astrological calculations, must now seem superstitious (as it did to many ancient thinkers), but it testified to the conviction that we could discover things about our future by reasoning about the past. Divination differs from inspiration. Cicero puts the distinction into his brother's mouth:

There are two kinds of divination: one, which is allied with art; the other, which is devoid of art. Those diviners employ art, who, having learnt the known by observation, seek the unknown by deduction. On the other hand those do without art who, unaided by reason or deduction or by signs which have been observed and recorded, forecast the future while under the influence of mental excitement, or of some free and unrestrained emotion. This condition often occurs to men while dreaming and sometimes to persons who prophesy while in a frenzy — like Bacis of Boeotia, Epimenides of Crete and the Sibyl of Erythraea. (Cicero, *De Divinatione*, 1.18)

Oracles and omens are more personal and far more ambiguous. Those who believe in oracles believe that the world is personal. Those who believe in augury are scientists, of a sort, with detailed records of auguries through the ages: 'there is nothing which length of time cannot accomplish and attain when aided by memory to receive and records to preserve. We may wonder at the variety of herbs that have been observed by physicians, of roots that are good for the bites of wild beasts, for eye affections, and for wounds, and though reason has never explained their force and nature, yet through their usefulness you have won approval for the medical art and for their discoverer' (*De Divinatione* 1.7.12–13). The distinction is not as clear as it might be: the means by which the auguries match the events appears to be merely the good will of the gods, and the records don't fully support the predictions: why should anyone have ever formed the hypothesis that a particular shape in a bull's heart had any relevance to the outcome of a battle (unless they were told so by a god)? Cicero observes in his own voice that there was little chance of Etruscan, Greek, Egyptian and Punic diviners ever agreeing on those rules: there is, as he says, no established practice (*De Divinatione* 2.12: Burkert 1992, p. 51).

Now the Chaldaeans, belonging as they do to the most ancient inhabitants of Babylonia, have about the same position among the divisions of the state as that occupied by the priests of Egypt; for being assigned to the service of the gods they spend their entire life in study, their greatest renown being in the field of astrology. But they occupy themselves largely with soothsaying as well, making predictions about future events, and in some cases by purifications, in others by sacrifices, and in others by some other charms they attempt to effect the averting of evil things and the fulfilment of the good. They are also skilled in soothsaying by the flight of birds, and they give out interpretations of both dreams and portents. They also show marked ability in making divinations from the observation of the entrails of animals, deeming that in this branch they are eminently successful. (Diodorus 2.29.2–3)

What Mediterranean commentators identified in the East (apart from the skills enumerated) was that their 'Magi' spent their time 'in the worship of the gods, in sacrifices and in prayers, implying that none but themselves have the ear of the gods'. They supposed that the world was full of spectres, which they could see and partly control (Diogenes *Lives* 1.7, after Cleitarchus [fl. 310 BC]) – a thought reminiscent of the remark attributed to Thales, that 'everything is full of gods' (Burkert 2004, p. 121). According to Diogenes Laertius's authorities, they held that the gods were fire, earth and water, and condemned the use of images, 'and especially the error of attributing to the divinities differences of sex'. Aristotle, in his dialogue *On Philosophy*, said that they believed 'in two principles, the good spirit and the evil spirit; the one called Zeus or Oromasdes, the other Hades or Arimanius' (Ross 1952, p. 79 [fr.6]). Diogenes went on to say that 'Clearchus of Soli in his tract *On Education* further makes the Gymnosophists [that is, Hindu or Buddhist ascetics] to be descended from the Magi; and some trace the Jews also to the same origin'.

These 'Magi', it seems, were what we now call 'Zoroastrians', and originated further east than the Mesopotamian kingdoms, probably among the Medes (who spoke an Indo-European language related to Latin, Greek, Persian and Sanskrit). That they analysed the physical world in terms of the three elements (leaving air, apparently, aside), and saw opposing principles at work in the world, called 'good' and 'evil', marks them as very different from those who invented Gilgamesh or the squabbling city gods. Behind those principles, Oramasdes (aka Ahura Mazda) and Arimanius (aka Angra Mainyu), lay Zurvan, Time, which engenders all things and to which all things return: our problem is whether we side with Truth (Oromasdes) or the Lie (Arimanius). That problem – of a fundamental dualism in existence, or a monism – I defer. The Magi described by Herodotus, it is fair to say, don't seem 'philosophical': they are Median magicians, and as treacherous and selfish as almost everyone in his History. But his sources were unfriendly ones. It is possible that Pherecydes of Syros picked up from the Magi the notion that the world begins from Time (along with 'Zas' and 'Chthonie': the heavenly and terrestrial principles), not just – as in Hesiod – from Emptiness. But the story may have had a Phoenician source, rather than a Zoroastrian. At any rate the Sidonians, according to Damascius (458–538 AD), set Time, Desire and Mist at the beginning, 'and from the union of Desire and Mist, as dual principles, emerged Air and Breeze, and from these two an egg was born, corresponding (so Damascius reckoned) to the intelligible intellect. . . . According to Mochus . . . at the beginning there was

Aither and Air, two principles themselves, from whom Oulamos was born, the intelligible god himself' (López-Ruiz 2010, p. 152, after Damascius, *De Principiis*, 125c). López-Ruiz points out that Oulamos is an identifiable Semitic name, meaning – roughly – remote time or eternity. Its Hebrew variant, *olam*, may be used for the Hebrew God. In other settings Time may be represented as a monster: a winged serpent with the heads of a lion, a bull and a man (López-Ruiz 2010, pp. 153–8) who is – perhaps – the enemy of God (whoever counts as God in the stories of whichever people). 'Time all things devours: birds, beasts, trees and flowers'. Eternity, on the other hand, contains all things. The two claims are almost identical. Metaphysical and moral debates can take place in code: whatever was meant at the time by all these symbols is now largely lost to us, except that we can guess they are not random choices.

According to Porphyry (fl.300 AD) Pythagoras of Samos had learnt rather more, whether directly from the Magi or from Pherecydes: 'above all things to speak the truth, for this alone deifies men'. For as he had learnt from the Magi, who call God Oremasdes, God's body is light, and his soul is truth (*Life of Pythagoras* 41: Guthrie 1987, p. 131). Not that we have much evidence that the Persians were consistently Zoroastrian:

> It is quite possible that Zoroaster's religion found receptive ears among the Achaemenids. But side by side with the spread of Zoroastrianism there remained throughout the Achaemenid era the traditional Indo-Iranian pantheon and cult. In fact, our evidence indicates that at least three different forms of religion coexisted simultaneously in Achaemenid Persia: Zoroastrian, Magian, and Persian. Each inherited the religious legacy that belonged to the Indo-Aryan group, but in time each moulded its own distinct religious identity and pattern. And if that is the case, then we can say that Herodotus has no contradictory statements or accounts, but interestingly enough demonstrates how the Persians and the Magians (who both claimed the Indo-Aryan legacy) each preserved separate identities in the various phases of their religions. (Nigosian 1993, p. 43)

Whatever was going on in Mesopotamia (and still further east) was no more consistent or coherent than whatever was happening around the Inner Sea.

Tales from the South

South of the Mediterranean Sea is the north coast of Africa. Herodotus attempted an ethnographic survey of the region, and concluded, among other speculations, that the goddess Athena was also to be found in Libya. Unfortunately, we have no record of what reasonings were involved in archaic Libyan thought. The ancient source of their thought and practice that the Greeks cheerfully acknowledged in Africa was the Egyptian. They perceived Egypt chiefly as the marshy delta of Lower Egypt ('a broad, flat country full of swamps' as far as Heliopolis, which is now buried beneath Cairo), into which the Nile flowed down from Upper Egypt through a narrow valley. Herodotus reckoned, correctly, that the land of Egypt – especially the Delta – had been washed down over thousands of years from Ethiopia, being black and crumbly unlike the soil and sand of Libya and Arabia. Those who travelled up the Nile would eventually reach Nubia, where Egypt mined its gold. Unlike the Mesopotamian milieu Egypt was united early, though its separate 'nomes' and cities retained distinctive pantheons and were sometimes independent.

Herodotus concluded that the Egyptians reversed the common practice of humankind (or at any rate of the Greeks), and were 'religious to excess', with an especial veneration for their sacred animals. He reckoned that it was they who originated the idea that there were twelve gods (which the Greeks called Olympian), including in that reckoning Heracles and leaving aside Poseidon (who came, Herodotus says, from Libya). But only Isis and Osiris were worshipped by all Egyptians (and Osiris, they said, was the Greek Dionysus). Of Heracles, who was also identified with the Phoenician god Melqart, I shall have more to say below. The supposed identity of Dionysus and Osiris – and a later identification even of Dionysus and of Yahweh (Plutarch, *Quaestiones conviviales*, 4.6.1–2; see Amzallag 2011 for an ingenious argument from the gods' shared character and symbology that the identity was acknowledged earlier) – raises the question how such identities were recognized or created. It might be easy to say that the 'chief of the gods', in whatever pantheon, was recognizably or conveniently one: Zeus, Baal and Ammon must be the same, even if different stories are told of them by different peoples. Inanna, Ishtar, Astarte, Aphrodite and

Venus – goddesses of sexual desire – could also be acknowledged as one and the same beneath all disguises. But why should Dionysus, the god of drunken ecstasy, and Osiris, the lord of the dead, be one[5]? How should Apollo (Horus) be his son? How could Yahweh and Dionysus ever have been equated, when 'Dionysiac Orgies' were what the Hebrews most detested in pagan Greek culture? And even if the Egyptian Ptah and the Greek Hephaistos were both imagined as Makers, can we ignore the obvious discrepancies, that Hephaistos was lame (because Zeus threw him out of heaven) and a metal worker, and Ptah was a healthy sculptor as well as the 'primordial mound' from which all worlds began? Ordinarily physical beings can be encountered in different guises and from different angles: we don't all know exactly the same things even about our friends and family. But 'divine beings', even if we suppose that they are real, don't seem to be simply physical, or to exist as locatable individuals. How then can we count how many there are, or be sure that we're counting correctly?

These questions lead on to metaphysical speculations about numbers, 'souls' or 'universals'. They may even indicate a larger metaphysical issue: whereas the Greek gods, as they appear in story and even more abstract speculation, are counted as discrete entities, who may take over one another's artefacts (as Apollo, so it was said, had accepted the lyre from Hermes) but remain distinct, Egyptian gods merge and re-emerge: the original ruler – till Isis extorted his real name from him – was 'Khepry in the morning, Re at midday, Atum in the evening' (Hornung 1982, p. 88). 'Amun' and 'Re', or 'Re' and 'Osiris', are sometimes two, and sometimes one (Hornung 1982, pp. 91, 93). In this, they are more like processes or events than countable, individual 'substances' – and maybe this is a better account of things in general. Storms, rivers, flames and rocks have transitory names – and so may living creatures: why should we be surprised that what is single, at one moment or one scale, is also plural on a different view?

Or consider the nature of moods, emotions, feelings, vices, virtues and many other aspects of our mental life. There is often no 'word for word' translation possible between different languages or dialects. Do the contentious words have much the same extension: are they applied, that is, to the same range of clearly visible events? Do they have the same intension: do they connect those events to 'just the same' aspects of the world and human life, or suggest the 'same' responses?

Is *thumos* the same as anger? Is *philia* the same as friendship, *time* as honour, *nous* as intellect? And what are anger, friendship, honour, intellect themselves? There are two errors possible: the first to assume that everyone is saying and thinking only what we would say and think ourselves, and that it is obvious that we can translate word for word from one tongue to another; the second to suppose, self-defeatingly, that nobody can understand a foreign tongue. Genuine conversation, even conversation with oneself, is more dynamic. So also is any attempt to think about the gods.

The metaphysical issue and the problem about translation are related to the status of such 'laws of logic' as the principles of identity, non-contradiction and excluded middle. The more immediate question might be the social or political: what difference did it make to Greeks, Egyptians, Phoenicians or Hebrews to think that it was the same or a different god that was worshipped? Part of the answer lies in what the worshippers thought it then right to do, whether in profane or sacred matters. What attitudes and feelings did the gods require, inspire or represent? Sometimes it might be enough to notice that a particular plant or animal or planet was sacred to what might otherwise seem different gods. Sometimes the point was rather that a similar ritual was required, or a similar disengagement from the rules of ordinarily profane existence. Osiris and Dionysus seem different (one represented as a living mummy, one as a feminized young man): yet both had died, been torn apart and been reborn, and both presided over mysteries that promised the same thing. Herodotus believed that the ceremonies were introduced to Greece by Cadmus the Tyrian 'and the followers whom he brought from Phoenicia into the country which is now called Boeotia', but that they originated in Egypt, along with almost all the names of the gods, first conveyed to 'the Pelasgi', the earlier inhabitants of Greece (Herodotus 5.58–61). He also proposed that the mysteries of Demeter (i.e. Isis) were brought to the Pelasgi by 'the daughters of Danaus', and called the Thesmophoria. Later Greeks inherited them, he says (though what exactly they were, he is too cautious or respectful to reveal). His claims about the rites of Dionysus have been vindicated by recent archaeological discoveries (see Burkert 2004, pp. 71–98): there was indeed a cult of Dionysus, grounded in Egyptian practice as well as ancient Pelasgian, that offered immortality, and a purification from both communal and individual sins – a cult that found expression from Sicily to Olbia (in what is now Ukraine), and that was associated with the name of Orpheus.

According to Diodorus 1.50.1–2, 'the [Egyptian] Thebans say that they are the earliest of all men and the first people among whom philosophy and the exact science of the stars were discovered, since their country enables them to observe more distinctly than others the rising and settings of the stars'. Modern Egyptologists do not agree that the Egyptians had much interest in the stars – though they seem to have shared a late antique conviction that the souls of the dead were stars (Hornung 1982, p. 81), and gave Sirius a rôle as the herald of the Nile flood. Diogenes Laertius has a longer account, partly drawn from Hecataeus of Miletus (550–476 BC), and Manetho of Heliopolis, an Egyptian historian of the third century BC.

> The philosophy of the Egyptians is described as follows so far as relates to the gods and to justice. They say that matter was the first principle, next the four elements were derived from matter, and thus living things of every species were produced. The sun and the moon are gods bearing the names of Osiris and Isis respectively; they make use of the beetle, the dragon, the hawk, and other creatures as symbols of divinity, according to Manetho in his *Epitome of Physical Doctrines*, and Hecataeus in the first book of his work *On the Egyptian Philosophy*. They also set up statues and temples to these sacred animals because they do not know the true form of the deity. They hold that the universe is created and perishable, and that it is spherical in shape. They say that the stars consist of fire, and that, according as the fire in them is mixed, so events happen upon earth; that the moon is eclipsed when it falls into the earth's shadow; that the soul survives death and passes into other bodies; that rain is caused by change in the atmosphere; of all other phenomena they give physical explanations, as related by Hecataeus and Aristagoras. They also laid down laws on the subject of justice, which they ascribed to Hermes; and they deified those animals which are serviceable to man. They also claimed to have invented geometry, astronomy, and arithmetic. Thus much concerning the invention of philosophy. (*Lives* 1.10–11)

Diogenes claimed that the Egyptians supposed that there were four elements – a belief also endorsed by Diodorus, who describes the five primary Egyptian gods (he says), as follows: Zeus is the spirit, animating all things; Hephaistos is fire; Demeter, earth; Oceane, water; and Athena air (Diodorus 1.12). There is no native evidence that the Egyptians acknowledged the four elements, let alone personified them (Hornung 1982, p. 80). Fire, Earth, Water, Air – and the animating Spirit (*pneuma*) – seem rather to be a Greek or Phoenician invention which became the default assumption about the stuff of which things were made, and so was identified, like the Olympians, in every one else's system. The Derveni papyrus also reckons that Zeus is the *pneuma* that rules everything (Burkert 2004, p. 121). The Stoics were later to hold a similar view. Maybe Manetho too was persuaded.

Diogenes's claim that the Egyptians 'deified those animals which are serviceable to man' is an hypothesis to explain what baffled non-Egyptians, and sometimes outraged them. The standard explanations were that the Olympians had taken the form of animals while fleeing Typhon, or else that the human king Osiris had organized his troops beneath heraldic standards, and finally that the Egyptians were only honouring the useful animals. Ps-Dionysius (a fifth century Christian Platonist) suggested instead that these images for divinity were selected precisely because they couldn't be taken literally:

> High-flown shapes could well mislead someone into thinking that the heavenly beings are golden or gleaming men, glamorous, wearing lustrous clothing, giving off flames which cause no harm, or that they have other similar beauties with which the word of God has fashioned the heavenly minds. It was to avoid this kind of misunderstanding among those incapable of rising above visible beauty that the pious theologians so wisely and upliftingly stooped to incongruous dissimilarities, for by doing so they took account of our inherent tendency toward the material and our willingness to be lazily satisfied by base images. At the same time they enabled that part of the soul which longs for the things above actually to rise up. Indeed the sheer crassness of the signs is a goad so that even the materially inclined cannot accept that it could be permitted or true that the celestial and divine sights could be conveyed by such shameful things. (Ps-Dionysius, *Celestial Hierarchy*, 141B: 1987, p. 150)

He hurriedly adds that we should also remember that 'there is nothing which lacks its own share of beauty, for as Scripture rightly says, "Everything is good"' (citing *Genesis* 1.31).

Whether the ancient Egyptians felt exactly this may be uncertain; however, that they used animal signs to signify particular attributes and habits in their deities, without literally supposing that the god Khepry, for example, had a scarab beetle for a head, seems true (see Hornung 1982, pp. 114–7). The images of their gods were coded messages, hieroglyphs – and hieroglyphs themselves were images, gods made manifest:

> The mixed form of their gods is nothing other than a hieroglyph, a way of 'writing' not the name but the nature and function of the deity in question. The Egyptians do not hesitate to call hieroglyphs 'gods', and even to equate individual signs in the script with particular gods; it is quite in keeping with their views to see images of the gods as signs in a metalanguage. As is true of every Egyptian hieroglyph, they are more than just ciphers or lifeless symbols; the god can inhabit them, his cult image will normally be in the same form, and his priests may assume his role by wearing animal masks. (Hornung 1982, p. 125)

Later 'Neo-Platonic' or 'Hermetic' accounts of Egyptian mysteries were more accurate than the earlier, literal-minded and Euhemerist accounts to be found in Hecataeus of Miletus (c550–c476 BC) and his imitators. Plutarch of Chaeronea was right to criticise the eponymous Euhemerus, probably of Messina (late fourth century BC), who

> drew up copies of an incredible and non-existent mythology and spread atheism over the whole inhabited earth by obliterating the gods of our belief and converting them all into names of generals, admirals, and kings, who, forsooth, lived in very ancient times and are recorded in gold letters at Panchon, which no foreigner and no Greek had ever happened to meet with, save only Euhemerus. (Plutarch, *On Isis and Osiris,* 355A-B: Baumgarten 1981, pp. 76–7)[6]

The images, and their associated rites, were intended to invoke, evoke, the presence of a god: to encourage in us that brightness and exaltation which is itself the god.

Ancient natural philosophy among both Greeks and barbarians took the form of an account of nature hidden in mythology, veiled for the most part in riddles and hints, or of a theology such as is found in mystery ceremonies in which what is spoke is less clear to the masses than what is unsaid, and what is unsaid gives cause for more speculation than what is said. This is evident from the Orphic poems and the accounts given by the Phrygians and Egyptians. But nothing does more to reveal what was in the mind of the ancients than the rites of initiation and the ritual acts that are performed in religious services and with symbolic intent. (Boys-Stones 2001, p. 108 citing Plutarch fr.157.16–25 Sandbach)

Expecting those images, those rites, and even the stories told around them 'to make sense' in any easily literal way is to mistake the case[7]. What we need – tradition says – is to awaken insight.

The wise men of Egypt, I think, also understood this, either by scientific or innate knowledge, and when they wished to signify something wisely, did not use the forms of letters which follow the order of words and propositions and imitate sounds and the enunciations of philosophical statements, but by drawing images and inscribing in their temples one particular image of each particular thing, they manifested the non-discursiveness of the intelligible world, that is, that every image is a kind of knowledge and wisdom and is a subject of statements, all together in one, and not discourse or deliberation. (Plotinus, *Ennead*, V.8 [31].6)[8]

So the sort of philosophy that the Egyptians created may have been associated with the 'mysteries' that late antique philosophy admired. What puzzled the earlier commentators, and led them to accept the Euhemerist interpretation of such important gods as Isis and Osiris (that Osiris was an Egyptian king of the distant past), was that the gods were mortal: not only did they have a beginning, as many other Mediterranean deities did, they would also have an end, when the primeval emptiness – symbolized as the serpent Apopis – was once more victorious. Then all differentiation will be at an end – an outcome that Stoic philosophers characterized as the conflagration:

This earth will return to the primeval water (Nun), to endless (flood) as in its first state. I [that is Atum] shall remain with Osiris after I have transformed myself into another snake which men do not know and the gods do not see. (*Book of the Dead* ch. 175, cited by Hornung 1982, p. 163)

Perhaps the Egyptians would have expected everything then to begin again, as the Stoics did: perhaps that is why the serpent is depicted as swallowing its own tail, as it lies wrapped round the universe of changing, differentiated things. Or else the world was finite in duration as well as in extent (the issue is as yet unsettled, even in modern physics). Any creator god (and any of the gods could be treated as the creator) can be described as 'one who made himself into millions' (Hornung 1982, p. 170; see further pp. 170–84). In that process, earth and sky are separated (as they are in Greek and many other myths), and room made for all the many million things.

> Heaven and earth were once a single form, but when they were separated from each other into two, they bore and delivered into the light all things: trees, winged creatures, beasts reared by the briny sea, and the human race. (Euripides fr.484 Nauck: López-Ruiz 2010, p. 36)

Outside and before that process, there is Nothing: the non-existent, Emptiness, which is not even space. Nor does that Nothing 'last for a long time', since 'then' there is no time. In speaking of that Nothing, it is possible to speak of it as 'One' – for Egyptian metaphysicians, so it seems, as also for the later Platonists, 'matter' (which is empty) and 'the One' (which is the source of everything) are equally indescribable, and almost equal. The One holds Beauty – which is Being – before itself as a veil (Plotinus, *Ennead*, I.6 [1].9). Matter itself can never itself be seen beneath the beautiful chains in which it is bound, the actual differentiated beings (*Ennead* I.8 [51].15). None of the things there are could exist without the One – but equally they couldn't exist without having room to do so.

> The undifferentiated one of the beginning differentiated himself through his work of creation, he 'made himself into millions'; mankind can experience him only in the multiplicity of the created, mortal, and changing gods. In them the Egyptians encounter an existent reality that does not need to be transcendent in order to be the greatest and the most perfect, unique and incomparable. (Hornung 1982, p. 185)

Does this imply that 'monotheists', on Egyptian terms, are mistaken? No single, nameable god can exhaust the fullness of created being. We may, on occasion, focus on a single 'god' or image, but must not then forget the other images, the other mortal gods. This is also a theme of Greek poetic thought: the core of many tragedies is that the hero is torn between two masters, two requirements (like Orestes), or has foolishly neglected one (like Pentheus or Hippolytus). In Greek thought, Zeus must be unbeatable (though there were stories that he had been challenged, and might possibly have been defeated and displaced), and there was therefore an overarching order that the lesser gods and demons must learn to respect and obey. The Egyptian pattern was different – and as shocking to Greek sensibility as the story the Cretans told (and earned themselves their reputation as perpetual liars): namely, that Zeus had died. The Egyptian mystery was that Osiris died, was dismembered – and reborn.

There is no single image of the divine – and certainly not humanity. The other shocking feature of Egyptian thought – sometimes treated as a joke and sometimes as a threat to civilized humanity – is that *animals* can be sacred, and seen as images of the divine. The Battle of Actium as the Roman poet, Virgil (70–19 BC), conceived it was not merely between opposing navies or rival would-be emperors: it was a vital stand against 'every kind of monstrous god and barking Anubis too' (Virgil, *Aeneid*, 8.698). Even the Hellenistic Jew who composed the *Wisdom of Solomon*, and insisted that 'God hates nothing that He has made (why else would He have made it?)' (*Wisdom of Solomon* 11.24), took pleasure in recounting how the very creatures that the Egyptians had foolishly worshipped, 'reptiles devoid of reason and mere vermin', were used to chastise them (ibid., 11.15–20).[9] Even Plutarch of Chaeronea (46–120 AD) thought that portraying the gods as animals must lead 'the weak and innocent into "superstition" (*deisidaimonia*), and the cynical and bold into "atheistic and bestial reasoning" (*atheos kai theriodes logismos*)' (see Gilhus 2006, p. 98, after Plutarch, *On Isis and Osiris*, 71).

But once it is agreed that the gods are active among us, and that every thing emerges equally from emptiness, why shouldn't non-human animals be recognized as images of the divine? Is it supposed that they would be bad examples, and that anyone who admires them would be bound to copy their behaviour? But non-Egyptian moralists, including those philosophers who placed most emphasis on the rational powers, have drawn morals from the behaviour of non-humans. And non-Egyptian diviners – far more so than Egyptians – have imagined that we could learn lessons about the future from their conduct, or their entrails. Presumably, it has been thought ridiculous to suppose that the gods could be like 'animals' because we'd rather forget that we are cannibals, and that is why – so Empedocles was to say – we have been condemned to continued life on earth (Empedocles 31B115DK: Waterfield 2000, p. 153). And that life is both good and bad.

> All those whom you have created dance before you – wild animals jump up, birds flutter their wings, fish leap in the water, and even the king joins, with the divine baboons, in the general jubilation. (Hornung 1982, pp. 202–3, after assorted Egyptian hymns)

Tales from the North

Herodotus supposes that of the three continents Asia, Africa and Europe, the last is by far the largest, stretching indefinitely to the north, and not even surrounded by the encircling Ocean in which other enquirers believed (see Strabo 1.1.8 [1929, vol. 1, p. 17]: 'the inhabited world is an island').

The initial spread of Neolithic agricultural technique and of Indo-European languages lies long before the place and period I am describing. More recently, the descent of Indo-European peoples into the peninsulas of Greece and Italy, or down through the eastern coasts to batter at Egypt, were recalled – by Greeks at any rate – as the return of the Sons of Heracles. It was also recognized that the Persians – though in some accounts these were the literal and moral enemy – were close kin. It is possible that the invaders brought with them more than horses, and more than a belief in the Eternal Sky: perhaps they brought the caste structure that has had its clearest form in India. Dumézil (1988, 1996), at any rate, detected signs of the distinctions in the mythology of Greece and the invented history of Rome: priestly and warrior castes presided over the property-owning caste as well as the caste of servants – and the great mass of aboriginal, 'untouchable', casteless peoples. Maybe this structure had some subliminal influence on the classes of Plato's Republic. But neither Greece nor Italy retained any strong tradition of a priestly caste distinguished from the armed nobility – though Diodorus mentions (1.28.5) a claim that the Athenians show their Egyptian origin by having three castes: the well-educated *eupatrids*, armed *geomoroi* and tool-using *demiourgoi*. Nor is there much sign, at least until the late Roman imperial period, of local and professional castes of the other sort familiar in Hindu India: *jati* as distinct from the four *varnas*. The axis of purity and pollution that determines Hindu hierarchy (and may also have been brought there by the Indo-European influx and influence) is not without its parallels in the Mediterranean world, but it does not have the same effects.

These features of the 'Northern' world were not remembered by Mediterranean enquirers. Indeed, it seems that enquirers were often none too happy to acknowledge any northern influence, whereas nineteenth century (Northern) scholars much preferred to suppose that the ancient Greeks and their culture came from the north (on which see Burkert 1992, pp. 1–6) – modern Greeks, some even suggested, could only be Levantine immigrants and 'Real Greeks' must be blondes! The ancient testimony is otherwise. Delos and Dodona had a tradition that missionaries had come with gifts from the Hyperboreans (that happy people from the back of the North Wind), and that the gifts still came regularly, passed on from tribe to tribe until they reached the shrines (Herodotus 4.33–6). But what the gifts amounted to, who knows? The island-city of Clazomenae, on the west coast of Anatolia, celebrated the annual arrival of Apollo from the Hyperboreans, in a chariot drawn by swans.[10] The Druids were sometimes mentioned alongside Magi and the Gymnosophists, as practising ascetics and esoteric sages, but any congruence between a Mediterranean thought and rumours of what northern tribes and peoples might believe was explained by saying – for example – that Zalmoxis was a sometime slave of Pythagoras, who deceived his fellow tribesmen, the Getae, into thinking that he had come back from the dead (Herodotus 4.94–6), and so convincing them that they were all immortal.

Is the ancient ambivalence about northern influence (by contrast with readiness to acknowledge Egyptian and Phoenician sources) to be explained by general unwillingness, on the part of coastal settlements, to investigate what was going on inland? Was it remembered that there had been past invasions (including the Amazon invasion of Attica – though some said they came from the East) which had assisted in the collapse of an earlier culture, and that in historical memory 'the Celts' succeeded in besieging both Delphi (279 BC) and Rome (390 BC)? Is it that 'the Scythians' (as the most general name for many different peoples, including – sometimes – Persians) were perceived as houseless wanderers, without any settled cities, and so 'uncivilized', having nothing to contribute to the Mediterranean world? Even Poseidonius of Apamea and Rhodes (135–51 BC) who seems to have visited the North, and talked to 'the Celts', emphasised the 'barbaric' aspects of their life, their duels to the death over trivialities, their nailing the heads of their enemies to the porches of their doors (see Kidd 1999, pp. 346–7). Or is it simply that mainstream Classical thought distrusted what 'the Scythians' were saying, not because they were Scythians but because believing them would turn the world upside down? What they were saying was that we were all immortal. Valerius Maximus is aggrieved that the Gauls are prepared to lend money, on condition that they be repaid 'in the Underworld': he would call them fools, except – (is it ironical?) – that Pythagoras agreed (2.6.10: 2004, p. 59; see also *Matthew* 6.19–20).

Some debts were sometimes acknowledged, at least by those disposed to accept the doctrine. Plato (*Charmides* 156 D) suggests that Socrates had learnt 'a charm' from a physician of the 'Thracian king Zalmoxis': no bodily ill, he said, could be cured without attending also to 'the soul'. Socrates chose to interpret 'charms' as arguments of the sort that philosophers now enjoy – but we should consider conversely whether those arguments are charms. That is what we need to counteract the effects of natural enchantments, the delusions pressed upon us by our bodily natures – that things happening here and now, at the human scale, to Me, are more important than what is happening 'in truth'. 'Just as the irrational part [even of the good man] is affected by incantations so he himself by counter-chants and counter-incantations will dissolve the powers on the other side' (Plotinus *Ennead* IV.4 [28].43). As Hilary Armstrong has written, 'philosophical discussion and reflection are not simply means for solving intellectual problems (though they are and must be that). They are also charms, counter-charms, for the deliverance of the soul' (Armstrong 1967, p. 260, after Plotinus *Ennead* V.3 [49].17).

Another visitor from the North, contemporaneous with Pythagoras, was Abaris (Herodotus 4.36; see also Porphyry, *Life of Pythagoras*, 29: Guthrie 1987, p. 129), who travelled around the lands of the

Greeks (including Italy) with an arrow, sent from the 'Hyperboreans' to cure the plague. Kingsley (2010) has argued that details given uncomprehendingly by Herodotus and other ancient sources make it likely that Abaris was an Avar, carrying a golden arrow as a symbol of his ambassadorial status – and also as a focus for the practice of entranced walking. This latter is attested in Mongol and Tibetan culture: a mental discipline that allows the walker to travel huge distances without growing tired or fretful. It was said – at any rate by Iamblichus (245–325 AD) – that he joined with Pythagoras in seeking to convert the tyrant Phalaris (notorious for his cruelties) to virtue. They both failed.

A stranger contact with the North was Aristeas of Proconnesus (an island city in the Propontis, between the Mediterranean and the Black Sea), in the seventh century BC: it is said that he vanished from his home after seeming to fall dead, and reappeared seven years later to deliver a poem, the *Arimaspea*, about his travels, 'possessed by Apollo', in the North. More oddly still, he reappeared 240 years later, in southern Italy, claiming to have been with Apollo, as a raven. The poem, long vanished except for snippets, seems to have described tribes in the vast North, bordering on Hyperborea, some from personal acquaintance, and some only by report. There in the North, he said, there were one-eyed men at war with gold-guarding griffins (very possibly the latter were inferred from the fossil remains of protoceratops, in the Gobi badlands, and the former were either inferred from elephant skulls – whose nasal cavity might suggest a single eye – or were the hairy hominids of legend: Mayor and Heaney 1993). There also were the Hyperboreans themselves, where Apollo dwells in winter. It has been argued both that Aristeas was an adventurer, and that he was a shaman (see Bolton 1962; West 2004). Most of us will probably believe that the *Arimaspea* was a collection of tall tales (even if told by Scythians), and that whoever appeared in Italy it wasn't the man from Proconnesus. What the story reminds us is that Apollo was Hyperborean, and that the North means immortality, and god-possession.

Apollo, as Kingsley (1999, pp. 87–92; 2010, pp. 119–22) observes, has often been misunderstood. According to Guthrie (1950, p. 73):

He is the very embodiment of the Hellenic spirit. Everything that marks off the Greek outlook from that of other peoples, and in particular from the barbarians who surrounded them – beauty of every sort, whether of art, music, poetry or youth, sanity and moderation – are all summed up in Apollo.

But far from being supremely 'rational', the god of seeing clearly and seeing whole, Apollo is associated with prophetic madness, dangerous riddles, plague, betrayal and the very distant. 'The oracles he gave out were full of riddles, full of ambiguities and traps' (Kingsley 1999, p. 87). He is 'a god of impossible enigmas' (Kingsley 2010, p. 43), and sometimes cruelty. His rivals, such as Marsyas, perish (in that case, flayed alive for losing a music contest by a trick). Those who are 'loved' by him are usually as unfortunate: Daphne becomes a laurel bush, Hyacinth and Coronis are both killed, and Cassandra will never be believed for all her accurate prophecies. As the patron of philosophy – for it was he who told Chairephon that Socrates was the wisest of mortal men, and so set Socrates upon the life-long quest that led to his execution (Plato, *Apology*, 21a) – it must be a kind of philosophy at once more dangerous and more obscure than moderns now remember. Pythagoras, so Abaris agreed, was an incarnation of Apollo – very much as a Tibetan lama may be a returning Buddha (see Kingsley 2010, pp. 39–41, 116–8) – but not because he could do geometry!

When the citizens of Cyme were required to hand over a rebel against Persia who had claimed sanctuary with them, they sent to the oracle of Apollo run by the Branchidae at Didyma[11], near Miletus, to ask if this would be allowed. On being told that it was, they asked again, and the same reply was given.

> Thereupon Aristodicus [a sceptical member of the delegation] deliberately did as follows. Going around the circuit of the temple he removed the sparrows and any other birds that were nesting in the temple. While he was engaged in this a voice is said to have issued from the sanctuary and reached Aristodicus, saying the following: 'Most sacrilegious of men, how dare you do these things? Why are you removing my suppliants from the temple?' Not disturbed by this, Aristodicus spoke as follows: 'O Lord, do you yourself go to the aid of suppliants in this way, and yet order the Cymaeans to surrender a suppliant?' The reply came in these words: 'Yes, I so bid you, in order that you may be rapidly destroyed as guilty of impiety, and so that in the future you will no longer ask the oracle about surrendering a suppliant'. (Herodotus 6.159)

The first implication is obvious: the god did not approve of surrendering a suppliant, any more than he approved of the behaviour of Glaucus of Sparta, who despite having the reputation of an honest man, seriously considered embezzling money left in his charge (and asked the oracle at Delphi if that was allowed: Herodotus 6.86). Even his hurriedly repenting for having asked the question did not satisfy Apollo. The second is that the god, by this account, was ready to goad enquirers to their deaths – as Delphi notoriously did to Croesus, telling him that he would destroy an empire if he made war on Persia (and omitting to mention that it would be his)[12]. We may believe that all such oracles were frauds, and that the cunning priests whose job it was to translate the oracle's ramblings were only playing politics. But the point is to notice what Apollo's worshippers expected: oracles weren't clear or unambiguous, nor did they get their authority from any rational thought, nor did the god intend to do us good. 'The lord whose oracle is in Delphi neither speaks nor suppresses, but indicates' (Heracleitos 22B93DK: Waterfield 2000, p. 40).

Does this fit his northern provenance? Our problem is that whereas the East and South were literate, we have no written testimony from the North to cover the Classical or pre-classical period. Nor can we be sure that later Scandinavian writings, for example, Snorri Sturluson's *Prose Edda* (thirteenth century AD), have any close relationship with earlier, 'Scythian', material. Sturluson treated Norse myths very much as Diodorus treated Egyptian myths: the gods were the heroes who fled from Troy, 'that goodliest of homes and haunts that ever have been'. But he also included more familiar, mythological motifs. The world began from the interplay of frost and fire in Ginnungagap, the Void, and the gods of proper order were late comers who constructed the present cosmos from the body of the murdered giant, Ymir. '[The sons of Bor] took Ymir and bore him into the middle of the Yawning Void, and made of him the earth: of his blood the sea and the waters; the land was made of his flesh, and the crags of his bones; gravel and stones they fashioned from his teeth and his grinders and from those bones that were broken' (Sturluson 1916, pp. 20–1).

We may also guess that their worshippers expected the world to end, and maybe to be renewed – as other peoples have expected too, drawing on the memory of disaster. 'An axe-age, a sword-age, shields shall be cloven; a wind-age, a wolf-age, ere the world totters' (Sturluson 1916, p. 79).

As the Romans pressed out into Gaul they 'recognized' some of the northern gods. The days of the week, as they are named in Germanic and in Romance tongues, record the imagined identities: Sun and Moon are easy; Tiu matches Mars, Woden Mercury, Thor Jupiter and Freya Venus. The identifications are not arbitrary, but may still be very misleading. None of the Aesir at first seem much like Apollo – except that Odin (or Woden) is the god of inspiration, of diseases and their cure, is always asking riddles; and Saga, goddess of story-telling, is his daughter. He also has two ravens (Hugin and Munin: that is, Thought and Memory) and two wolves (Geri and Freki: Greedy and Avaricious) as companions. Apollo is also Lykeios, 'wolfish'. His mother Leto arrived in Delos (which as a floating island was neither land nor sea) from Hyperborea in the form of a wolf, and accompanied by wolves (Bridgman 2005, pp. 69–70). Like Apollo, Odin holds us to our word – but was himself a betrayer. If Apollo came out of the North, then perhaps he was once like Odin (see Grimm 1882, vol. 1, p. 147). Or else, as Kingsley has proposed, the Hyperboreans were Mongols, whose god was the Eternal Sky.

Neither suggestion is simply a slight historical hypothesis. Who can tell what routes ideas travel by, or why one imagined god may pick up traits from another? Both draw attention to aspects of an obviously 'Greek' god that are obscured as long as we imagine that the Greeks were 'unique' or 'rational' in the ways we now expect. Both also suggest that there is something to be said for madness and inspiration, however harsh they seem.

Tales from the past

The eruption of Santorini, which is recalled in myth as a revolt against the gods, and which has sometimes been blamed for the end of the Minoan Era, in fact happened rather earlier (in 1636 BC, according to evidence from a buried olive-tree) than the more general collapse of Mediterranean civilization half a millennium later. The explanation for that collapse may be cumulative, and climatic: several years of drought damaged local crops, and set tribes wandering. The Hittite empire disintegrated, and its capital Hattusa was sacked, and thoroughly forgotten. 'The Peoples of the Sea' were met and defeated by the Egyptian armies, but settled along the coast of Palestine (and were later known as Philistines). Northern tribes descended into Greece, calling themselves the Sons of Heracles. The people of Israel took refuge for a while in Egypt (and eventually escaped again). The memory of earlier days faded into myth.

The world of the ancient Mediterranean was influenced in the aftermath by Tyrrhenians, Phoenicians and Greeks: all these peoples traded widely and settled themselves in colonies from Gades to Olbia. The Tyrrhenians are mostly remembered as Etruscans – an Italian society whose art suggests a happy domesticity, but of whom we know almost nothing. These various peoples, successors to the second millennium empires, learnt history from Egypt, Mesopotamia and the Anatolian kingdoms. What the Phoenicians made of this we do not know: their records have been lost, by normal attrition, and deliberate destruction. When Rome obliterated Carthage, in 146 BC, they handed the library over to the kingdom of Numidia, but it does not seem that the texts survived the later wars between Rome and King Jugurtha. Juba II, who finally inherited the kingdom (and also Mauretania) as a vassal king, was an assiduous scholar and natural historian, but such fragments of his work as have survived do not include a distinctive Phoenician philosophy. Nor did Cleitomachus (formerly known as Hasdrubal), a Carthaginian philosopher who survived the fall of Carthage by having migrated to Athens to study with Carneades some years before, record Phoenician history or philosophy. The legend of Carthage's foundation was that Elissa of Tyre, the widow of a priest of Melqart murdered by her brother, was its first ruler, and that she burnt herself alive rather than be remarried to a native king – the story was remodelled by the Roman poet Virgil. What notions of honour, or the afterlife, lay behind this imagined choice we do not know.

It is possible that the *Phoenician History* (see Baumgarten 1981), attributed to Sanchuniathon of Berytus (putatively, writing around the time of the Trojan War) by his purported translator Herennius Philo of Byblos, recorded a genuine tradition, though it was more likely Philo than Sanchuniathon that interpreted the stories about the gods as stories about mortal heroes. Other authors refer to Sanchuniathon – but say nothing that they could not have copied from Philo. On the other hand, the names that Philo offers in his theogony have been confirmed as Phoenician in much older inscriptions, and he may have been right to suggest that the earliest gods of Phoenicia were the fixed and planetary stars. His Euhemeristic account of Ouranos, Kronos and Zeus (as a dysfunctional family) could be derived from Hesiod rather than any Phoenician source, but might also be evidence of the way that the older Hittite story was transmitted from Anatolia. Euhemeristic explanation of mythology may have had a beginning with Hecataeus of Miletus, and Miletus was a *polis* much influenced by the Phoenicians. Perhaps Euhemerism was a Phoenician practice. Just possibly, they worshipped sun, moon, stars and the elements at first, and added assorted generals, admirals, kings and innovators to the pantheon only later. 'So, says Polybius, each one of the gods came to honour because he discovered something useful to man' (Strabo 1.2.15: 1929, vol. 1, p. 87). But even those philosophers – Numenius, Porphyry, Iamblichus – who were Phoenician in ancestry and original habitation (Apamea on the Orontes, Tyre and Syrian Chalcis respectively) were not certainly Phoenician in their language or philosophy, and neither were they Euhemerists.

The nearest we can otherwise come to the Phoenician story is from the writings of their relatives, the Hebrews: speaking a different dialect of a common tongue. That Hebrew story is significant in its own right, not merely as a way of re-imagining Phoenician thought. 'The history of the Near East in the Roman period in no way supports the notion that the common use of a group of Semitic languages (Aramaic in its various dialects, Hebrew and – perhaps still – Phoenician) instilled any sense of a common ethnic or cultural identity in its various peoples' (Millar 1997, p. 252). There must nonetheless have been some common history, and a folk-memory of catastrophe, interpreted differently by different peoples. In Mesopotamian story, the great Flood was engineered by the gods because they were irritated by human noise. In the Hebrew story – as also in the Greek – the Flood was a response to human wickedness, as also were later disasters. Sodom and Gomorrah were destroyed, the Hebrew writings said, because of their brutal inhospitality, their lack of compassion for strangers and the poor. 'This was the iniquity of your sister Sodom: she and her daughters had pride of wealth and food in plenty, comfort and ease, and yet she never helped the poor and wretched' (*Ezekiel* 16.49). One crime is relevant for Carthaginian history: the sacrifice of children as burnt offerings to their gods (see also Baumgarten 1981, pp. 221, 244–52). In Greek legend, such sacrifices were also cannibalistic, and the gods were revolted. That was the occasion for Deucalion's

Flood. In the Hebrew story, Abraham showed that he too was ready to sacrifice his son to God – if that was what his God required: the concluding moral was that God did not, after all, require it (*Genesis* 22.1–18). The test wasn't only of Abraham's obedient faith, but also of God's compassion. What he was *not* being asked to do was obey his God's command rather than the moral law: 'the moral law' (i.e. the customs of his day) in fact required the murder.[13]

The Hebrews thought of themselves as having returned from exile: in the earliest days, from Egypt, where their ancestors had taken refuge during a famine, and in later, historical time, from Babylon. This too was a theme familiar to the Greeks: the Sons of Heracles, as they defined themselves, were returning both to mainland Greece and to other coastal regions, because Heracles had been there before them, and laid a claim on the land. Like the Hebrews, they tried to make the indigenous peoples into serfs (or killed them): 'hewers of wood and drawers of water' (*Joshua* 9.22–7). The Lacedaimonians, as the most prominent of 'Dorian' peoples, successfully enslaved the people they found, as 'helots', and conducted a permanent war against their serfs. The Hebrews were less successful in intimidating all Canaanites, and less successful in battle against established cities. It paid better, in the end, to trade than seek to kill. And they did retain a memory that they had themselves been slaves in Egypt, and should therefore be more kind. Some Greeks, like the Athenians, preferred to say that they had never left, that they were the indigenous peoples – though Herodotus records a story that there was a Phoenician settlement in Athens, absorbed into the Athenian people (Herodotus 5.57). In this the Athenians were like the settled Phoenician townships, such as Tyre and Sidon. Suano (2003) has intriguingly suggested that the various peoples remembered in Egypt as 'the Peoples of the Sea' were escaped slaves, refugees and rebels from the collapsing Hittite Empire. There was a general folk memory of having escaped from tyranny, not only among the Hebrews. And it was the bonds of trade that saved the post-imperial age from descending entirely into a pirate age.

The Hebrews remembered, or invented, a story that Abram's father, Terah, had migrated from Ur of the Chaldees, and Abram (later to be called Abraham) in his turn from Haran in northern Palestine (*Genesis* 11.31–12.9). That is, they abandoned city life, and the astrological religion with which Chaldeans were associated, to live as pastoral nomads. Abraham and his kin wandered round Palestine, and even down to Egypt, leaving shrines and memories for the returning Hebrews. Philo of Alexandria (fl.40 AD), in his massive attempt to make philosophical capital out of the Hebrew Scriptures (without denying their historicity), makes the migration a claim about the proper order of philosophy.

> Pray do not spin airy fables about moon or sun or the objects in the sky and in the universe so far removed from us and so varied in their natures, until you have scrutinized and come to know yourselves. After that we may perhaps believe you when you hold forth on other subjects: but before you establish who you yourselves are do not think that you will ever become capable of acting as judges or trustworthy witnesses in the other matters. (Philo, *De Migratione Abrahamis*, 1.38: (1929–62), vol. 4, p. 211)

Philo also equated Terah with Socrates, 'for the latter grew old in the most accurate study by which he could hope to know himself, never once directing his philosophical speculations to the subjects beyond himself. But he was really a man; but Terah is the principle itself which is proposed to every one' (Philo, *De Somniis*, 1.55f: (1929–62), vol. 5, pp. 325f., after *Genesis* 11.31–12.6; see Gruen 2002, p. 229).

There are Mesopotamian traces in the Hebrew Scriptures, whether these were from Abram's day or from the Babylonian Exile (when the peoples of the southern kingdom of Judah were relocated – like many other peoples – by the current imperial power, until Cyrus the Persian took Babylon, and allowed them to return). Even the detail that Adam was created as a gardener may recall the tale that human beings were made for the servile work that the junior gods didn't like! It is also likely that the God of the Hebrews once had a female partner, like the Baalim of their Phoenician cousins, that he had, like Marduk, defeated 'Rahab' or 'the dragon in the deep' (*Job* 26.12; *Isaiah* 51.9; *Psalm* 89.10) and remade her body into the ordered realm we know. Once upon a time the Hebrews felt like other peoples, Greek and Phoenician both, about the springs and spinneys of their land. Consider the story of the Aramaean commander, Naaman, who begged the prophet Elisha (nineth century BC) to cure him of 'leprosy' (2 *Kings* 5.1–14). Elisha, without bothering to meet him, told him to go and bathe in the river Jordan. Naaman was offended at the idea that the Jordan might have any extra power than 'Abana and Pharpar, rivers of Damascus', but decided to try the experiment, and was cured. The Greeks would have attributed the cure to the local river-god, or possibly to the magic cloak that Elisha had inherited from his master, the still scarier prophet Elijah. In the Hebrew Scriptures, Elisha has been given the power of Yahweh to heal or kill: Yahweh is Lord – by experimental proof – in a manner that doesn't allow any lesser power to get the credit (see Urbach 1979, pp. 102–3). What happens in the world happens by Yahweh's will, and that can be discovered by watching to see what happens: most notably, arrogance leads to disaster (as Herodotus agreed).

Both Hebrews and Greeks tried to make sense of their half-remembered past, by obsessive genealogizing – locating all present towns and peoples within a genealogy that would explain and justify their presence. Both recalled a time when 'there were giants', or 'demi-gods', the product of liaisons between 'the sons of God' and 'the daughters of men'. For the Hebrews, all these perished in the Flood. The Greeks suggested that Zeus engineered the Theban and the Trojan Wars not merely because there were 'enough born, even too many' (Blake 'Four Zoas' 7.121–2: 1966, p. 323), but specifically to eliminate the race of 'heroes' or remove them from contention (Burkert 1992, p. 101–3, after Hesiod, *Catalogues*, fr.204.96ff). Even though it was Zeus who had scattered his seed to make heroes, with some intention of taming the wild places of the world, he had concluded that most of his heroic offspring did more harm than good. Sometimes this was because they were driven mad by Hera, but often they were simply proud and greedy. The stories summarized by Apollodorus agree with those of Herodotus, that people, especially powerful people, are so strenuous in their own immediate self-interest, so prone to taking violent offence at any imagined slight, that they routinely ruined themselves, their families and their cities. Even the victors of the Trojan War were ruined, returning home to find their cities in rebellion, and their wives – except Penelope – unfaithful. Once upon a time the gods were visible, on occasion, and took a part in human history. There might be occasional and ambiguous signs that they still were – but when Poseidon spitefully blocked the harbour of the Phaeacians – the gatekeepers, it seems, of the Other World in which Odysseus and others wandered – there were no further intrusions. Zeus and the Fates from then on acted impartially, and there was to be no escape. So also the Hebrews recalled an earlier day in which God might walk in the Garden, or Abraham argue with Him, as a man might speak to a friend. Nowadays was different, and might be very much worse. Fortunately, there were reforming law-givers in their past: Minos, like Moses, brought down laws from his conversation with the god – Minos from Zeus on Mount Ida, Moses from Yahweh on Mount Sinai. Lycurgus founded the Spartan constitution, in partial imitation of earlier Cretan models. Successive reformers in Athens abolished older tribal and familial loyalties in favour of new local demes and fellowships. Good Order was a necessary, vital measure to restrain a foolish 'self-interest'.

Hebrews and Greeks alike could fall into the trap of one-man rule, whether the rulers were labelled kings or tyrants. They often could not trust themselves, it seems, to keep to the law they had sworn to, or to stay uncorrupted. Better therefore, they thought, allow one man the power to punish and control, even though that man could also be foolishly 'self-interested' or insane. Better, the Hebrews decided in defiance of the prophet Samuel's warning (*1 Samuel* 8.11–22), to have a king to represent them to the other nations. The northern tribes soon broke away from Jerusalem, and endured a succession of short-lived dynasties (almost as short indeed as the Greek tyrants managed) until the Assyrian Empire dismantled the northern kingdom (Israel), and took most of its people away from Palestine in about 720 BC. The Davidic line lasted longer in the southern kingdom (Judah) until the Babylonian Empire did the same to them. When Babylon fell to the Persians, Cyrus – and Darius after him – restored Jerusalem, and the returning Hebrews established their uniquely theocratic order in obedience, they said, to Truth. At one of the debates encouraged by King Darius between three members of his bodyguards, enquiring what was strongest, Zerubbabel – a Jewish soon-to-be statesman who was serving the Persian king as a bodyguard or page – replied first by pointing out – a little pertly – that however powerful the King might be he would do anything to please his favourite concubine, and then by advancing instead the claim for Truth herself:

> Truth is great and stronger than all else. The whole earth calls on truth; the sky praises her. All created things shake and tremble; with her there is no injustice. There is injustice in wine, in kings, in women, in all men, and in all their works, and so forth. There

is no truth in them; they shall perish in their injustice. But truth abides and is strong for ever; she lives and rules for ever and ever. With her there is no favouritism or partiality; she chooses to do justice rather than what is unjust and evil. All approve her works; in her judgments there is no injustice. Hers are strength and royalty, the authority and majesty of all ages. Praise be to the God of truth! (*1 Esdras* 4.35–40)

All the people, it was said, agreed that the Truth trumped pretty women, royal power and drink, and Darius fulfilled his promise to restore Jerusalem and its people. Commentators are mostly convinced that the story is a fable. The tag line about the greatness of truth is a familiar aphorism – recorded indeed in the *Institutions of Ptahhotep*: 'truth is great; it endures; it is firmly established'. This is also said of Justice (Delcor 1989, pp. 491–2).

Three morals remain from the story. The first is observed by Gruen (1998, pp. 162–7), who points out that King Darius emerges as drunken, tyrannous and besotted (but strangely and untypically ready to accept these jibes from his young staff): the principal moral, he suggests, is that the Jews obtained their freedom by their cynical and courageous attitude to power. The second related moral is that the Hebrews, unlike the Hellenes, built their remembered past around the experience of defeat, enslavement, exile: whereas the common imagined past of the Hellenes was the heroic age, the imagined past of the Hebrews was of a nation regularly restored as long as it sought to follow 'truth'. The third moral – or the third puzzle – is to understand what they meant by 'truth'. Neither Hebrews nor Hellenes meant any mere correspondence of word and world: speaking the truth is not necessarily just to say of what is that it is. *Aletheia*, by a familiar pun, is what is not-hidden or not-forgotten. *Emeth* is 'enduring loyalty' (Berkovits 1969, p. 291), what can be relied upon, a judgement or attitude not perverted by self-interest or stupidity.

There was another imagined history that had effects at least on philosophical theorists, if not on the general population. Diodorus (1.8.1–8) records the familiar theme, also reported by Plato in his *Protagoras*, and Lucretius in his great poem *On the Nature of Things*:

The first men to be born led an undisciplined and bestial life, setting out one by one to secure their sustenance and taking for their food both the tenderest herbs and the fruits of wild trees. Then, since they were attacked by the wild beasts, they came to each other's aid, being instructed by expediency, and when gathered together in this way by reason of their fear, they gradually came to recognize their mutual characteristics. And though the sounds which they made were at first unintelligible and indistinct, yet gradually they came to give articulation to their speech, and by agreeing with one another upon symbols for each thing which presented itself to them, made known among themselves the significance which was to be attached to each term. But since groups of this kind arose over every part of the inhabited world, not all men had the same language, inasmuch as every group organized the elements of its speech by mere chance. This is the explanation of the present existence of every conceivable kind of language, and, furthermore, out of these first groups to be formed came all the original nations of the world. Now the first men, since none of the things useful for life had yet been discovered, led a wretched existence, having no clothing to cover them, knowing not the use of dwelling and fire, and also being totally ignorant of cultivated food. For since they also even neglected the harvesting of the wild food, they laid by no store of its fruits against their needs; consequently large numbers of them perished in the winters because of the cold and the lack of food. Little by little, however, experience taught them both to take to the caves in winter and to store such fruits as could be preserved. And when they had become acquainted with fire and other useful things, the arts also and whatever else is capable of furthering man's social life were gradually discovered. Indeed, speaking generally, in all things it was necessity itself that became man's teacher, supplying in appropriate fashion instruction in every matter to a creature which was well endowed by nature and had, as its assistants for every purpose, hands and speech and sagacity of mind.

The story is a fable, resting only on what might be imagined true, without any attempt to see and understand how contemporary 'savages' lived, or even how 'wild beasts' lived. If our actual ancestors were ever thus ignorant and alone, they died. Since they didn't – or lived at least quite long enough to bear and rear their children – we know that they were not ignorant and alone. Neither sociality nor language can be invented in quite that way. If our ancestors once lived a 'bestial life', it was not undisciplined, nor solitary, nor even very short. Why then should this implausible story still seem more 'rational' than a folk memory of peoples bound by the natural lusts and affections, and familiar from their beginning with the supplies that 'nature' offered? We may suspect that presently established powers found it convenient to suggest that there was no alternative to Leviathan, and that a 'state-less' society was a contradiction.

CHAPTER THREE

Inspired thinkers

Seeking the unseen

The poets who were the first to speak for Greece supposed that Something came out of Nothing and became, through slow degrees, the world of human, Greek experience: mortals stumbled through the world in fear of beautiful or horrid presences, but not without their mortal dignity. The all-seeing Sky demanded that people keep their promises and offer hospitality to all. Zeus Xenios, Zeus Horkios (God of Strangers, God of Oaths) would not leave treachery unavenged, nor allow mere mortals to rise up too high for long. Back in the age of Kronos we did what we desired, but now live under discipline. The stories the poets told were also scandalous, as though the powers were vast and lustful children, shaped in the imagination of those who thought success would be to conquer their enemies and feast in comfort. Later Platonists were to allegorize the stories or recover their original meanings, and thereby inspire first Aristobulos of Paneas (fl. 160 BC) and then Philo, both Alexandrian Jews, to find new, philosophical, meanings in the Torah.

Xenophanes of Colophon despised the myths. No image of Zeus as man-like, bull-like or a golden rain, could be acceptable, and nor could Zeus be moved by lusts and angers of a lesser kind. Such stories were projections.

If cows and horses or lions had hands, or could draw with their hands and make things as men can, horses would have drawn horse-like gods, cows cow-like gods. (Xenophanes 21B15DK: Waterfield 2000, p. 27)

It is a thought more powerful than is commonly understood: as David Hume also enquired, 'what peculiar privilege has this little agitation of the brain which we call "thought" that we must thus make it the model of the whole universe?'[1] And why, correspondingly, should we imagine that creatures like us can internalize and understand the workings of the world? Only if there is a god in us, is that remotely plausible.

Elsewhere on the Mediterranean shore, similarly indignant prophets – both Hebrews and the Magi – denied that God could be pictured (but was not humanity itself somehow made in His image?), or that He had a beginning. God could only be known as the God of Justice, and the people of Israel were self-defined as His alone, while the other nations served, at best, His servants. Not that the Hebrews were unanimously monotheistic: as before, the prophets' denunciation of infanticide, ritual prostitution and the worship of Phoenician Baalim showed otherwise. The Jews who returned from Babylon reconstructed their lives, and their history, in obedience to a vision, and slowly worked out how to maintain it when the Seleucid monarchs, heirs to Alexander, sought to integrate them into a Hellenistic Empire.

Later generations were to acknowledge the Hebrews as a 'nation of philosophers', self-dedicated to living as philosophers should, by God's laws, not the king's nor any mob's commands (there were some less accurate, and also some more hostile accounts: see Gruen 1998, pp. 41–72). It may not be obvious at first that Greek philosophers were saying the same as Hebrew prophets. But Xenophanes' Principle had some effect: we shouldn't project our qualities on to the origin of all things. If there can't be creatures like us till late in the world's development, we can't explain its origin by saying that something like us created it. Or if we suppose, conversely, that the properties we have are images or echoes of the Creator's nature, we would have to acknowledge that everything else is just as much an image or an echo. Neither the apophatic nor the kataphatic way (to use a later distinction: *apophasis* rejects all descriptions of the Creator; *kataphasis* imagines properties purified or exalted) gives us any good reason to suppose that God is more human than non-human, even in being 'rational' (Cleanthes was to disagree: Long and Sedley [hereafter LS] 1987, p. 326: 54I). The same applies to every other description of the Origin of things. If Thales was right to say that *water* was the root of things, it was not *watery* water, common water, that he meant. Maybe he only meant, like Heracleitos of Ephesus (fl.500 BC), that 'everything flows'; maybe he only sought the most obvious image for that Thing 'in which we live and move and have our being' (*Acts* 17.28, after Epimenides' *Cretica*). Maybe he only meant that everything depends on water. Maybe he had noticed that Egypt – and especially the Delta – was the gift of the Nile, that water generated soil. But probably his chief goal was a moral and religious one, not merely (or at all) a cosmological. According to Cicero, he said that 'men ought to believe that everything they see is filled with gods, for all would then be purer, just as they feel the power of religion most deeply when they are performing religious rites' (Cicero, *De Legibus*, 2.10 (26): Liebeschuetz 1979, p. 49).

The poets had known that the gods 'took shapes' that were not essentially their own, that they spoke another language, breathed a different air, and yet were not entirely alien. Everything reflected deity. Philosophers like Xenophanes insisted instead that deity was utterly unlike everything, and hence was indescribable. Truth lies in the depths, so Democritus of Abdera (c460–357 BC) declared (and also *Ecclesiastes* 7.24: 'whatever has happened lies beyond our grasp, deep down, deeper than man can fathom'). And 'nature loves to hide', according to Heracleitos (22B123DK: Waterfield 2000, p. 40). The aphorisms are ones that now seem obvious: how things really are, and how they seem to us, to anyone, are not necessarily, or at all, the same. The world as creatures like us experience it didn't exist until we did, and how things 'really are' (or would be in our absence) is outside our sphere of knowledge. The thought was consciously paradoxical. The Greek word that we translate as 'truth' is *Aletheia*, and a stream of puns makes clear that the Greeks could, if they chose, hear this as 'the Unhidden', or as 'the Unforgotten' (see Heidegger 1949, pp. 330ff; Clark 1991, pp. 48–54: *lanthanein* is to escape notice; *lethe* is forgetfulness). The Truth that lies in the Democritean depths, the Nature that loves to hide, are paradoxical because 'the Truth' should rather be what does not hide, the obvious. The truth is what we cannot escape because it never sets, because there is no other thing than truth to take its place (as darkness replaces light) – as Heracleitos said (22B16DK: Waterfield 2000, p. 42). The Truth is the all-seeing sky in which – and not just under which – we live. The notion that we can't escape the sky is also mentioned in Xenophon's *Anabasis*, as a reason not to forget our oaths (2.5.6).

And yet the truth is hidden (Democritus 68B117DK: Waterfield 2000, p. 176). We can't evade it, but it can evade us. Really, Democritus declared, we know nothing; all that we perceive is only true by custom. Different customs generate different sense-worlds, different stories, but the truth over-all is only 'atoms and the void'. In a later age, this 'atomism' – which had, so Poseidonius said (Strabo 16.2.24: see Gruen 2011, pp. 121, 343), been formulated first by Mochus of Sidon (a Phoenician) – can be hailed as a brilliant anticipation of current physical theory. Modern physicalists also speak as if the common human world were a complete illusion (sometimes even denying that there is any consciousness to be deceived) in which case the words and writings that propound the theory are an illusion too (more obviously so because they depend upon particular human languages to be perceived at all). Democritus was more careful, acknowledging that the very reasons that he had for thinking that the senses did not show us Truth were drawn from what the senses showed us. His atomism was less a physical theory than a mystical conclusion. Like other, earlier sages, he is said to have travelled widely in the East, and frequented graveyards to contemplate, no doubt, his dissolution (Diogenes, *Lives*, 9.38). Persons (like taste, temperature and colours) exist 'by convention': 'really' there are only atoms and the void. All ordinary objects are composed, without remainder, of atomic simples. Because there could be no infinite regress of parts, there must be unrestricted, simple singulars (atoms), without the characters of their complex products. As before, the real world, the explanans, could not itself possess the characters it was invoked to explain – but if it didn't, where did those characters come from?

Democritean atomism was no more a 'scientific hypothesis' than the Heracleitean fire, or the Hebrew God: none depended simply on observation, nor on calculation of what would follow for our experience if the hypothesis were either true or false. Neither were the other 'Ionians' engaged in anything much like science. Thales might suggest that the ultimate stuff was 'water', Anaximenes (fl.

546 BC) that it was 'air', and Heracleitos 'fire', but none, at best, were doing more than gesture towards the notion of something not yet determinate: the fluid, the undefined, the infinite, as Anaximander (c609–c546 BC) said (12A9DK: Waterfield 2000, p. 14). For there to be anything – any particular place or temperature or humidity or solidity – there must 'first' be the dimension on which such particularities are measured. Particularities, it came to seem, were constituted by the conjunction of Unlimited and Limit. Whether the stuff of things was really changed by the imposition remained an issue. Whether the forms that manifested in that stuff had any separate substance of their own was also to be disputed. At one extreme, a remark by Chuang Tzu may indicate an implication of the doctrine:

> Suppose a master foundryman is casting his metal and the metal leaps up and says, 'I must be made into the best sword'. The master foundryman would certainly consider the metal as evil. And if simply because I possess a body by chance, I were to say 'Nothing but a man! Nothing but a man!' the Creator would certainly regard me as evil. If I regard the universe as a great furnace and creation as a master foundryman, why should anywhere I go not be all right? (Chan 1963, p. 197)

On another occasion, Chuang Tzu enquired why he should be expected to grieve because the stuff that had been shaped into his wife now had a different shape. What real substance do individual forms have, whether the real stuff is a homogenous continuum or a cloud of atomic bits? The thought was explicit in a Sicilian thinker: 'no mortal thing has a beginning, nor does it end in death and obliteration; there is only a mixing and then a separating of what was mixed' (Empedocles 31B8DK: Waterfield 2000, p. 145).

This is not to suggest that China and the Mediterranean world communicated (though maybe they did). Nor is it to suggest that the Ionians drew the same moral as Chuang Tzu. It is only to emphasize that 'the Ionians' were not 'scientists', nor even 'naturalists', in the modern sense. They might, like Daoists in China, have an interest in observing what occurred. They might even – also like Daoists – have some radical views about the proper ordering of human affairs: in particular, could anything – on their philosophical view – be considered really polluting? When visitors found Heracleitos 'in the kitchen' (euphemistically: at the earth closet), they were embarrassed: he called them in, saying – as Thales had also said – that there were gods even 'there' (Aristotle, *De Partibus Animalium,* 1.645a15f). And corpses were nothing more – and also nothing less – than dung (22B96DK: Waterfield 2000, p. 46).

Their theories were not lisping attempts at modern science, but meditations on the transience of commonsensical subjects, and the strangeness of what comes 'before' our world. Their provenance is also worth recalling: Abdera, Clazomenae, Colophon, Ephesus and Miletus are near neighbours by the Gulf of Izmir, on the west coast of Turkey. Thales at least had Phoenician contacts: he may even have been influenced by Mochus of Sidon (West 1971, 28–36; 1997, p. 101). Heracleitos' oddities are rather like Ezekiel's, or Isaiah's:

I asked Isaiah what made him go naked and barefoot three years? He answer'd: 'the same thing that made our friend Diogenes, the Grecian.' I then asked Ezekiel why he ate dung, & lay so long on his right & left side? He answered, 'the desire of raising other men into a perception of the infinite: this the North American tribes practise, & is he honest who resists his genius or conscience only for the sake of present ease or gratification?' (Blake, 'Marriage of Heaven and Hell', $13: 1966, p. 154, after *Isaiah* 20.2–5, *Ezekiel* 4.4–15)[2]

Sicilians and Italians

Xenophanes left Colophon, in protest at its corruption or on its fall to Persia. In Italy, it was later said, he taught Parmenides of Elea (fifth century BC: that city being where the Phocaeans – also Ionians – settled in their flight from the Persian conquest). According to Aristotle (*Metaphysics* 1.986b20), Xenophanes was the first of the Eleatic tribe 'to postulate a unity [but] made nothing clear'. They were at least alike in dismissing 'common sense', and reaching towards an apophatic account of 'unity'. 'It is necessary', said Parmenides, 'to say and think that Being is' (28B6DK)[3]. One possible interpretation amounts to no more than the duty of being truthful, that of what is we should say that it is. Even this, though it sounds banal, is significant: why, after all, not lie, tell stories, hide away from truth? But Parmenides had more to conclude than that. Among the 'truths by convention', things we agree to reckon true but that are 'in truth' deceptive, are claims about change and possibility. Other things than are – we suppose – might be; other things than are are not; some things come to be and others cease. How can this be? What *isn't*, isn't, and so cannot be spoken of, or described. There is no such thing as nothing. There can be no void, no Nothing; nor can there be 'nothings', fictions; nor can things come to be or ever have been Nothing. Does this mean that the many things we call 'imaginary' (unicorns, chimeras and a perfect city) are real after all? Or that we are not saying or thinking anything when we pretend to think or speak of 'them': 'deaf and blind at once, dazed, undiscriminating hordes'? Parmenides concluded that there can be neither void, nor change, nor difference. The Way of Truth requires us to think that Being is, and never could be otherwise. Falsehood is also impossible – it is a claim that surfaces in several different philosophies. All and only what can be 'thought' is real. Reality is what can be thought without contradiction, and thinking is the only route to knowledge: we need to divorce ourselves from our misleading senses, and make 'thinking', 'reason', the mistress of our credulity. Some have greeted this as the dawn of 'rational' or 'intellectual' enquiry. But we shouldn't conclude that Parmenides wished us to rely on our individual human reason. Why, after all, should we? Why should we suppose that we have 'a faculty of calm and balanced reasoning'? (Kingsley 2003, p. 141). Why should we imagine that anything we have would lead to truth?

There is a problem in saying simultaneously that falsehood is impossible and that we are all deceived. And perhaps a later age was right to revert to the Egyptian insight: 'for the Egyptians the world emerges from the one, because the non-existent is one' (Hornung 1982, p. 253), and that non-existent is also the nothingness, the void, that surrounds the cosmos[4]. What was Parmenides really inspired to say? Are we to understand – as later syncretists did – that all that can be said of the one real is '*estin*', rather as the only name that the God of the Hebrews offers Moses is '*Eh'je asher eh'je*', 'I am the one that is' (or else 'I am whatever I am': the exact meaning, as I shall observe, is debatable)? It is, and must be always, everywhere, unchanging, and every other thought is an error. Or are we to understand that *everything* that we experience and believe is real, that our error is that we forget the Truth that is imaged or

represented in our experience?[5] Can this be simply the conclusion
of an abstract argument, or must one undertake the ascetic practice
that lies behind the story if one is ever to understand?
'Parmenides' inspiration': this was, indeed, exactly as he presented
it. A goddess brought him the revelation, and welcomed him into
another world, on the edge of the land of the dead.

> The goddess received me kindly. Taking in her hand my right
> hand spoke and addressed me with these words: 'Young man,
> you have reached my abode as the companion of immortal
> charioteers and of the mares which carry you. You are welcome.
> It was no ill fate that prompted you to travel this way, which
> is indeed far from mortal men, beyond their beaten paths; no,
> it was Right and Justice. You must learn everything – both the
> steady heart of well-rounded truth, and the beliefs of mortals,
> in which there is no true trust'. (Parmenides 28B1DK, 22–30:
> Waterfield 2000, pp. 57–8)

The goddess in question, Kingsley has suggested, was Persephone,
queen of the Underworld, and the patron of Phocaea (from which
the citizens of Elea came), and Parmenides was remembering or
imagining a near-death experience. Later poets and philosophers
acknowledged her as the figure of Philosophy, whether in mortal
guise (as Plato's Diotima of Mantinea, in his *Symposium*) or
immortal (as the one who visited Boethius in his cell). Kingsley
has suggested that Parmenides is depicting something more
than argument: he is recounting real experience, engendered by
'incubation'. By deliberately excluding sense experience and lying
still, the mind may become aware of its own unchanging being,
may actually notice that it is 'thinking' (and incidentally may very
well hear a constant hissing, as of serpents: we call it tinnitus). As
Kingsley observes, it takes long discipline or a sudden jolt to notice
what we are doing, and also what we aren't (2003, pp. 515–17).
    Much of the Parmenidean argument now looks to us like
sophistry, as it did to Plato, who spelt out – especially in *The
Sophist* – the ways in which we might after all be wrong, and how
what didn't 'exist' or wasn't 'true' might still, in a way, be thinkable.
Sophistries are not without their uses: they enable us to make the
distinctions that we need to make if we are to cope with living in
the everyday. Seneca (4 BC–65 AD) thought it ridiculous to spend

time on fallacies (as that 'mouse' is a syllable and mice eat cheese, so at least some syllables eat cheese). But that very absurdity points to the important thesis that there is more to the world than words. Parmenides' argument does more than identify some problems with the copula. If he was right, then the Truth which loves to hide is stranger than even Heracleitos or Democritus supposed. If we know nothing about reality (as Democritus said), how can we claim that it is composed of individual simples scattered across space and changing over time? Once we close our eyes to seeming, we have no reason left to think that there are several things at all, or that Space and Time are more than ways we seem, to ourselves, to see. If we *can* know a truth – as Parmenides said we could – it could not be by ordinary experience. Reason alone declares what Is. This, for Parmenides, is the One.

But what are 'reason' and 'intellect'? The easier conclusion is that Parmenides had discovered logic, a process whereby we journey towards the truth by considering what cannot be the case, eliminating the impossible until we must accept whatever's left. By thinking through the implications of what is said and done, we are closer to finding ways of testing them. By putting aside our personal or parochial wishes, we have a chance of finding what would persuade just anyone. That seems to be what Plato conceived as a proper dialectic: to test hypotheses against each other and against the basic rules of logic, and so at length prevent good arguments from escaping or being forgotten.

But this is to set Parmenides himself aside. All we can learn from him, on this account, is a method, while discarding what he himself concluded (which suggests that his method was mistaken). It is also to miss the point. Zeno of Elea (c490–c430 BC) used dialectical reason to undermine the commonsense alternatives to Parmenides' account. The very notion of change, so Zeno argued, involved inescapable paradox. To change completely, it was necessary to change half-way: and each half-way stage could then be treated as something to be completed, and there be another half-way stage to achieve first. Achilles could never overtake the tortoise since the latter would always have moved on when Achilles arrived where the tortoise had been before; the arrow could never reach its target, nor ever move at all, since at any instant it occupied no greater space than its own length. In order to loosen our grip on common sense Zeno, it was said, invented dialectic: that remained its secret purpose. Zeno, by the way, was one of those who perished as philosophers were meant to do: defying a tyrant with such courage that, after his murder, the tyrant was overthrown (Diogenes, *Lives*, 9.26–7). That fact should make us doubt any reinterpretation of his philosophy as logic-chopping or the pursuit of paradox[6]: the vision he sought to live by was an inspiration. Nowadays, Zeno's puzzles may still be puzzling: but – at best – they are only ways of suggesting better analyses of change and difference. Few commentators consider whether the point was different: that change and difference are indeed absurd, that there is nowhere else than Here.

One further – and misleading – way of grasping the Parmenidean claim is to suppose that he is speaking about the four-dimensional (or n-dimensional) plenum in which many rationalists have believed, and found courage in believing. Everything that ever happens is a fixed element of one single whole: our distinctions of past and future are no more significant than distinguishing left and right. The cosmos hangs, unchangingly, in emptiness, 'like the body of a well-rounded sphere, everywhere of equal intensity from the centre' (Parmenides 28B8DK, 43–4: Waterfield 2000, p. 60). KRS inferred that in making 'all reality a finite sphere', he must be contradicting himself: 'must there not be real empty space beyond the limits of the sphere', as the Stoics supposed? (KRS 1983, p. 252). A better conclusion must be that the point of mentioning 'a sphere' is to exploit the notion of something whose surface is everywhere the 'same distance' from the centre. The sphere that Parmenides describes is even more tightly managed: there are no inner layers closer to the centre than the outer. Or as later thinkers expressed it: 'God is a circle whose centre is everywhere and whose circumference nowhere'[7]. That is, Parmenides is not describing a plenum but a presence everywhere the same, containing all things without any break or difference or loss. 'We are in the center of the world always, moment after moment' (Adams 2010, p. 54, citing Suzuki 1970, p. 31). We cannot escape from it, and all the worlds of our imagining are here (see also *Psalm* 139.7–12). This view finds philosophical formulation in the Talmudic saying, 'Why is God called "the Place" (*hamaqom*)? Because the universe is located in Him, not He in the universe'. ([*Midrash*] *Genesis* R.68: Maccoby 2002, p. 24; see also Urbach 1979, pp. 49, 68) Two other figures of the Sicilian and South Italian group, one earlier and one later than Parmenides, are still less amenable to redescription, namely Pythagoras (fl. 530 BC) and

Empedocles (fl. 450 BC). According to one account, a Pythagorean, Ameinias, first introduced Parmenides to the practice of *hesychia*, stillness (Diogenes, *Lives*, 9.21; see Kingsley 1999, p. 162, 173–83). Both made important contributions to our science, and both were professed prophets, even shamanic seers. Both claimed to remember their past lives. Both claimed to be embarked for godhead. Both puzzle us.

The main problem in identifying what Pythagoras in particular taught or thought is that his doctrine was developed by his many followers, and often associated with cultic myths and practices – commonly labelled 'Orphic' – which we do not understand. He came from Samos – an island city off the coast of Turkey – and had, like other Ionian philosophers, Phoenician or Tyrrhenian connections. 'It is said that he [Pythagoras] learned the mathematical sciences from the Egyptians, Chaldeans and Phoenicians; for of old the Egyptians excelled, in geometry, the Phoenicians in numbers and proportions, and the Chaldeans of astronomical theorems, divine rites, and worship of the Gods; other secrets concerning the course of life he received and learned from the Magi' (Porphyry, *Life of Pythagoras*, 1–2, 6: Guthrie 1987, pp. 123–4). How much Pythagoras himself was concerned with mathematics we don't know, nor what precisely was meant by some of the rules of his school. For example: 'wretches, utter wretches, keep your hands off beans!' (Empedocles 31B141DK: Waterfield 2000, p. 154). It has been suggested that some Greeks of southern Italy were suffering from favism, involving a bad reaction to eating beans, or that dried beans were used in selecting rulers[8], or that '*kuamoi*' in fact means 'testicles' (Aulus Gellius 4.11, 9–10), or that beans were thought as alive as animals, or simply that they were taboo. We cannot even be certain that Pythagoras renounced animal sacrifice, despite the long association of Pythagoreanism with a bloodless diet. Being a Pythagorean is living the Pythagorean life, not necessarily accepting a particular stock of doctrines (Huffman 1993, pp. 10–11), but we may not even be sure what a 'Pythagorean life' was. He came to stand for a whole tradition of philosophical and scientific thought, and was transformed accordingly in each new generation (see Ferguson 2010). He influenced Parmenides, but also, Thrasyllus of Mendes said (a first century Egyptian who bequeathed us the standard ordering of Plato's dialogues), Democritus (Diogenes, *Lives*, 9.38).

There were seemingly three things that Pythagoreans originally embraced: the significance of number, the immortality of the soul and that the wise should rule the city. 'Orphic' and 'Pythagorean' mysteries constituted a long-running alternative to the mainstream 'Classical' opinion (which was that individual, bodily, mortal beings leave only shadows of themselves behind). They also helped identify a distinct class, 'the wise', who knew more than the seven sages. Pythagoras won the city of Croton over, whether by charismatic authority or the allegiance of select disciples. Even after the violent overthrow of that brief rule, one of his followers, Archytas (428–347 BC), as well as being an innovative mathematician and inventor, was elected governor of Tarentum seven times (and taught Plato something of both cosmology and politics). Even if much of the Pythagorean arithmetic was no more than numerology, dependent on the magic or symbolic properties of numbers from one to ten, they pointed towards a possibility that later ages have developed: the road to understanding is through arithmetic, even though that understanding slowly revealed some shockingly (and literally) irrational aspects of the world of number. Pythagoras was more astute than some who held the same faith later on: how should we learn the gods' language if we were not gods ourselves? If we are not, how could we expect to know more than our senses tell us? The God of mathematicians was born, and so was the thought that mathematicians could aspire to godhead. Even Aristotle, who liked numbers less than Plato, said 'as sight takes in light from the surrounding air, so does the soul from mathematics' (Diogenes, *Lives*, 5.17).

Later stories suggested that Pythagoras was acknowledged, by the northern traveller Abaris, as an incarnation of Hyperborean Apollo. But the commoner association of 'Orphism' was with Egypt:

> Orpheus, for instance, brought from Egypt most of his mystic ceremonies, the orgiastic rites that accompanied his wanderings, and his fabulous account of his experiences in Hades. For the rite of Osiris is the same as that of Dionysus and that of Isis very similar to that of Demeter, the names alone having been interchanged; and the punishments in Hades of the unrighteous, the Fields of the Righteous, and the fantastic conceptions, current among the many, which are figments of the imagination — all these were introduced by Orpheus in imitation of the Egyptian funeral customs. (Diodorus 1.96.4–5)

Modern critics who insist that Pythagoras cannot have been both a real philosopher and a believer in reincarnation display their bias, especially when they add that he could have had no 'reason' for such a belief. If he thought he remembered earlier lives, that was a reason. If both Egypt and the North agreed that there were immortal souls (including ones with knowledge of what they did) that too can count as a reason. But the principal reason for suspecting that there was indeed 'a god' (i.e. an immortal spirit) present in human life – as Democritus also thought (68A167DK: Waterfield 2000, p. 216) – may have been, precisely, that we have godlike thoughts. Three sorts of people visit the Games, Pythagoras said: traders, for cash; athletes, for honour; and 'spectators' to admire what happens (Cicero, *Tuscalan Disputations*, 5.3.9; Diogenes *Lives* 8.8). The last class was the superior – which strikes many as odd, believing as we do that there is no more to be seen at the Games than athletic competitions, and that 'mere spectators' are parasites on the action. But the word is *theoria*, and the Games are seen as sacred. The best life is to contemplate the action of the gods around us, not only at the common festivals. So also Plutarch of Chaeronea:

> I am delighted with Diogenes, who, when he saw his host in Sparta preparing with much ado for a certain festival, said, 'Does not a good man consider every day a festival?' and a very splendid one, to be sure, if we are sound of mind. For the universe is a most holy temple and most worthy of a god; into it man is introduced through birth as a spectator, not of hand-made or immovable images, but of those sensible representations of knowable things that the divine mind, says Plato, has revealed, representations which have innate within themselves the beginnings of life and motion, sun and moon and stars, rivers which ever discharge fresh water, and earth which sends forth nourishment for plants and animals. Since life is a most perfect initiation into these things and a ritual celebration of them, it should be full of tranquillity and joy, and not in the manner of the vulgar, who wait for the festivals of Cronus and of Zeus and the Panathenaea and other days of the kind, at which to enjoy and refresh themselves, paying the wages of hired laughter to mimes and dancers. . . . By spending the greater part of life in lamentation and heaviness of heart and carking cares men shame the festivals with which the god supplies us and in which he initiates us. (Plutarch, *De Tranquillitate Animi*, ch.20: 1936–9, vol. 6, p. 239)

Empedocles too is seen through a haze of later confusions, which culminate in the notion that he was a Darwinian before his time, unjustly criticized by Aristotle. That he also proclaimed himself a god in exile, and – supposedly – killed himself by jumping into a volcano are puzzles most ignore. His cosmology is taken to be naturalistic: the four elemental states are earth, air, fire and water, ceaselessly combined and separated by the twin influence of Love and Strife – or Attraction and Repulsion. When the cosmos settled into inhabitable form, it produced fragmentary life-forms, combined at random, and only some of these survived to breed whole-natured forms. 'Wherever everything turned out as it would have if it were happening for a purpose (*heneka tou*), there the creatures survived, being accidentally compounded in a suitable way; but where this did not happen, the creatures perished and are perishing still, as Empedocles says of his "man-faced ox-progeny"' (Aristotle, *Physics*, 2.198b29ff). Aristotle's criticism of the notion that there ever could have been such fragments (separate heads or hands or organs), or that current life-forms are merely 'accidental' combinations, was enough to establish immanent forms and final causes as a vital feature of biology and cosmology for centuries. We can rewrite the Empedoclean story to make it agree with Neo-Darwinian theory (which does not suppose that the first living things were fragments – though there is some force in the idea that eucaryotic cells and multicellular organisms in general are the products of symbiosis: see Margulis and Sagan 1997), but both Neo-Darwinian theory and the re-imagined Empedoclean story find it difficult to explain how life began at all. Natural selection only operates when there are already entities that reproduce themselves with variations, and so cannot explain the first emergence of such creatures.[9] It may be that Empedocles derived his idea of fragmentary life-forms from the fragmentary fossils that were the principal evidence of floods and of mythological chimeras. But we are probably mistaking his actual, moral intention: the story was not told to explain the present world, but to interpret it, as a battle between the forces of Love and Strife, Combination and Disassociation.

Love, naturally, has been reckoned the better part, but this too is a mistake. Back in the earlier years, only Aphrodite ruled, and there was peace: 'their altar was not drenched by the unspeakable slaughters of bulls, but this was held among men the greatest defilement – to tear out the life from noble limbs and eat them' (Porphyry, *On Abstinence*, 4.21). But even before those days, before there was a cosmos of our sort at all, we had committed some dreadful sin, and been exiled here. Long ago, we were gods, and some of us – Empedocles said – remember this. In realizing our imprisonment, he presented himself to Acragas in Sicily as 'an immortal god, mortal no more' (31B112DK: Waterfield 2000, p. 140). So also Hesiod's gods may be condemned to lie frozen by the Styx when they break their oath (*Theogony* 775–806). Zuntz's aphorism is almost correct: 'the banished god described by Hesiod is – Man' (Zuntz 1971, p. 267). Almost correct, but not exactly: for the point Empedocles is making is that the banished god isn't essentially human, even if it may be born among humans 'as prophets, singers of hymns, healers and leaders' (Empedocles 31B146DK: Waterfield 2000, p. 141) – and among beasts as lions, or laurels among trees (31B127DK). 'Will you not end the terrible sounds of your murder? Do you not see that in your thoughtlessness you are eating one another?' (Empedocles 31B136DK: Waterfield 2000, pp. 153–4). Modern commentators do not usually care for this. Thus, KRS:

> If [Empedocles] thinks of man as fallen god (or divine spirit), this is *surely* because he sees an affinity between him and the god of *On Nature*, the Sphere, which transcends the difference between them. The affinity *doubtless* lies in their shared capacity for thought. It is in this that Empedocles sees perfection, as is suggested both by his association of 'holy mind' with divinity, and by his notion that blood, the stuff with which we think, is a nearly equal mixture of the four elements, which are *of course* equally mixed in the Sphere. (KRS 1983, p. 320: my emphases)

Terms like 'surely, 'doubtless' and 'of course' should worry us. It is at least strange to be so quick to equate 'the heart, nourished in the ebb and flow of seas of blood . . . the main seat of what men call understanding' (Empedocles 31B105DK: Waterfield 2000, p. 158) with 'the only mind, sacred and inexpressibly vast, rushing through the whole world with swift thoughts' (31B134DK: Waterfield 2000, p. 151). That the blood around men's hearts is what *they* call understanding is not to say that their thoughts are spotless! The question again is: what is meant by 'thought' (*nous, noema, phren*)? The awakening eye may have nothing at all to do with 'reasoning', nor need we suppose any special affinity between 'what men call thought' and the thoughts of the most high.

It is also not so clear that Aphrodite is unambiguously good, and Strife (or Ares) evil, as Aristotle supposed (Aristotle, *Metaphysics,* 1.985a4–7; see Kingsley 2003, pp. 416, 588). The principles of attraction and repulsion keep the world in motion, so that the elements are sometimes mingled together, sometimes dissociated. But dissociation may be exactly what we now need, to help us return from exile, and it may be Aphrodite's charm that has enticed us into forgetful mingling with each other, here. We compound our folly and reinforce our forgetfulness by killing and eating each other. But this depends on attraction, not repulsion: our wish to kill and eat is not so different from our wish to mate and breed – in both cases we relish getting involved! Conversely, when Empedocles speaks of himself as 'putting [his] trust in the insanities of strife' (31B115DK, 13: Waterfield 2000, p. 154) he may not be describing the cause or condition of his exile but a recipe for his return (Kingsley 2003, p. 432, *pace* Plotinus *Ennead* IV.8 [6].1; but see Osborne 2005). 'His hope was not that his own soul would be drawn back into chaos through Love. His hope was for his soul's immortality' (Kingsley 2003, p. 401, 588). 'Strife' is dissociation, purification: what Plotinus himself calls 'the flight of the pure to the pure (*phuge monou pros monon*)' (*Ennead* VI.9 [9].11, 51).[10]

Interestingly, as Kingsley (2003, p. 443) points out, the Arabic translation and adaptation of Plotinus' *Enneads* is closer to Empedocles' vision (and also truer to other aspects of Plotinus):

> When he came down to this world he came as a help to those souls whose minds have become contaminated and mixed. And he became like a madman – calling out to people at the top of his voice and urging them to reject this world and what is in it and go back to their own original, sublime and noble realm. (Kingsley 2003, p. 443, quoting *Theology of Aristotle* 1.31)

Philosophers and Jews

Ionians, by many modern accounts, were more like modern philosophers – chiefly in that on the one hand they offered reasons for what they said, and on the other, that they described a universe which had no reasons. The aphorism can be questioned, as well as the premises of the claim: is it odd to suppose that we should have reasons for our beliefs, and yet also believe that the universe as a whole exists and changes for no reason, that 'final causes' apply only in the case of 'reasoning individuals' like us? On the other hand, it does seem strange to insist either that we operate on entirely different principles than the cosmos of which we are a part, or else that what we do with our lives depends entirely on mechanistic causes (as though I were writing and you were reading *only* because of neurochemical exchanges in our respective brains). Most of the ancients were persuaded, like Zeno of Citium (c334–c262 BC), that the world was 'alive' and 'intelligent', because we clearly were (Cicero, *On the Nature of the Gods*, 2.22: LS 1987, p. 325 [54G]). Anaxagoras of Clazomenae (500–428 BC) was barred from Athens for suggesting that the sun was a red-hot stone (a little larger than the Peloponnese), but he was also nicknamed 'the Mind', for insisting that it was Mind (or *Nous*) that governed all things, and claimed the sky as his fatherland (Diogenes, *Lives*, 2.6–7).

The other feature of 'Ionian' thought that is often praised is that they acknowledged, in various ways, that things are always changing. This, it is supposed, is of the essence of modernity. But the fact that things are 'fluid' does not mean that there is no order, no commanding presence. Heracleitos, in identifying that order, that *logos*, as the thunderbolt (22B64DK: Waterfield 2000, p. 42) was not speaking 'mythologically', but had no better reason for his faith than Hesiod or Anaxagoras.

Certainly the Ionian philosophers were often practical people, and so were the Italians. Both groups were political reformers, critical of the customs of their day. Heracleitos anticipated later moralists by spurning the delights of Ephesos, and ended his days, it was said, as a grass-eating misanthrope. Others attempted to discover or imagine how societies, especially civil societies, had formed, and how they might be better managed. Democritus, whose theories inspired the atomists, could more plausibly be counted as the founder of social contract theory: just as there were individual singulars, the atoms, so were there – at least by convention – individual persons, frightened and attracted into larger masses. Pythagoras was the ascetical reformer of the Greek city of Croton. Zeno of Elea died by torture after being captured delivering arms to a local liberation movement. Anaxagoras was a friend and adviser to Pericles of Athens (and suffered as a result). Archytas of Tarentum was more successful, being elected seven times to lead his city. Most philosophers gradually concluded, as had Heracleitos, that the fall of cities, the decay of morals was a universal fate; only small groups of friends, or even solitaries, could live well. But even in that despair they offered guidance. We should remember Epictetus' warning (55–135 AD: a sometime slave of one of Nero's nastier henchmen), that one who pretends to 'teach philosophy' without the knowledge, virtue and the strength of soul to cope with distressed and corrupted souls, 'and above all the counsel of God advising him to occupy this office' is a vulgarizer of the mysteries, a quack doctor.

> The affair is momentous, it is full of mystery, not a chance gift, nor given to all comers. . . . You are opening up a doctor's office although you possess no equipment other than drugs, but when or how these drugs are applied you neither know nor have ever taken the trouble to learn. . . . Why do you play at hazard in matters of the utmost moment? If you find the principles of philosophy entertaining sit down and turn them over in your mind all by yourself, but don't ever call yourself a philosopher. (Epictetus, *Discourses*, 3.16)

The lessons that philosophers ought to rehearse, so Epictetus said, are the primacy of individual moral choice, the unimportance of body, rank and estate, and the knowledge of what is their own. The slave (which is Epictetus) here agreed with the emperor (Marcus Aurelius [121–180 AD]): it was our own souls only that we could save (if that). Self-deprecatingly, Epictetus acknowledged that he and his disciples were not properly 'philosophers': Jews in word and not in deed, '*parabaptistai*' and not 'dyed-in-the wool' (*Discourses* 2.9.21). That association – strange to modern readers – of 'true philosophy' and the Jewish way of life – is worth recalling, and explaining.

First, more historical background: during the sixth century BC, while the Ionian cities were sending colonies towards the Black Sea and the Western Mediterranean, the kingdom of Judah (the southern inheritor of the united Hebrew Kingdom of David and Solomon) was conquered by Nebuchadnezzar of Babylon, and its people resettled in Mesopotamia. The Babylonian Empire was overthrown in turn by an alliance of Medes and Persians, and Cyrus of Persia gave the Jewish community permission to return to Judah, and rebuild the temple. This was happening over roughly the same period as the Phocaeans fled from Ionia and founded Elea. The return to Judah did not gather force until Darius (550–486 BC), and many Hebrews remained in Babylon, or Egypt, or still further afield. The earlier conquest of the northern successor state, Israel, by the Assyrian Empire, in the late eighth century BC, and the evacuation of its people (namely the 'lost ten tribes' of Israel) had also scattered Hebrews across the middle east. Some had remained in what became known as Samaria, and retained a separate tradition of the Hebrews' early years in Palestine after their escape from Egypt, and – so they said – the original Aaronite priesthood.[11] The full story of the Hebrew Diaspora will never be written: the exiles seem not to have been much noticed in the chronicles of other peoples. With the Return, things changed.

The returning exiles were determined to rebuild the temple in Jerusalem, and to reconstruct their history. This is when the Hebrew Bible took its canonical shape – not because the exiles wrote the various books that composed it (that would be to imagine unprecedented literary and theological genius in a band of would-be theocrats!) but because they collected and reshaped the older stories, including the diatribes of northern and southern prophets, court records, dietary and ritual regulations, philosophical speculations, folk tales, and popular songs and proverbs. These writings provided the rules and subject matter for Rabbinical and Christian argument for centuries, and still lie in the background of the Western and Orthodox Minds. Ancient commentators during the Hellenistic and Late Antique period, even in the Greek tradition, thought well of them – though they conflated what they knew of Jews with their image of other exotic sages. Magi, Gymnosophists and Jews were all identified as ascetics, devoted to the cultivation of a strictly monotheistic tendency: 'nations of philosophers'. It does not seem that pagan philosophers paid much attention to the actual Hebrew texts, even in their Greek translation, but some of their practices were acclaimed. Aristotle's successor Theophrastus of Lesbos (371–287 BC), though he disliked their sacrifices, praised Jews because they talked to each other about God, gazed at the stars, and called upon God through their prayers (Porphyry, *On Abstinence,* 2.26; see also Hengel 1974, p. 256). Another pupil of Aristotle, Clearchus of Soli (fl.320 BC), wrote a work *On Sleep,* in which Aristotle himself is impressed by a learned Jew – or at any rate by someone from Syria identified as a descendant of an Indian philosophical sect of the sort 'called Calanoi by the Indians but Jews by the Syrians' (Gruen 2011, pp. 311–12). Possibly these witnesses, and others, were talking about that branch of Hebrew thought and practice that was later to be called Essene. Later commentators even suggested that the Greek philosophers, including Plato and Pythagoras, had learnt their trade and teachings from the Books of Moses. 'What is Plato but an Atticizing Moses?' enquired Numenius of Syrian Apamea (Eusebius, *Praeparatio*, 9.6.9: 1903, p. 209; see also Momigliano 1975, p. 147), a second century Platonist.

There are three Biblical themes that deserve special attention: the story of creation, the demand for justice and theodicy.

'In the beginning God made the heavens and the earth' (*Genesis* 1.1). The term represented here by the expression 'God' was originally '*Elohim*': a plural form apparently indicating One Alone. This shifts to '*Yahweh Elohim*' at *Genesis* 2.4b. It is generally agreed that the stories recorded in those first two chapters have different human authors: the 'Priestly' and the 'Yahwistic' sources identified elsewhere in the Bible. But they were all incorporated into the canon, in the belief that they all mattered. This first sentence of the Torah already makes clear the difference between the Jewish view and the general Mediterranean account that I have described before. The Creator does not emerge late on in history, from Nothingness. He has – so far – no character, no family, no back story, whatever other stories may once have been suggested. Nor does He employ any biological or manufactured implements. His Word is enough to create both heaven (later equated with the realm of Forms) and earth (the phenomenal realm we seem to ourselves to inhabit), and to give form to the otherwise formless. The first readers of the document did not start blind: the claim is that it was *their* God, the God they met in cult and story, who had created all things. Berkovits (1969) has argued that the different titles assigned to that one God have different associations: as Yahweh He is transcendent, unlike all other, created, things; as 'Yahweh your Elohim' He is involved with His people Israel, concerned for their survival and their welfare, and requiring obedience from them; as 'the Lord of Hosts [He] judges; [as] the Holy One of Israel [He] saves' (Berkovits 1969, p. 144). In His absolute Otherness, the God that the Jews addressed resembles the One of the philosophers, but though that One pulls us towards itself, and its emissaries may lay down laws for us, it is not involved in the details of our lives. Even in thinking of a more accessible folk-divinity, there is a difference: Minos may talk to Zeus as well as Moses may talk to Yahweh, but we have no record of that conversation – and Abraham, Moses and the other Hebrew prophets actually dared argue with their Lord.

So the claim is not simply that an unknown something made the heavens and the earth, and established, step by step, its order. Neither does the story of our fall, in *Genesis* 2, refer to an unknown Creator. The claim is that the god acknowledged in Israel's own back story – the one who brought them out from Egypt – is the Lord of all things: not a tribal spirit or civic icon, but the universal maker. It is a grandiose claim: the Greeks were prepared to acknowledge that other peoples worshipped Zeus, Athena, Aphrodite and the rest under different names and with different rituals. Mostly, they thought that the others had got things subtly or not so subtly wrong: the 'real form' of the gods must be much more like the human, for example, than the Egyptians thought. But any favourites that the gods might have had better beware – there were always other gods very likely to take offence, and just as powerful. The Hebrew claim – despite the obvious appearances – was that any calamity that the Hebrews suffered was allowed by Yahweh, or even imposed by Him. There was no other power in the world or out of it that could compete. 'I form the light, and create darkness: I make peace, and create evil: I the Lord do all these things' (*Isaiah* 45.7). In this matter, the Hebrews disagreed with the Chaldaeans (that the stars were rulers), and with the disciples of Zoroaster (that there were two equal and opposite principles in the world, the good and the evil).

So what did Yahweh their Elohim require of them, and why did they have to suffer fresh calamities once rescued out of Egypt and delivered to a land 'flowing with milk and honey'? The Romans, faced by lesser public disasters, were agreed that their gods must be angry with them – for neglecting the public rituals. The solution would be to restore the temples and the neglected statues (Liebeschuetz 1979, p. 56). The answer of the Hebrew prophets, confirmed in the post-exilic reworking of their history, was that the people – especially, but not only, the kings of Israel and Judah and their courtiers – had offended against justice. They had neglected the instructions to take care of orphans and widows, strangers and slaves, and to spare the wild things of their country. They had neglected the rule of Jubilee, to cancel debts every seven years (*Deuteronomy* 15.1–12), and in the fiftieth to liberate all slaves and return lands to their original tenants (*Leviticus* 25).

> When your brother-Israelite is reduced to poverty and cannot support himself in the community, you shall assist him as you would an alien or a stranger, and he shall live with you. You shall not charge him interest on a loan, either by deducting it in advance from the capital sum, or by adding it on repayment. You shall fear your God, and your brother shall live with you; you shall not deduct interest when advancing him money nor add interest to the payment due for food supplied on credit. I am the Lord your God who brought you out of Egypt to give you the land of Canaan and to become your God. (*Leviticus* 25.35–8)

It was in this, as the Hebrews conceived the case, that Yahweh differed from Baal Shamin, the God of the Phoenicians, who might otherwise seem much the same (see Teixidor 1977, pp. 28–9). When Ahab, king of Samaria (?883–863 BC), much desired a vineyard belonging to one Naboth of Jezreel, his wife Jezebel (a daughter of the king of Sidon) arranged for Naboth to be falsely accused and stoned to death, so allowing Ahab to take the vineyard. In doing so she conceived that this was the right of a king, hampered only by the odd customs of her husband's people. The God of Elijah the Tishbite judged quite otherwise (*I Kings* 21.1–29).

Some centuries later the Christian apologist, Lactantius (c240–c320 AD), insisted that 'neither the Greeks nor the Romans could possess justice, because they had men differing from one another by many degrees, from the poor to the rich, from the humble to the powerful . . . for where all are not equally matched there is no equity; and inequality itself excludes justice' (Liebeschuetz 1979, p. 272, quoting Lactantius, *Divine Institutes,* 5.15). Charitable aid is to be given according to need, not because of any social ties between client and patron (*Divine Institutes* 6.10–12, criticizing Cicero, *De Officiis,* 2.18).

We learn further from Ezekiel (c622–c570 BC) what it is to reject the laws: the man of violence 'obeys none of them, he feasts at mountain shrines, he dishonours another man's wife, he oppresses the unfortunate and the poor, he is a robber, he does not return the debtor's pledge, he lifts his eyes to idols and joins in abominable rites; he lends both at discount and at interest. Such a man shall not live' (*Ezekiel* 18.10ff).[12] Consider also the offence (*2 Kings* 23.10) of passing children through the fire 'to Molech' (or 'as a burnt offering'). Consider again the iniquity of Sodom. The Bible's claim is that our possession of the land (and anything else we think we own) is conditional.

So also Jeremiah (c650–c580 BC): 'You keep saying "This place is the temple of the Lord, the temple of the Lord, the temple of the Lord!" This catchword of yours is a lie; put no trust in it. Mend your ways and your doings, deal fairly with one another, do not oppress the alien, the orphan, and the widow, shed no innocent blood in this place, do not run after other gods to your own ruin' (*Jeremiah* 7.4). The command is heard in earlier centuries. 'What does the Lord require of you, but to do justly, and to love mercy, and to walk humbly with your god?' (*Micah* 6.8: a sixth century prophet in the southern kingdom). Amos, in the eighth century, similarly denounced those 'who grind the destitute and plunder the humble . . . that [they] may buy the poor for silver and the destitute for a pair of shoes' (*Amos* 8.4–6). So also Ezekiel, in words that also have implications for our treatment of the non-human:

> These were the words of the Lord to me: Prophesy, man, against the shepherds of Israel; prophesy and say to them, You shepherds, these are the words of the Lord God: How I hate the shepherds of Israel who care only for themselves! Should not the shepherd care for the sheep? You consume the milk, wear the wool, and slaughter the fat beasts, but you don't feed the sheep. You have not encouraged the weary, tended the sick, bandaged the hurt, recovered the straggler, or searched for the lost; and even the strong you have driven with ruthless severity. . . . I will dismiss those shepherds: they shall care only for themselves no longer; I will rescue my sheep from their jaws, and they shall feed on them no longer'. (*Ezekiel* 34.1ff; cf. *Leviticus* 25.46, 53)

The union of justice and mercy is not a paradox: the justice is to be done on the oppressor, and mercy granted to the oppressed. But there may be confusion, when the very same people are both the oppressed and the oppressors. Sorting that out may demand a radical re-visioning of all creation. And that creates a difficulty for Abrahamic theism which does not exist for the more usual Mediterranean sort. The challenge usually (and mistakenly) attributed to Epicurus identifies the so-called problem of evil: 'Is God willing to prevent evil, but not able? Then is he impotent. Is he able, but not willing? Then is he malevolent. Is he both able and willing? Whence then is evil?' The argument is badly formed, but may still speak to us. Whereas Zeus is himself bound not to disturb destiny, and makes no claim to universal benevolence, the God of the Hebrews is holy and supreme in power. That holiness – though there is an association with notions of purity and separation – is shown chiefly, as Berkovits (1969, pp. 141–223; see also Harrington 2001, pp. 27–8) has argued, in His ongoing concern for the weak, and the demand He makes on His followers to share that care. 'Ye shall be holy for I the Lord your God am holy' (*Leviticus* 19.2). That is why He rebukes and punishes His people – but why in that case does He not do more to show His own compassion? Why do so many innocents suffer, and so much?

This is the crux of the *Book of Job*, written sometime between the sixth and fourth centuries BC, and reflecting earlier complaints against the gods. Job was a wealthy Edomite, pious in all his doings, and Satan, 'the Adversary', came to the court of God to suggest that Job was only pious because God favoured him: withdraw the favour, and he would rebel. God accordingly permitted Satan to take a hand: destroying Job's goods, his children and his health. Job nonetheless rejected his wife's urging 'to curse God and die', retained his piety and was rewarded at last with new goods, new children and his lasting health. No doubt this – that suffering is a test of our fidelity – was the moral often drawn, as in the English folk song:

> Now Job he was a patient man, the richest in the East.
> When he was brought to poverty, his sorrows soon increased.
> He bore them all most patiently, from sin he did refrain.
> He always trusted in the Lord. He soon got rich again.

The rest of the story is not so comforting. In fact, though Job does not curse God, he does complain. He bears his sorrows, in fact, impatiently, and resents the efforts of his 'friends' to assure him that he must have sinned to incur such dreadful misfortune. In the end God answers Job 'out of the whirlwind', rebukes his friends and vindicates Job, precisely, for his complaints. Job is right, we are told, to demand that the Judge of all the world do justice, and right to insist that what has happened to him is wrong (*Job* 42.7; see Berkovits 1969, pp. 250–1).[13] If there is an intellectual answer to the problem, it lies in the proposition that the Creator plays fair by all His creatures, and 'gives to [them] His boundary so that each may become fully itself' (Glatzer 1969, p. 63), whether it be Satan, or Leviathan, or Job. God's power 'is revealed in His ability to restrain himself from destroying the wicked' (Harrington 2001, p. 25). He will disentangle 'good' from 'evil' only at the end of time. Then it will be true that 'mercy and truth are met together; righteousness and peace have kissed each other' (*Psalm* 85.10). Till then we live in hope (and faith), 'not having received the promises but having seen them from afar' (after *Hebrews* 11.13). The claim is that Justice will prevail, and not that the present world is just – and in this the Hebrews differed from other 'Classical' philosophers.

That the Jews were a 'nation of philosophers', as many pagans said, may have rested in the belief that they were consistent in their devotion to an unimaginable God, and that they were loyal to the expectation of another world than this, whether that was an apocalyptic future or an unearthly heaven. The Hebrews themselves remembered, mostly, that they were to be 'a kingdom of priests and a holy nation' (*Exodus* 19.6; see Harrington 2001, p. 162), to similar effect. But we can also see that Rabbinic Judaism, at any rate, encouraged a more familiar sort of philosophy, in the intensely dialectical elaboration of their laws and stories, and a refusal ever to close off the discussion. This too is a sort of philosophy.

According to the Babylonian Talmud, the Rabbi Eliezer ben Hurcanus, nicknamed the Great (c50–c120 AD), was in dispute with the other Rabbis on a point of law. After performing several miracles (and still failing to convince them),

> Rabbi Eliezer then said to the Sages: 'If the *halakhah* is in accordance with me, may a proof come from Heaven.' Then a heavenly voice went forth and said, 'What have you to do with Rabbi Eliezer? The *halakhah* is according to him in every place.' Then Rabbi Joshua rose up on his feet, and said, 'It [the Torah] is not in the heavens (*Deuteronomy* 30.12)'. What did he mean by quoting this? Said Rabbi Jeremiah, 'He meant that since the Torah has been given already on Mount Sinai, we do not pay attention to a heavenly voice; for Thou has [sic] written in Thy Torah, "Decide according to the majority" (*Exodus* 23.2)'.

Rabbi Nathan met the prophet Elijah. He asked him, 'What was the Holy One, Blessed be He, doing in that hour?' Said Elijah, 'He was laughing, and saying "My children have defeated me, my children have defeated me"'. (*Bava Metzia* [Babylonian Talmud] 59a–59b: Maccoby 2002, pp. 173–4)

God Himself, in short, will hold by His own word, to give His creatures a say. Perhaps we sometimes wish He wouldn't.

CHAPTER FOUR

Travellers and stay-at-homes

Custom, dictat and advantage

Plato's attacks upon the fourth-century Sophists (a title that once meant only 'experts') left his successors sure that 'sophistry' was consciously amoral. Some later experts, similarly claiming that there are no knowable objective values, thence conclude that 'success' is all that matters. Those who are prepared to serve *all* masters who will pay them well, or do anything (however distasteful, undignified or 'immoral') to achieve their ends, are bound to be distrusted – even by those who buy them: why should they stay bought? Those who equate the 'moral' with the 'socially acceptable' are hardly better. But though Plato had a point, it may be that the Sophists did as well.

Inspired and evangelical thinkers set out to change the world, but even less pretentious people have a mission. Some Sophists were only what they said they were: teachers of useful arts, like Hippias of Elis (fl. c420 BC), who boasted that he had himself made all his clothes, his tools and ornaments, and could teach others how to do so too (as well as making speeches and composing poems). But the mechanical crafts were mostly taught by locals, to their apprentices, by practice more than book learning. Sophists were better known for teaching the arts of persuasion. Where the prize was a man's life or livelihood, such arts were at once desirable and dangerous. The civil peace is delicate: how many contests can it endure, and how readily can it allow advantages to those rich enough to pay? Consider how we feel about mercenary soldiers, ready to teach anyone how to fight a war: their art may be real, and some of their causes just, but do they know which ones are just, or why? And even if the cause is just, will civil war achieve it? Gorgias of Leontini (c485–380 BC), who figures as a Sceptic in later commentaries, may have meant well. Later biographers suggested that he had been a pupil of Empedocles, and himself taught Antisthenes the Cynic (c445–c365 BC). Like many other philosophers, he served on an embassy to foreign powers (in his case, Athens, in 427 BC), where maybe he met Socrates.

The arts of persuasion were important, especially in democratic cities, where the citizens made decisions no longer governed by ancestral dictat. Ostwald (1969) associates the use of '*nomos*' as the term of choice for what we consider 'laws' with the rise of democracy: in place of dictats from above, or *thesmoi*, the Athenians preferred to think of their laws as consensual, changeable customs. This may not be the only usage, nor the only distinction: Sophocles, in his *Antigone*, prefers instead to contrast ancestral *nomoi* with the dictates of the current ruler, Creon (who has ordered the body of Antigone's brother to lie unburied, and who comes, too late, to realize that there are higher laws than his). Even ancestral laws need interpreting – as Rabbinic speculation proves – and even tyrants can, sometimes, be persuaded to change their minds. But the arts of persuasion do have a special relevance when it is an assembly that needs to be convinced, and an assembly little disposed to do all and only what has been done before.

According to Herodotus, there was a brief debate among the Persians seeking to overthrow a Magian usurper, whether they might lie to achieve their goals. Darius declared that those who tell the truth and those who lie are seeking the same end – namely, to succeed – and that there is therefore nothing amiss with crafty lying (Herodotus 3.70). This was to defy the lessons taught all Persian youth: to ride, to draw the bow and to tell the truth. Lying was regarded as the most disgraceful thing of all (Herodotus 1.136–8). Herodotus had a moral message: the gradual erosion of Persian decencies and moral strength by greed. Darius, once he was King, also arranged a debate about the proper treatment of our dead.

What price would the Greeks take if they would eat the dead bodies of their fathers? What price would the Indians 'called Callatiae' take for burning the bodies up instead of eating them? In each case, they said no price would be enough (3.38). Does it follow that custom is king (and that the customs of the land and people must always be respected), or that kings may rule by fiat?

Darius and his successors acknowledged no restraints. Even the founder of the earlier Median dynasty, Deiokes, by Herodotus's account, only established himself as a seemingly honest arbitrator to get his hands on power (1.96–8). If even the seemingly just are aiming only at their own advantage, why should we blame the unjust? And why should we expect that anyone should be just? The best we can expect is a pretence of virtue.

Herodotus also tells of Amasis, who made himself king of Egypt (2.172). Finding that the Egyptians despised him for his common birth, he had a foot-bath (in which the courtiers had vomited and pissed, as well as washing their feet) made into a golden statue, to which they paid great reverence. Pointing this out to them, he insisted that he too should now be reverenced: what mattered was the function, not the stuff. The story reverses a Hebraic argument, in which the prophet Isaiah (c760–c690 BC) mocked those who cut down a tree and shape it for different aims: 'some of it he takes and warms himself; some he kindles and bakes bread on it; and some he makes into a god and prostrates himself, shaping it into an idol and bowing down before it' (*Isaiah* 44.15–16; see also *Wisdom of Solomon* 13.11–14.10; 15.7–13). What we control can hardly be a god (see also Gruen 1998, pp. 215–6, quoting the *Letter of Aristeas*, written in Alexandria sometime in the last two centuries BC). Conversely, there can hardly be 'anything more wretched than for a man to be in thrall to what he himself has made' (Augustine, *City of God*, 8.23: 1998, p. 347; see Fowden 1986, p. 210).

Commentators might contrast *nomos* and *thesmos* (from the same root as *theos*), or else nature and convention. But there are at least three sorts of law: the customs that a community makes up over many years; the natural impulses that guide most individuals; and also the ideal of justice, as something other than 'the way of kings'. King David (c1040–c970 BC), it was said, desired the wife of his immigrant Hittite commander, and when he had got her pregnant, sought her husband's death (by having him ordered into the front line of battle). Knowing of this, the prophet Nathan came to court and told a story:

> There were once two men in the same city, one rich and the other poor. The rich man had large flocks and herds, but the poor man had nothing of his own except one little ewe lamb. He reared it himself, and it grew up in his house with his own sons. . . . It was like a daughter to him. One day a traveller came to the rich man's house, and he, too mean to take something from his own flocks and herds to serve his guest, took the poor man's lamb and served up that.

David exclaimed in anger that the man deserved to die, and Nathan answered: 'You are the man' (2 *Samuel* 11.1–12.25).

The point of telling this story is both to emphasise the Hebrew tradition of telling truth to power in a way that would not have been dared in the courts of tyrants or Great Kings, and to show a different mode of argument. Nathan's story is not an allegory, and its relevance to David's crimes is not direct. But the story displays the arrogance of power in a way no argument from first principles would do. Persuasion by example is sometimes as legitimate, and as powerful, as persuasion by principle (as if Nathan had asked David what he meant by 'justice', or pointed to a pre-existing law about how to treat ewe lambs).

Sophists were not only selling the skills that citizens needed to survive and prosper in an argumentative society. They had a particular vision of the world and of humanity, that we could make up new customs, and that we would do so when it seemed advantageous. Those who feared their influence were motivated both by their wish to retain inherited customs and by their – reasonable – fear of what could be done by rulers who acknowledged no restraints. It was not only tyrants or Great Kings who should be feared. When the retired Athenian general Thucydides, writing a history of his country's downfall in the late fifth century BC, described the arguments the Athenian envoys used to the doomed island-community of Melos (which Athens was to conquer and despoil), he attributed to them a division between the laws of nature and of custom: it was 'natural' that the strong should rule the weak (Thucydides 5.84–116). Custom alone, and fictions about the gods, demanded any respect for those without defence: 'realists' understood that no-one had any motive but his own success, and would do anything that might secure it.

> Justice removed, what are kingdoms but great bands of robbers? What are bands of robbers themselves but little kingdoms? (Augustine, *City of God*, 4.4: 1998, p. 147)

There might be a reply to this, without invoking the laws of God: the Athenians assumed that they knew what 'success' was, and that all exchanges must be zero-sum games, with winners and losers. If this is false, then Athenian 'realism' was misguided, and a better way, less likely to go wrong, would be to cooperate. They might have made new customs rather than relying on the dogma that everyone will always act for his/her own 'advantage'. Better that one understand one's own 'advantage' better. Better to treat others as one would oneself prefer – and that is, with respect. But even such new customs might not have restrained their 'natural' impulses. Maybe it does take laws delivered by Minos, or by Moses.

Diodorus, writing about the ancient Egyptian system, expressed surprise that the Pharaoh could not do just as he pleased, and that he seemed happy to accept this discipline.

> The hours of both the day and night were laid out according to a plan, and at the specified hours it was absolutely required of the [Egyptian] king that he should do what the laws stipulated and not what he thought best. . . . For there was a set time not only for his holding audiences or rendering judgments, but even for his taking a walk, bathing, and sleeping with his wife, and, in a word, for every act of his life. . . . Strange as it may appear that the king did not have the entire control of his daily fare, far more remarkable still was the fact that kings were not allowed to render any legal decision or transact any business at random or to punish anyone through malice or in anger or for any other unjust reason, but only in accordance with the established laws relative to each offence. And in following the dictates of custom in these matters, so far were they from being indignant or taking offence in their souls, that, on the contrary, they actually held that they led a most happy life; for they believed that all other men, in thoughtlessly following their natural passions, commit many acts which bring them injuries and perils, and that

oftentimes some who realize that they are about to commit a sin nevertheless do base acts when overpowered by love or hatred or some other passion, while they, on the other hand, by virtue of their having cultivated a manner of life which had been chosen before all others by the most prudent of all men, fell into the fewest mistakes. (Diodorus 1.70.3–71.3)

Similar rules applied to the High Priest in Jerusalem, and the *flamen dialis* in Rome (see Harrington 2001, p. 61). What we might reckon a strict morality is originally a way of preserving a link with the divine, attempting to be 'pure' as it is pure.

Protagoras and Socrates

The two greatest Sophists were something more than mercenaries: namely Protagoras (481–411 BC) and Socrates (469–399 BC). Both Plato and Xenophon of Athens (c430–354 BC) were at pains to distance their friend, Socrates, from any 'sophistic movement', but his contemporaries saw little difference. Even Plato was ambivalent. In *The Sophist*, his 'Eleatic Stranger' guides the conversation to develop several accounts of what 'a Sophist' is – and all of them apply to Socrates. One unacknowledged difference was that Socrates was an Athenian patriot, and the others were homeless foreigners. Sophists, typically, travelled, and sought pay for their efforts; 'unlike most philosophers [Socrates] had no need to travel, except when required to go on an expedition' (Diogenes, *Lives, 2.22*), and relied on his investments (according to Aristoxenus of Tarentum (fl.335 BC): *Lives* 2.20)[1]. But all subverted ancestral certainties. All showed off their talents to annoy and to amuse. Oddly, the main argument against thinking Socrates a Sophist may be in *The Clouds*, an unsuccessful comedy of Aristophanes that helped to poison men's minds against him. Aristophanes placed in his characters' mouths a number of metaphors that took centre stage in Plato's dialogues. The Socratic thinker 'looks away' from earthly things to contemplate eternal entities that are not the city's gods, and practises a spiritual midwifery, encouraging his acolytes to give birth to new ideas – Plato's addition in *Theaetetus* being that midwives judge which infants can be reared. Socrates, in brief, had higher goals than Sophists.

But first consider the more 'sophistical' or argumentative side of his work. The ideas most closely tied to the historical Socrates are first, that he only knew that he knew nothing, and second, a 'Socratic Paradox', that no-one does wrong willingly: to act at all is to do what one thinks good (seemingly agreeing in this with Herodotus's Darius). If one nonetheless does ill, it must have been through ignorance. It follows that 'wrong-doers' need only be taught their error, and that no-one should be spared that teaching. To avoid punishment for one's wrong-doing is like avoiding necessary medicine, or wilfully preferring error (but why punishment rather than education?). True friends should denounce each other, so as to be better informed about the bad effects of what they've done. Socrates assumed that it is always better not to be deceived, and that even the pain of realizing that one was deceived (but that one still has no better notion of the truth than that one hasn't found it) is a good. His interlocutors did not always agree, but were sometimes coaxed into a more tolerant frame of mind than when they took it for granted that they had things right. A third theme, that it was better to *suffer* than to *act* unjustly, better to be oppressed than an oppressor, is perhaps no paradox, but only what all virtuous persons must agree, even if they don't know why.

Protagoras denied that there was any available Truth beyond what people said. In effect, he agreed that he too knew only that he knew nothing – except what it would be better to believe! 'Man was the Measure of all things': this amounts to a rejection of the earlier revelation, that the truth 'lies in the depths'. Truth, once again, is obvious, but what is obvious to one need not be so to another. The choice between conflicting 'truths' must be made on other grounds than that one side was 'truer'.

At first sight, *pace* Parmenides, it seems obvious that some thoughts are false, some things that we imagine or seem to see are figments. But all such figments, all such fantasies, may still be present realities, even though we misunderstand them. To insist that Orestes didn't 'really' see the Furies who beset him after he had killed his mother won't be a successful therapeutic strategy, whereas exorcism may. Heracles 'made a mistake' in killing his wife and children, supposing that they were monstrous enemies, but what he saw was 'real to him' (until the madness passed). Even if what we perceive are shadows (as Plato was to suggest), they are at least real shadows. We may pretend that only material objects have causal powers (as Stoic philosophers said), but this is paradoxical: the statement that this is so is not itself (as the Stoics knew) material, and yet it has effects that are not the same as the physical effects of the breath's disturbing the air. 'A sentence uttered makes a world appear where all things happen as it says they do' (Auden 'Words': 1976, pp. 473–4). We can change worlds by speaking, like magicians (see Hornung 1982, pp. 207–10). Empedocles dispelled the murderous rage of a dinner guest by uttering a line of Homer (Kingsley 1995, p. 247, after Iamblichus, *Life of Pythagoras,* 113) – most likely the passage that Plotinus also mentions (*Ennead* VI.5 [23].7, 9f), when Athena tugs Achilles by the hair to recall him to good sense (*Iliad* 1.197–222). Not all rhetoric is simply about winning. Not all agreements are con-tricks. Sometimes words can make a better world and are not to be judged on whether they were first true or false.

> Where faith in a fact can help create the fact, that would be an insane logic which should say that faith running ahead of scientific evidence is 'the lowest kind of immorality' into which a thinking being can fall. (James 1919, p. 25)

One interpretation of Hebrew thought, remember, is that justice is to come, rather than being present. God Himself, and His Kingdom, are, in a way, 'not yet', and the name the Hebrews claimed for Him (namely *Eh'je asher eh'je*) means something different from 'He Who Is' (as most philosophers in the Hellenic tradition thought). It means, so Bloch has argued, 'I will be who I will', just as the God of Job – or His justice – is a promise rather than a fact (see Bloch 1986, pp. 1235–6).[2] This is not to say that God's Justice is not a reality, but only that the world is not yet just: if it were up to us to decide what would be just, there would be nothing to hope for.

Protagoras's aim was to enable people to maintain a 'better' peace, to find some laws and doctrines that they could maintain together. Such a consensus would not have greater claims to being 'true', but would avoid the pains of war. The civil peace was best maintained by mutual persuasion, not by any caste or clan that had an undisputed line to God. Or maybe not. The story is told that one pupil agreed to pay him for his teaching when he had won his first court-case. When the pupil delayed payment, Protagoras threatened court proceedings, pointing out that if the pupil lost, he would have to pay by the court's judgement, and if he won, he would have to pay by the agreement (Diogenes *Lives* 9.56). The reply was that if the pupil won he need not pay, but if he lost he also need not pay (by the court, and the agreement, respectively). The story sounds like satire, but is revealing: persuasive arguments depend on premises, and can always be turned round. What matters in the end is what 'we' can agree, and not what is 'really true'.

Socrates disagreed – but maybe there is not much difference in effect between those who agree that the *real* truth is unknown and those who abandon any wish to know it? The question in either case must then be what assumptions we should act upon here-now. If 'truth-in-the-depths' is beyond our reach, and all we see in the well are our reflections, we had better hang on to whatever peace we have. We should judge our governors and teachers by the standards that we use to select any tradesman: their competence in doing what they profess, and their honesty in settling on the price. At least, we should be cautious about obeying people whose motives, goals and manners we don't know. Does it follow that we should govern our own lives, ignoring the usual authorities? But if the usual authorities turn out unreliable, we ourselves are unreliable for exactly the same reason. None of us – apparently – know what we mean by justice, virtue, honour or success, and none of us have any clear idea of what to do. Why then trust ourselves any more than the authorities? Believing in oneself is as foolish a superstition as believing in Joanna Southcott (Chesterton 1961, p. 5). So also Philo of Alexandria: 'if we mistakenly trust our private reasonings we shall construct and build the city of the mind that destroys the truth' (*Legum Allegoriarum* 3.228: 2005, p. 151). A mind that fancies 'itself competent by its own abilities to judge what was expedient, and to assent to all sorts of apparent facts, as if they really had solid truth in them' is drunk, and not in a good way (Philo *De Ebrietate* 41, citing *Genesis* 19.3).

Philo went on to mock philosophers' trust in the fallible instruments of 'reason' and 'experience', pointing out that 'about these very things, and about the different ways of life, and about the ends to which all actions ought to be referred, and about ten thousand other things which logical, and moral, and natural philosophy comprehends, there have been an unspeakable number of discussions, as to which, up to the present time, there is no agreement whatever among all these philosophers who have examined into such subjects' (*De Ebrietate* 48). He was closer to the Socratic spirit in this than are those who imagine that Socrates urged us to doubt everyone but ourselves.

By this account, both Socrates and Protagoras praised tolerance. Both were concerned to disillusion those who thought they had a path to truth so certain that they could afford to ignore tradition and their friends' opinion. The better 'truth' was what we could, for a while, agree upon. But there remains a difference. It is often now imagined that it is 'objective moralism', the belief that there are real truths of value, which must lead to 'expert rule', and that 'democracy' depends upon the assumption that the 'right road' merely means the one that most of us approve. This is mistaken. Protagoras professed to help cities achieve a 'better' state, one they could approve, and Socrates reminded them of the simple rules they actually would use when choosing between builders, cobblers, doctors and the rest. Socrates, in effect, asked people to trust their common sense in deciding between their would-be rulers, not to obey them merely because they claimed to know the truth, and not to be too sure we knew the truth ourselves. Protagoras suggested that the best rulers would be the ones best able to convince the populace to keep the peace. It does not follow that the Socratic choice would be for aristocracy, the Protagorean for democracy, but rather the reverse. The weak are best protected by an *ancient* order that the strong may think they can afford to lose. That Socrates was a defender of the élite, and Protagoras of all the struggling masses, is absurd: Socrates, on the contrary, attacked the élite, and Protagoras sold them weapons. Both, it seems, offended powerful parties, and were respectively killed and evicted by the Athenians. Both might not unreasonably claim to have intended to do good, if only by curing people of their conceit. But whereas the Protagorean conclusion is that we should be content with ignorance, the Socratic pursuit of truth continues, all the more vigorously when our earlier thoughts are silenced. Only when we are dumbstruck by our own incompetence is there much chance of hearing what the Truth will tell us.

Were there other reasons for the Athenians to be suspicious, of Socrates as well as other Sophists? Were their cosmological speculations most feared? The fate of Anaxagoras (imprisoned, threatened with death, and finally dismissed from Athens) fits similar stories about the anger felt by established or conventional thinkers at the attempt to dethrone Zeus in favour of Whirligig (as Aristophanes alleges Socrates intended). This seems to suggest, to moderns, that philosophers were secular scientists, at odds with a superstition. This theme reappears in discussing later centuries: it is supposed, for example, that a Christian mob murdered Hypatia, in 415 AD, because she was a rationalist (and a woman). The truth is otherwise: few moderns who now mourn Hypatia endorse her probable beliefs, which were mostly Pythagorean. The violence of Alexandrian – or more broadly Egyptian – mobs was a familiar theme, and Hypatia, sadly, paid a price – perhaps at Cyril of Alexandria's instigation (see Damascius 1999, pp. 129–31 [43A-E]). But neither she, nor Socrates, nor even Anaxagoras were 'naturalists' or 'rationalists'. Why the Athenians chose, if they did, to censure the suggestion that the sun was a red-hot stone had more to do with politics than religion, as also in the case of Socrates. It was convenient to condemn some individuals. The story goes (Diogenes, *Lives*, 7.43) that the Athenians repented promptly of their treatment of Socrates: the accusers all ended badly. Anaxagoras, worn down by disapproval and the death of his sons, killed himself. The citizens of Lampsacus, where he had retired, gave school boys – at his request – an annual holiday in his honour. Did they honour him because or in spite of his cosmology? Was the issue ever really about the actual nature of the earth, the sun, the stars? What difference would it make to the normal pieties of Mediterranean cities that it was Whirligig who ruled the world 'instead of Zeus'? Both Whirligig and Zeus, after all, were bound by Destiny, and in either case we lived on the wheel of fortune, without any assurance that we shall survive for long, or that we shall ever know 'the truth'. The real danger to civil peace lay in the idea that nothing could matter to us but our immediate profit, and the answer lay in devotion to the laws and customs of an established city. Shame and a sense of justice, as Protagoras is made to argue in Plato's dialogue *Protagoras*, are what is needed to preserve the city. Or maybe Socrates was needed, and the love he felt for Athens – a love the greater because it was not uncritical.

The dramatic date of Plato's dialogue, *Protagoras*, also deserves some notice: it seems to be set in the late 420s, just after the great plague. In that disaster, so Thucydides says, both shame and a sense of justice lapsed.

Men who had hitherto concealed what they took pleasure in, now grew bolder. For, seeing the sudden change - how the rich died in a moment, and those who had nothing immediately inherited their property - they reflected that life and riches were alike transitory, and they resolved to enjoy themselves while they could, and to think only of pleasure. Who would be willing to sacrifice himself to the law of honour when he knew not whether he would ever live to be held in honour? The pleasure of the moment and any sort of thing which conduced to it took the place both of honour and of expediency. No fear of Gods or law of man deterred a criminal. (Thucydides 2.53: 2004, pp. 90–1)

Protagoras himself had visited Athens at least twice, in the 430s as well as the 420s, and Plato probably composed his dialogue as a pastiche of both occasions, and his own interpretation of what Socrates would have said. But the subtext had more force than we now feel: the debate was not an abstract one, but about what could be done to restore or create the peace. Can we rely on educated emotions, or should we attempt a careful hedonic calculation of our every act and ordinance, or is there something else to be done, in the name of an unknown virtue? It is also noticeable that the Athenians present at the debate, held in the house of a young man who wasted his wealth on Sophists, all failed to help Athens. Whether or not virtue can be taught, the young Athenians present did not learn it. Perhaps Plato was right to suggest, in another dialogue, that this needed divine intervention (*Meno* 99e: see Walsh 1984).

Purity and the practice of death

Plato was chiefly responsible for recreating Socrates as one made immortal by his contact with true Beauty, and later commentators have disagreed about the accuracy of his portrayal, even about the extent to which Plato presented 'his own' philosophy in his dialogues. But there were many other post-Socratics, variously acting out the role that Socrates had created or transformed. Phaedo of Elis (fl.380 BC) carried on the logical enquiries that have since pleased logicians. Aristippus of Cyrene (435–356 BC) sought to identify true pleasures more delightful and long-lasting than those of fashionable Athens. Antisthenes (445–365 BC), and after him Diogenes the Cynic (412–323 BC, from Sinope, on the Black Sea), whom Plato described as Socrates run mad, followed Heracleitos' lead by rejecting civilization in favour of the wild (except that they stayed in cities). Pyrrho of Elis (360–270 BC) tried to 'strip himself of human nature' so far as not to agree that anything that happened was either good or bad. It was in the end these radicals who captured the name of 'true philosophers', although it was Plato's theories that most, in the end, purveyed.

Much of what we nowadays label 'Socrates' is owed to Plato, and even more is owed to our own version of 'philosophy'. Precisely because they are both icons, we attribute to them whatever we care about in 'philosophy'. The issue is not primarily 'historical'. We can paint Socrates as an apologist for the Few: almost all the characters he seeks to influence in Plato's dialogues, and even the ones for whom he professes most affection, turn out 'badly'. Were these really his friends and followers, and did they act out the plans he encouraged in them? Maybe the Athenian people were quite right to fear and dislike him, because he subverted ancestral pieties in favour of the oligarchic party. Or did Plato wish to show that he had tried to influence those upstarts for the better (but had failed)?

One other notion that Plato attributed to him, in the dialogue describing his last day, *Phaedo*, is that philosophy is the practice of death, and that this is why philosophers should not mind dying. The conversation on that day is mostly with Pythagoreans, though they do not seem to be much influenced by Pythagoras's own convictions. The aphorism is partly confirmed by Socrates' habit of falling, as it seems, into a trance, and his obedience to an inner voice, a *daimon*. It is easy to explain all this away: his trances were absorption in a line of thought, and the inner voice was his conscience or intuition. 'The practice of death' is only a grandiose title for the habit of thinking about a larger world than is present to us through our senses, a way of discounting any immediate pains or pleasures in favour of a rational grasp of consequences, for others and for ourselves. Anything more than that, we can suppose, is merely what later, more superstitious ages added.

But we should acknowledge our own superstitions: that each of us is competent to reason our way to truth and good behaviour, and that we can identify ourselves entirely with particular human bodies. These are the errors that Socrates – maybe – spent his life rebutting. Even the Aristophanic parody detached Socrates from the everyday: the insult '*meteorolesches*', sky chatterer, is close to an older label with shamanic associations, 'sky walker', *aithrobates* (see Kingsley 1999, p. 245; 2010, pp. 94–5). Though Aristophanes sets up a debate between the Worse and the Better Cause, and suggests that Socrates, like other Sophists, is teaching people to win their contests (in court or in the assembly), this is not the central image of his play, which has Socrates hauled up in a basket, far from the distracting earth. Neither is the notion that Socrates was a secular student of nature. Instead we can imagine Socrates as a sort of prophet, doing the god's work of unsettling people with riddles, and liable to be 'god-caught' at inconvenient moments.

So maybe Socrates was Apollo's servant, not simply 'Classical'. Maybe what he told his friends on his last day is indeed what he supposed: that he was, like Pythagoras, Empedocles and the rest, an immortal spirit, with nothing to fear from the end of his mortal body. Maybe his conviction rested not on argument but on experience, supported by familiar ascetic practices.

Sophists were not the only travellers to offer settled citizens a service. There were also exorcists, diviners, purifiers, of the sort denounced by the Hippocratic authors as 'Magi, purifiers, begging priests and quacks'. Plato had his imagined city make laws against their pretences (*Laws* 10.909a8–b7), and causes Adeimantus to denounce them, as giving the rich a chance – as they suppose – of evading punishment (*Republic* 2.364b–366b). So in a later age, Protestant reformers denounced the sale of 'indulgences' and 'cheap forgiveness'. In both cases, the acknowledged corruptions did not imply that there was no chance of forgiveness, nor even that ritual could play no part in it. In *The Symposium*, it is Diotima (hired to purify the city after the great plague) who teaches Socrates, and not he who shows that she doesn't know what she's doing. Love, she says, is a desire to be remade immortal.

What, after all, is exorcism but the attempt to dispel curses, to rid the patient of his destructive demons? (see *Laws* 9.854b). Epimenides the Cretan employed animal sacrifices in every Athenian parish with a view to restoring the city: Porphyry could reject those methods (as serving only to feed such demons as required blood) without disputing the need for purification. Porphyry's master, Plotinus, mocked sectarian attempts to cure disease by exorcising demons and the use of charms (*Ennead* II.9 [33].14). But he too acknowledged that we needed ways to dispel the coarse enchantments of the world, the flesh and the devil. Those arts include 'a magical art of love', erotic sorcery, used by those who apply by contact to different people magical substances designed to draw them together and with a love-force implanted in them; they join one soul to another, as if they were training together plants set at intervals. They use as well figures with power in them, and by putting themselves in the right postures they quietly bring powers upon themselves, since they are within one universe and work upon one universe. . . . And there is a natural drawing power in spells wrought by the tune and the particular intonation and posture of the magician – for these things attract, as pitiable figures and voices attract; for it is the irrational soul – not the power of choice or the reason – which is charmed by music, and this kind of magic causes no surprise: people even like being enchanted, even if this is not exactly what they demand from the musicians. (*Ennead* IV.4 [28].40, 11f)

Socrates' one claim to expertise was that he was a match-maker, and that he sought to seduce the young into rethinking what they had thought – a claim sufficiently alarming that Plato put considerable effort into disarming the suggestion that Socrates was a sexual predator. The words that Plato put in Socrates' mouth on his last day are usually now ignored:

The body is a source of countless distractions by reason of the mere requirement of food, and is liable also to diseases which overtake and impede us in the pursuit of truth: it fills us full of loves, and lusts, and fears, and fancies of all kinds, and endless foolery, and in very truth, as men say, takes away from us the power of thinking at all. Whence come wars, and fightings, and factions? Whence but from the body and the lusts of the body? All wars are occasioned by the love of money, and money has to be acquired for the sake of the body and in slavish ministration to it; and by reason of all these impediments we have no time to give to philosophy; and, last and worst of all, even if the body allows us leisure and we betake ourselves to some speculation, it is always breaking in upon us, causing turmoil and confusion in our inquiries, and so amazing us that we are prevented from seeing the truth. It has been proved to us by experience that if we would have pure knowledge of anything we must be quit of the body - the soul by herself must behold things by themselves: and then we shall attain that which we desire, and of which we say that we are lovers - wisdom; not while we live, but, as the argument shows, only after death; for if while in company with the body the soul cannot have pure knowledge, one of two things follows - either knowledge is not to be attained at all, or, if at all, after death. (*Phaedo* 66bff)

The claim is indeed at odds with the 'Classical' worldview. The commoner assumption was that bodies were the only, or the more significant, realities, and that only in youthful bodies could we glimpse the divine. Ugliness, old age, senility and death were obvious evils, and after death, if anything survived, there were only mournful shadows. Even the Hebrews were uncertain that there was any return from Sheol. The Mysteries offered an alternative, that we could escape not merely from this body but from the wheel of fortune. Maybe Socrates only meant to use these themes as metaphors, to suggest that we would do better to think of other things than our immediate bodily needs and wishes. We would be happier if our own immediate happiness was not all that mattered. 'Memory' – by which is meant the impersonal memory of science and of tradition – 'is exalted because it is the power that makes it possible for men to escape time and return to the divine state' (Vernant 1983, p. 88). By remembering that there is a larger and older world than mine I can realize both that the world can go on without me (and one day will) and that in awareness of that world I can find a sort of immortality. But maybe Socrates expected a literal immortality, of the very same sort as allowed Pythagoras to claim to have had earlier incarnations: to have escaped, and yet to have returned to the Wheel to help the rest of us.

Socrates was not, in Plato's eyes, a Sophist, a sexual predator nor yet a professional exorcist. But he was willing to use those dangerous tools in the service of his gospel. To know the truth, to live the life of God, we have to put ourselves aside, to silence that vulgar, chattering goblin who poses as our ego. We have to submit to correction:

Refutation is the greatest and chiefest of purifications, and he who has not been refuted, though he be the Great King himself, is in an awful state of impurity; he is uninstructed and deformed in those things in which to be truly blessed he ought to be fairest and purest. (*Sophist* 227c, 228a-d, 230d; on the further history of this trope, see Boyle 2002)

Exorcists were not the only ones to be concerned with 'purity'. Though there was no priestly caste in most Mediterranean cities, many priesthoods were inherited, and those families were partly separated from the mass of the population. In Israel, the priestly families could marry out, but at the price of their priesthood. The office – in Israel and elsewhere – carried some privileges, but also many penalties and restrictions. Priests – and especially, in Israel, the High Priest – must be free of all pollution.

Purity also defines the gods. By establishing a place, a lineage, a person who could be judged 'clean', or 'pure', there could be a link between the gods and us – like Pharaoh or the High Priest. The people at large could afford impurities because at least there was someone, somewhere close, to be our advocate. To be 'holy' is to be separate, untouched by common things, and 'holy men' must stay like that, their status at risk from sickness, sex or contact with the dead.

Rules about the handling of dead bodies, about contagious diseases and about sexual intercourse are helpful. Contagion, after all, is something that affects us still. The brutal regulations that are given in *Leviticus* and brutally enforced, for example, in *Numbers* are still bound to strike us as appalling.

> When the Israelites were in Shittim, the people began to have intercourse with Moabite women, who invited them to the sacrifices offered to their gods. (*Numbers* 25.1–2)

The Lord, it is said, was angry, and ordered the killing of any who had worshipped 'the Baal of Peor'. Seizing the occasion, Phinehas, son of Eleazar and grandson of Aaron, the high priest, took a spear and killed one couple, 'pinning them together'. The Lord, it is said, approved and granted Phinehas and his line a covenant forever, 'because he showed his zeal for his God and made expiation for the Israelites' (*Numbers* 25.13)[3]. After the killing, the plague which had attacked the Israelites was brought to a stop, though twenty thousand had already died (*Numbers* 25.8). Though later Rabbis did not doubt that Phinehas was right, they were disturbed that 'due process' had not been followed, and were cautious in the morals they drew from the story. Philo preferred to allegorize it entirely, seeing Phinehas as that Reason which – like Heracles – refuses the wiles of Pleasure (see Feldman 2002). But the merely historical message should not be forgotten. *Deuteronomy* may have been composed some centuries later, to indicate where the people of Israel went wrong as they moved into Palestine, but it is of a piece with the earlier writings.

> When the Lord your God brings you into the land that you are about to enter and occupy, and he clears away many nations before you - the Hittites, the Girgashites, the Amorites, the Canaanites, the Perizzites, the Hivites, and the Jebusites, even nations mightier and more numerous than you - and when the Lord gives them over to you and you defeat them, then you must utterly destroy them. Make no covenant with them and show them no mercy. Do not intermarry with them, giving your daughters to their sons or taking their daughters for your sons, for that would turn away your children from following me, to serve other gods. Then the anger of the Lord would be kindled against you, and he would destroy you quickly. But this is how you must deal with them: break down their altars, smash their pillars, hew down their sacred poles and burn their idols with fire. (*Deuteronomy* 7:1–6; see also *Psalm* 106.34–39)

Such brutal regulations may indeed have been the only way at the time to halt a sexually transmitted plague, just as the dietary rules of the Torah may have been important for medical and hygienic reasons. But the actual reasons offered have to do with 'holiness'. The plague was not the reason that promiscuity was wrong, but God's judgement on the wrong already done. The people of Israel were to have nothing to do with the earlier peoples and their customs. They were forbidden to profit from their conquests, whether by making slaves or taking ransom. The defeated were to be dedicated to the God. This was not a practice peculiar to the incoming Hebrews. Mesopotamian Empires had done as much, though they did not openly claim that the defeated peoples were wicked.

> A famous parallel is provided by the Moabite Stone, erected by the ninth-century king Mesha: 'And Chemosh said to me, "Go, take Nebo from Israel". So I went by night and fought against it from the break of dawn until noon, taking it and slaying all, seven thousand men, boys, women, girls, and maid-servants, for I had devoted them to destruction for (the god) Ashtar-Chemosh'. (Collins 2003, p. 5; see also Stern 1991)[4]

Is keeping the people and the priesthood 'pure' simply ethnocentrism, rationalized as devotion to the god of a peculiar people? The question arises for the Hebrews as it did for Euthyphro, in Plato's dialogue (on which more below): what is it that God or the gods desire of us? At first, Euthyphro can only repeat himself: 'Let me simply say that piety or holiness is learning how to please the gods in word and deed, by prayers and sacrifices' (Plato, *Euthyphro*, 14b). These 'prayers and sacrifices' include attempts to purify, to set things right. They are not merely ceremonial. We don't do the gods any good – but we can please them, can be what they wish us to be. And what they wish is our cooperation in making 'many and fair things', things they love (*Euthyphro* 14a).

The answer devised by the Hebrews was that 'holiness', *qadosh*, involved compassion: to be holy, it was not enough to enforce a sexual or dietary distance from the peoples round about, merely to make a distinction. The distinction was to be made because those peoples had done 'abominable things' (*Leviticus* 18.27–9): chiefly, in that passage from *Leviticus*, they had had sexual relations with anyone or anything they pleased, and 'surrendered their children to Molech'. But those were not the only abominations. The reiterated rule is that the people of Israel are to be holy. They are not to steal or cheat or keep back an employee's wages, nor deprive the poor and the stranger of the chance to glean the harvest, nor 'treat the deaf with contempt nor put an obstruction in the way of the blind' (*Leviticus* 19.9–14).

> You shall not pervert justice, either by favouring the poor or by subservience to the great . . . You shall not nurse hatred against your brother. . . . You shall not seek revenge, or cherish anger toward your kinsfolk; you shall love your neighbour as a man like yourself. I am the Lord. (*Leviticus* 19.15–18)

So how can it be right to kill the wicked, if wickedness is shown in the willingness to kill? Conversely, how can it be right not to oppose that wickedness, even to the death? Whatever we do or fail to do, it sometimes seems, we're wrong, and need some absolution.

When other peoples encountered the Mosaic Law, they usually distinguished 'ritual' from strictly 'ethical' commands, and mostly commended the latter while mocking most of the former (see Harrington 2001, p. 165). We can suspect that 'holiness' was reinterpreted, and that it did originally amount much more to 'purity' and distance from a disturbing world. Olympian gods like Artemis cannot stay beside their dying followers: 'easily do you leave our long intimacy', said Hippolytus, unhappily, to the goddess who most represented 'purity' to him (Euripides, *Hippolytus,* 1437ff). The practice of death advised in Plato's *Phaedo* is not that different from the practice of his *Symposium*: to try to see beauty bare, stripped of flesh and colours and all that mortal nonsense (*Symposium* 211e). So also in *Theaetetus*, where we are told that our duty and our joy should be to get more like God: 'wherefore we ought to fly away from earth to heaven as quickly as we can; and to fly away means to become like God, as far as this is possible; and to become like him, means to become holy, just, and wise' (*Theaetetus* 176b).

> God ought to be to us the measure of all things, and not man, as men commonly say: the words are far more true of Him. And he who would be dear to God must, as far as is possible, be like Him and such as He is. Wherefore the temperate man is the friend of God, for he is like Him; and the intemperate or unjust man is unlike Him, and different from Him. And the same applies to other things; and this is the conclusion, which is also the noblest and truest of all sayings, that for the good man to offer sacrifice to the Gods, and hold converse with them by means of prayers and offerings and every kind of service, is the noblest and best of all things, and also the most conducive to a happy life, and very fit and meet. But with the bad man, the opposite of this is true: for the bad man has an impure soul, whereas the good is pure; and from one who is polluted, neither a good man nor God can without impropriety receive gifts. Wherefore the unholy do only waste their much service upon the Gods, but when offered by any holy man, such service is most acceptable to them. (Plato, *Laws,* 4.716cff, tr. Benjamin Jowett)

That all this was not just *Plato's* opinion is suggested by Xenophon's account of Socrates:

> I think that to want nothing is to resemble the gods, and that to want as little as possible is to make the nearest approach to the gods; that the Divine nature is perfection, and that to be nearest to the Divine nature is to be nearest to perfection. (Xenophon, *Memorabilia,* 1.6.11)

But if we get closer to God by stripping and shedding things (which is the metaphor that later Platonists also used: see Clark 2008), what exactly is it that remains? And is there some reason not to rise too far from the merely human? Phinehas, son of Eliezer did, let us suppose, what rationally he should: he took prompt action against open disobedience of a sort that, at the time, threatened disaster for the people. But we prefer our heroes to have more doubts than he had. The later writers were right to hope that mercy would temper judgement. Being like God, and doing what God does, may require us to divest ourselves of error, and to stay unsullied by 'the world, the flesh and the devil', but it also must mean love. Pagan and Hebrew both, in the end, agreed.

> It does no good at all to say 'Look to God', unless one also teaches how one is to look. . . . In reality it is virtue which goes before us to the goal and, when it comes to exist in the soul along with wisdom, shows God; but God, if you talk about him without true virtue, is only a name. Again, despising the universe and the gods in it and the other noble things is certainly not becoming good. . . . For anyone who feels affection for anything at all shows kindness to all that is akin to the object of his affection, and to the children of the father that he loves. But every soul is a child of That Father. (*Ennead* II.9 [33].15, 33–16.10)[5]

CHAPTER FIVE

Divine Plato

Reading the dialogues

No history of ancient thought can avoid the mountain mass of Plato, but in his own day the massiveness of what he was and did was far less obvious. We see him as the founder of a distinctive 'Platonic' school, and as responsible for making Athens into 'the School of Hellas', the place where all aspiring philosophers would have to go to study. In later years, there would be other such 'University Cities' (including Alexandria, Antioch, Constantinople, Pergamum, Rhodes and Rome), but there were already other Schools, whose words and actions have not been as well preserved. Though Plato was inspired by Socrates, it may be that he went elsewhere for doctrines.

> When Socrates was gone, he attached himself to Cratylus the Heraclitean, and to Hermogenes who professed the philosophy of Parmenides. Then at the age of twenty-eight, according to Hermodorus, he withdrew to Megara to Euclides, with certain other disciples of Socrates. Next he proceeded to Cyrene on a visit to Theodorus the mathematician, thence to Italy to see the Pythagorean philosophers Philolaus and Eurytus, and thence to Egypt. (Diogenes, *Lives*, 3.6; see also Cicero *De Re Publica* I.10, p. 19)

Nor were these travels only in his youth. Even later, when he was famous, he was not always to be found in Athens.

When enthusiastic young men were competing to get to Athens so that they could have Plato as their teacher, he himself was studying under Egyptian elders and travelling along the endless shores of the Nile and through its vast plains, its widespread exotic regions, and the twisting paths of its canals. So I am hardly surprised that he went over to Italy, where he learned about the principles and teachings of Pythagoras from Archytas of Tarentum, and from Timaeus, Arion, and Echecrates at Locri. (Valerius Maximus 2004, p. 283: 8.7 ext.3)

That he visited Lower Egypt may be no more than the usual claim. That he visited Italy and Sicily, and returned in the hope of educating the Syracusan ruler, is likelier to be true. Also, that he learnt from Archytas and from the writings of Philolaus of Croton (c470–c385 BC: see Huffman 1993). That he learnt from 'Timaeus of Locri' may be a faulty inference: most scholars suspect that Timaeus, in the dialogue of that name, is as much a figment as 'the Eleatic Stranger' of *The Sophist* and *The Statesman*, or 'the Athenian Stranger' of *The Laws*. But even if there was no actual Timaeus, the cosmology offered under his name is distinctively different from others of Plato's imaginings (some said it was copied from Philolaus), and was influential both in the Middle Ages and, especially, in the Renaissance. This story indicates a wider truth: in Plato's dialogues, many differing traditions met, and many differing traditions also grew. If we had more than fragments of Parmenides, Empedocles, Philolaus, Democritus and many others of his predecessors, we might have a different view of his achievement. Similarly, if Aristotle's esoteric writings were not so voluminous, and we had more of Poseidonius the Stoic (from Apamea in Syria by birth, but resident in Rhodes) instead. The difficulty of approaching Plato (and also Aristotle) is the opposite of the problems we face with other, fragmented authors: we easily suppose that we therefore understand them better. But the fact that we don't have the other texts means that we also lack the context for what they wrote, what exactly they were writing against, and why. Plato was correct, in *Phaedrus* and elsewhere, to say that writings, on their own, are easily misunderstood, especially if we don't practise what their authors preached. So also in the Hebraic tradition, the oral teaching is the medium through which the written is to be interpreted (Harrington 2001, pp. 140–2). 'The Talmud is essentially an activity, not a book: you engage in it, rather than read it as you would a piece of literature' (Solomon 2009, p. xviii). The same should be true when reading any philosophy.

The Letters attributed – perhaps falsely – to Plato (especially the second and seventh) deny that any of Plato's writings describe his own philosophy. But this is because such philosophical truths can never be conveyed in the written word, rather than that Plato disowned the views he attributed to Socrates. A conventional account – though one that scholars feel less certain about than once they did – is that the shorter – and maybe earlier – dialogues, typified by a relative simplicity of diction and uncertain outcome, may show us something of the 'real' Socrates, a man devoted to the demolition of misplaced certainties. Typically, he enquires what people mean by 'courage', 'piety', 'friendship' or 'virtue', and rejects their usual attempt to answer him by giving examples of each kind. Without some principle, he suggests, we cannot understand how to extend the list, say, of courageous actions. When they respond by offering a criterion, he answers by adducing other examples that are recognizably, say, courageous but do not fit the criterion, or recognizably not, but do. The dialogue will then conclude with the rueful admission that we don't know what we mean. There is an unacknowledged contradiction: if we can recognize an act of courage before we can voice a criterion, and use that recognition to rebut an hypothesis, then we don't, after all, need to articulate what we know very well: most of us can recognize our friends, but rather few of us can manage to *describe* them well enough for others to do so too! It can be even worse: in his dialogue with Euthyphro, Socrates can be made to seem corrupt (Geach 1966).

Euthyphro is sure that his father has committed a grave wrong – and most of us will agree that he has (namely, throwing a hired labourer, one of Euthyphro's dependants, into a ditch to die because he had killed a slave in a drunken brawl). The event occurred in Naxos some years earlier when Euthyphro's family farmed there as Athenian colonists, but the case could not be considered then. Athens had been under the rule of the Thirty, or engaged – after the restoration of the democracy – in codifying the ancient laws. Now that these have been settled, Euthyphro intends to take the case to the *Archon Basileus* (on the very day that Socrates himself has been called before that official to answer a charge of blasphemy). Socrates subverts his certainties by raising doubts about the way, at Socrates' behest, Euthyphro explains himself. It is true that there was, especially for Greeks, a serious issue here: did Euthyphro owe his father so much respect as to forbid his taking action against him, even in this case? And was Socrates himself to be blamed – as Aristophanes and his accusers blamed him – for setting sons against their fathers? Plato himself depicts him – in *Gorgias* – as arguing, exactly, that it is our duty to bring a prosecution even against our friends, if they've done wrong. So one purpose of *Euthyphro* may be to defuse that charge (Rosen 1968).

> Rhetoric is of no use to us in helping a man to excuse his own injustice, or that of his parents or friends, or children or country; but may be of use to anyone who holds that instead of excusing he ought to accuse - himself above all, and in the next degree his family or any of his friends who may be doing wrong; he should bring to light the iniquity and not conceal it, that so the wrong-doer may suffer and be made whole; he should force himself and others not to shrink, but with closed eyes like brave men to let the physician operate with knife or searing iron, not regarding the pain, in the hope of attaining the good and the honourable; let him who has done things worthy of stripes, allow himself to be scourged, if of bonds, to be bound, if of a fine, to be fined, if of exile, to be exiled, if of death, to die, himself being the first to accuse himself *and his own relations*, and using rhetoric to this end, that his and their unjust actions may be made manifest, and that they themselves may be delivered from injustice, which is the greatest evil. (Plato, *Gorgias*, 480bff: my emphasis)

Certainly this is a shocking thought, especially as regards the relations of sons and fathers, which were clearly stressful in ancient Greece (and also something to joke about). The standard impossible question was 'Have you stopped beating your father yet?' (Diogenes *Lives* 2.135; see also Aristotle *Nicomachean Ethics* 7.1149b8–13). Whitlock (1994) and Zhu (2002) have pointed to the analogous dispute in Confucian ethics, and the significance for Chinese and Greek alike of filial piety. According to Xenophon, Socrates advised his son (who was at odds with his mother) that he ought to honour his parents above all:

> 'From whomsoever a man receives a favour' [said Lamprocles], 'whether friend or enemy, and does not endeavour to make a return for it, he is in my opinion unjust'. 'If such, then, be the

case,' pursued Socrates, 'ingratitude must be manifest injustice?' Lamprocles expressed his assent. 'The greater benefits, therefore, a person has received, and makes no return, the more unjust he must be.' He assented to this position also. 'Whom, then,' asked Socrates, 'can we find receiving greater benefits from any persons than children receive from their parents? children whom their parents have brought from non-existence into existence, to view so many beautiful objects, and to share in so many blessings, as the gods grant to men'. (*Memorabilia* 2.2.2–3)

The Athenian Stranger of *The Laws* likewise endorses laws prescribing filial obedience, and in *The Republic*, Socrates rejects the stories of Zeus and Kronos, Kronos and Ouranos, to which Euthyphro appeals[1], saying that even if they were true, the young should not be told about them. But the conflict is unreal. The same argument, from gratitude for existence, is used in *Crito* to explain why Socrates thinks himself obliged to submit to the Athenian decision (that he be executed), but this obligation did not require him to stay silent and not interrogate the Athenians! He had, he said, a greater obligation to obey the god Apollo, and fulfilled both, by questioning them but permitting them to kill him. And even in *The Laws* there is a set procedure for Euthyphro's dilemma:

[If a son wants to file a charge,] this is the law the son must observe. First of all he must go to the eldest Guardians of the laws and explain his father's misfortune, and they, after due investigation, must advise him whether to bring the charge or not. If they advise that he should, they must come forward as witnesses for the prosecution and plead on his behalf. (Plato, *Laws*, 11.929e)[2]

Which is very much what Euthyphro was actually set on doing – though it is possible, and even probable, that we are to understand that Socrates – himself an unofficial Guardian of the laws – persuaded him to go away and think about it (Diogenes *Lives* 2.29). Could he trust either the *Archon* or an Athenian jury to reach a sound decision? Reading the text requires us to stay alert enough to read behind it.[3]

In longer dialogues that remain the triumphant apex of philosophical literature (such as *Meno*, *Phaedo*, *Phaedrus*, *Symposium* and *Republic*), Plato more openly subverts some apparently Socratic axioms. First, he devises a psychology that makes it possible for people to do wrong knowingly. Human action can stem from other roots than reason, and it is not ignorance only that produces evil. In the schematic psychology of Buddhism, Anger, Lust and Ignorance are to blame – and Plato thought so too (though extending 'anger', *thumos*, to cover false ambition). Second, he noticed Socrates' reliance on an unarticulated knowledge of what counts as courage, justice and the rest. We can assess the accuracy of a suggested criterion because we can already discriminate, rather as we can say whether a suggested name is the one that we've forgotten. Third, he spoke more firmly of the kind of being such kinds must have (and thereby also gave an answer to the Parmenidean puzzles). In brief, he outlined what has since been called the Theory of Forms (though we need not think that there was ever a single, well-formed theory), which I shall sketch below. Fourth, he admitted – which is indeed implied in the Socratic practice – that 'right opinion' and a sound upbringing may spare the city many evils that 'free-thinkers' bring. During this middle period he also tried to play a practical part in Syracusan politics, and failed – with what effect on his morale, who knows?

A third class of dialogues (identified by stylistic complexity, and a smaller role for the dramatic Socrates) employ a new technique of definition seeking: homing in on a disputed concept by successive, strange dichotomies. A statesman, for example, is defined as a sort of herdsman of tame, gregarious animals, specifically those land-dwelling, walking, hornless, endogamous and bipedal animals that we call human. The nearest thing to the Statesman is the swineherd. A slightly different cut might instead have identified us as featherless bipeds, and the Statesman's nearest kin, by unspoken analogy, as a gooseherd. This sort of dichotomizing definition was mocked in contemporary comedy, and more seriously criticised by Aristotle (as indeed, implicitly, by Plato). Some late commentators have concluded that Plato at last abandoned any Theory of Forms (if it was his to hold), and also at last betrayed the spirit of his master. Socrates, it is said, would have been convicted by the thought police of Plato's last imaginings, in *The Laws*. Atheists, he suggests, and those who think that the gods don't care about us, are enemies of civil peace, and should be converted, exiled or executed.

The idea that Plato radically changed his mind and methods, and became, in his last days, at once an analytical philosopher and an inquisitor, is too modern a thought to be convincing. Earlier critics saw no sign of any change of heart, even if the details of the exposition changed. That we owe obedience to the laws of our land as to our parents and originals is an idea to be found from the (early?) *Crito* to the (late?) *Laws*. That the statesman is a sort of herdsman is an idea attributed to Socrates himself by Xenophon (*Memorabilia* 1.2.32). Socrates was never praised as a 'free-thinker', bent on his own way, but as an obedient servant of the gods. This too is confirmed by Xenophon. 'Do you not see', he is said to have asked a young man inclined to neglect popular religion, 'that the oldest and wisest of human communities, the oldest and wisest cities and nations, are the most respectful to the gods, and that the wisest age of man is the most observant of their worship?' (*Memorabilia* 1.4.16). The possibility that kings might become philosophers is as much to be hoped for at the end as at the beginning, and as little to be expected.

Nor is the once accepted dating of Plato's dialogues certain. The fact that he was apparently writing or re-writing *The Laws* when he died does not establish that this was his last work: authors often revise or reconsider or even merely re-read their early works. Maybe in any case *The Laws*, whenever it was written, should be read first, as stating the political problem faced by fourth-century Greeks (Zuckert 2009). Maybe – as Diogenes also records (*Lives* 3.38) – it was *Phaedrus* or at least an early version that was Plato's first attempt.[4] It is also said that he wrote other dialogues while Socrates was still living: 'on hearing Plato read the *Lysis*, Socrates exclaimed, "By Heracles, what a number of lies this young man is telling about me!" For he has included in the dialogue much that Socrates never said' (*Lives* 3.35). What the lies were – or what those who told this story thought they were – Diogenes does not say. At least we cannot be sure that what Plato wrote is either true to the historical Socrates or entirely what Plato himself believed. The dialogues are works of art as well as of philosophy – and neither art nor philosophy is always wholly clear. The principal effect of Plato's work, in many differing schools, lies not in his chronology, nor even in his ideas, but in the figure of Socrates, and his delight in argument.

Forms

But a belief in Forms, and the Immortality of the Soul, is what is usually meant by Platonism, and it is not uncommon for historians and theologians alike to suggest that it is all the fault of Platonism, and the Greeks, that the modern industrial complex ravages the earth and patriarchalists despise the womanly sentiments (or else it's the fault of the Jews). Even a brief acquaintance with Platonism's critics might reveal that it was more often they who despised the sentiments, as well as the earth and our fellows. Platonists, historically, have usually been the ones to consider our duties to those not of our species. When a sparrow took refuge with him from a hawk, Xenocrates, the third head of the Academy, stroked it and let it go, declaring that a suppliant must not be betrayed (Diogenes, *Lives*, 4.10). Both pagan and Abrahamic Platonists have found corporeal nature sacramental. Plotinus was vegetarian, refused medicines made from animals, and denounced those 'gnostics' who despised the earth. Porphyry, his pupil, was until recently the only 'professional philosopher' to write at length in favour of 'the rights of beasts' (Porphyry 2000). Nor was this at odds with Plato, who caused his Athenian Stranger to lay down these rules for his imagined city:

> The earth is their parent: let them tend her more carefully than children do their mother. For she is a goddess and their queen, and they are her mortal subjects. Such also are the feelings which they ought to entertain to the gods and demi-gods of the country. (Plato, *Laws*, 5.740)

This may, admittedly, have more to do with the earth, the landscape, as it is for its human inhabitants, suffused with ceremonial and memory, than with the earth of its many non-human residents. What is to be valued is the house of memory, with its hero shrines and named geological features. Though Socrates, in *Phaedrus*, pretends that he is only at home in the city, he knows the valley of the Ilyssus well and refers without apology to the meaning conveyed by cicadas and oracular trees. The living earth is our mother, and disrespecting our mother is a really bad idea.

So what is 'the Theory of Forms'? It has at least three roots: in speaking of what there is, of how we know it, and what we should do. First, it is an answer to the challenge posed by the twin hypotheses that everything changes and that nothing does. The answer is that there must be unchanging forms if anything is to change. If nothing at all were ever 'the same' from one instant to another, or 'the same' in different places, there could not even be instants or those different places. Rationality requires that there be real beings present at many different points in space and time. Even if such samenesses were *only* immanent, possessed by those several points and never to be found outside them, they would be quite real (the term *eidos* is sometimes reserved for immanent forms, *idea* for the transcendent). Even to say that there is nothing in common between This and That except that we employ the *same* name for it (say, 'dog') implicitly assumes both that there is a speaker who is the *same*, and that there is a word that is and means the *same* in many instances. Nominalism, as it was later called, is literally unspeakable: those who believe it must, to be consistent, eventually resort to gestures. Platonic realism differs from more immanent varieties in admitting that there are unrealised entities, kinds such that there are no particular instances, and that there must be if we are to think. The mathematical entities that Pythagoras – perhaps – discerned cannot be equated with their images in the sand or stone. Truths about circles and triangles would still be true even if there never had been material geometric figures, and even though the ones there are aren't altogether what those truths decree. Most working mathematicians are still Platonists at heart. Some of the greatest of them have been *dogmatic* Platonists:

> The Platonistic view is the only one tenable. Thereby I mean the view that mathematics describes a non-sensual reality, which exists independently of the human mind and is only perceived, and probably perceived very incompletely, by the human mind. (Gödel 1995, pp. 322–3)

As to how we know these things, or any others: Plato saw that we already know a great deal that we cannot wholly say, or prove. He saw that we could never find evidence for any thought at all unless we already knew what counted as evidence and what as true. How could you reliably recognize a picture of Antisthenes if you have never met him in the flesh? How can we recognize the truth unless we already know at least what the truth must look like? The question then arises: how? How is it that creatures such as we should have devices for discovering truths, or ever be able to articulate them? Modern attempts to suggest that evolutionary theory can explain it fail: natural selection cannot, in its nature, ever select for creatures able to look up aloft, *meteorolescheis*, and to get those things right. It can select for creatures able to avoid immediate danger or recognize swift advantages: there is an immediate pay-off there. But even if a variation capable of accurate cloud-watching did appear (and how?) – it would not be preferred to the far more practical ground-watchers. Long-distance gains have little effect on evolution. Plato's answer seems the only hope: we have the capacity to see such truths because we carry the image of truth in us, and we do so not by chance and natural selection, but from our origin, which is also the world's origin. We could never work out truths by sense alone, and we have the wherewithal to work them out because we are offspring of the self-same intellect that engenders the ordered universe.

And what should we do? The forms themselves are what is to be admired. There are no forms of disease or devilry except the forms of health and righteousness from which the unhealthy and malicious deviate: to be diseased is simply not to be healthy, in however many ways we might fall ill or fail. The standards to which particulars approximate are the ways in which pure Beauty can be known; the goals to which we yearn are the ways pure Good is qualified for our particular beings. The truth of ethical propositions is as unchanging as the truth of mathematics, but far more difficult to identify – except that even the truths of mathematics depend on those of ethics. Only if it is *true* that mathematical elegance is a form of beauty, that beauty is a standard to which we ought to bend, will it prove true (in any but a trivial sense) that Pythagoras's theorem (or any other) is a truth to be obeyed. And why should we concern ourselves with beauty? That, said Aristotle, is a blind man's question (Diogenes *Lives* 5.20). However abstract or pedantic Platonic Forms may seem, especially when they are identified with Numbers, we should remember that they are the objects of passionate love. They are Beauty in its several forms, and derive their being from the Good Itself.

The soul, or at any rate the mind, shares in eternal being. That is to say, we can regard the most important part of ourselves as indestructible, precisely because it has no content and no substance except the eternal objects that it contemplates. By identifying myself with eternal truths I know myself, that self at least, immortal. What matters about Plato, what he minded about, must be forever. More metaphysically, the immortal Mind in me is just the same as the immortal Mind in you. That mind, in fact, is a god – though the way a particular corporeal being thinks is only intermittently, and waveringly, the immortal mind. We do not always think the truth: when we do, there is one thought in each of us, and that thought will survive our mortal bodies. This may be all that Plato's actual arguments for immortality could show (if they show this much), but he probably wanted more. He suggested that there were real immortal, *individual* souls who were condemned to live our earthly lives until they had sufficiently purified their emotions and their thought.

So why, if the theory has so many and so great advantages, did anyone dismiss it? One unimportant reason is doubtless only to avoid there being unchanging standards by which we are judged. More seriously, some have thought that there was a contradiction in the usual idea of Forms. This argument, commonly known as the Third Man, is found in Plato's dialogue *Parmenides*, as well as in Aristotle's writings (e.g. *Metaphysics* 1.990b17): it was, in short, a commonplace. Suppose, the argument goes, that we postulate a Form for every class of things that are rightly called by the same name (as it might be the Ideal Human); such a Form will itself be Human (if it were not, what could be?), and there will 'therefore' be a further Form, the Ideal Meta-Human, in parallel with the newly enlarged class composed of all the particular humans plus the Ideal Human. The argument is then repeated to create the Ideal Meta-Meta-Human, and so forever. Better, obviously, not to begin, but what is the beginning? The conventional claim is that Plato seems to have committed himself to two conflicting notions: first, that every real class of things must manifest or share or imitate one form which is distinct from any or all of that class (Monroe was beautiful, but was not beauty); second, that such a form itself – and paradigmatically – is of the same class as its avatars or mimics. In other words:

1 Nothing that is predicatively f is identical with the Form it manifests.

2 The Form manifested by any such particulars itself is f.

It is unnecessary (indeed it is fatal) to abandon the idea that the Form itself is f (if justice itself is not just, nothing could be just). Nor is it necessary (indeed it is fatal) to abandon the idea that there is an F that every f-thing manifests (if there is no justice, nothing could be just). The fallacy in the argument is to assume that 'being f' must always be 'being predicatively f'. Everything derivatively moist, by an analogy, is such because it's covered in liquid: is liquid itself moist, and what is the hyperliquid film that covers it? The simple answer is that liquid is moist essentially: liquid is, identically, moisture. Just so the Ideal Human is essentially and identically Human, and we particular beings manifest It. We 'are', by partial participation, what It *is*.

The goddess told Parmenides that mortals were wandering backwards and forwards, trapped between the paths of being and non being (Parmenides 22B7DK: Waterfield 2000, p. 59), as though at a t-junction. It was necessary, she said, to choose – and since only one path, that of being, was real there couldn't, really, be any other choice. There are echoes here of the Choice of Heracles, challenged to go with Virtue or with Pleasure (see Xenophon *Memorabilia* 2.1.21–34). Whether Parmenides intended to allow any credit to those who could not go with the goddess, but stayed on their 'backward-turning' path, we can't be sure. Plato provided them with a sort of answer: our ordinary judgements and perceptions are always 'rolling around (*kulindeitai*) between being and non-being' (*Republic* 5.479d4), and '*doxa*', opinion, is the appropriate faculty for dealing with this fluid and ambiguous world. What's 'really real' is all that can be 'known', because it's pure and unchanging. But we still need, somehow, to discriminate within the realm of what isn't 'really real' between the better and the worse, the more-or-less correct and the almost-entirely false.

That ordinary judgements 'roll between being and non-being' has an easy interpretation: sometimes they are mostly true, and sometimes false (see Crombie 1963). That Socrates is standing upright may be true at one moment, and false at another. Insofar as it is not always true, it is not an appropriate object of 'knowledge', *episteme*, and also because it need not ever be true at all, and so could not be required by the whole network of knowledge. What cannot be affirmed as necessary is not known. Whatever cognitive faculty is relevant to recognizing that the claim is, on occasion, more or less correct is not fully 'intellectual'. There may be other features that also render it incognizable: what counts, exactly, as 'upright'? Far away from here, there are men whose heads *do* grow beneath their shoulders, since they are standing 'upside down' on the other side of the world. All the way round the earth people are standing upright, yet angled in different directions.

Sometimes Socrates was standing, sometimes speaking, some-times – even – snub-nosed, and yet not always, nor by necessity.

So Socrates himself, and not only what was said about him, was also 'rolling between being and non-being', between sharing and not-sharing in whatever property. The same seems true of everything phenomenal – and what then can we say are the things that are thus changeable? What is it that is sometimes one thing and sometimes another, sometimes being x and sometimes not? What sort of being can it have? Is it anything?

This may be a necessary confusion: the sort of mind-numbing riddle that – in other traditions – is the beginning of a sort of wisdom. We should attend more sympathetically to such dialogues as *Cratylus* and *Euthydemus*. In the former, familiar words are deconstructed by random etymologies (so that *aletheia* becomes 'a godly wandering'). In the latter, wildly fallacious arguments – including ones that seem to show how falsehood is impossible, and that anyone who knows anything at all must actually know everything – are greeted with mounting hostility by Socrates' young companion, but with continued respect by Socrates himself (see Levenson 1997). Confusion and not clarity may be the goal: the moment when we find ourselves entirely at a standstill, knowing that we know nothing.

> Intellect also, then, has one power for thinking, by which it looks at the things in itself, and one by which it looks at what transcends it by a direct awareness and reception, by which also before it saw only, and by seeing acquired intellect and is one. And that first one is the contemplation of Intellect in its right mind, and the other is Intellect in love, when it goes out of its mind 'drunk with the nectar'; then it falls in love, simplified into happiness by having its fill, and it is better for it to be drunk with a drunkenness like this than to be more respectably sober. (Plotinus, *Ennead*, VI.7 [38].35)

Two worlds or one

The most famous allegory in all philosophy, lovingly adopted by philosophers and artists who know almost nothing else of Plato, is the story of the cave (*Republic* 7.514–18). We are to imagine that there are people chained to their seats in a dark cave, watching a shadowplay on the wall before them. They have never known anything else, and spend their time working out the shadow-patterns, not knowing what is causing them. In fact, there are puppeteers on a ledge behind them, casting the shadows with the help of a fire behind. What would happen if one of the prisoners were freed from his chains and led back through the cave, observing the puppeteers as he passed, and so at last made his way out into the sunlit lands? Would he not be dazzled and confused to see the 'real things' of which the puppets – and their shadows – were no more than images? And what if he then went down again to enlighten his companions? Would they be willing to believe him? Or would they not rather notice that he was himself confused and stumbling in the sudden dark, and despise him for his follies? That, said Plato's Socrates, is our condition. We see no more than shadows, and resist the stories told by those who have escaped the cave.

In Indian tradition, the notion that this life is an illusion was explored with more imaginative sympathy (see O'Flaherty 1984). The Mediterranean peoples were likelier to assume that material bodies were real, or even the only realities, and that visionaries were dreamers. But even materialists must think that we are deluded, and that the mere phenomena are not what do the work. 'We see the sun rise and set, but we think of the earth as moving round the sun' (Frankfurt et al., 1949, p. 20). A merely material understanding of reality informs us that there are bodies with definite spatial locations, enduring through a common temporal order. In the merely material world, there are no privileged places, times or scales: there is nowhere that is uniquely here, no time that is uniquely now, no reason to suggest that the human scale of things is especially important. In the merely material world, there are no 'secondary qualities' such as colour or taste or texture, and such 'primary qualities' as are associated with those phenomena are not like them. Once upon a time, before there were living creatures with distinctive senses, the world was – literally – without form, and void.

> We may, if we like, by our reasonings, unwind things back to that black and jointless continuity of space and moving clouds of swarming atoms which science calls the only real world. But all the while the world we feel and live in will be that which our ancestors and we, by slowly cumulating strokes of choice, have extricated out of this, like sculptors, by simply rejecting

certain portions of the given stuff. Other sculptors, other statues from the same stone! Other minds, other worlds from the same monotonous and inexpressive chaos! My world is but one in a million alike embedded, alike real to those who may abstract them. How different must be the worlds in the consciousness of ant, cuttlefish or crab! (James 1890, vol. 1, pp. 288f)

Another way of making the point is to consider how Chaldaean astronomers might at first have made their predictions, by identifying lights in the sky and ordering them into convenient diagrams. Once that has been done, it is possible to record their movements over the days and seasons – even over decades and centuries. But until the astronomers had some material model of the stars and planets (or at least the planetary spheres), they could not have understood just why those 'decorations in the sky' were moving as they did (Plato, *Republic,* 7.529). The Antikythera Mechanism seems to have been used to predict lunar and solar eclipses, on the basis of observed regularities, without any need of an explanation for those motions. It may even be that the use of epicyclic spheres to explain planetary motion was extrapolated from the interlocking gears of such devices:

In other words, epicycles were not a philosophical innovation but a mechanical one. Once Greek astronomers realized how well epicyclic gearing in devices such as the Antikythera mechanism replicated the cyclic variations of celestial bodies, they could have incorporated the concept into their own geometrical models of the cosmos. (Marchant 2010, after Evans, J., Carman, C. C. & Thorndike, *A.S.J.Hist.Astron.* 41, 1–39 [2010])

As Vitruvius remarked, 'an attentive examination of human inventions often leads to a knowledge of the general laws of nature' (*On Architecture* 1.6.2).[5]

Poseidonius and Archimedes both built astrolabes that may have been intended as genuine models of stellar motions (Cicero, *On the Nature of Gods,* 2.88; *Republic* 1.21). But even the material model cannot itself be the final answer, as though there were material objects that just happened to move in whatever ways they do. A properly 'scientific' analysis must put numbers to the motions: how fast do they move, and in what relation to each other? And this too won't work very well as long as we have mistaken assumptions derived from our sense experience: finding ourselves, and in a way quite truly, at the centre of the world, we imagine that the stars and planets are orbiting around us. The effect is that we must devise quite ugly and unmeaning models to permit the wandering, 'planetary', bodies to dodge back and forth in their motions, and must suppose that the material of the outermost sphere of the 'fixed stars' is made of alien stuff (or be torn apart by its speed). Plato's demand for beauty in our equations was not vindicated until first Copernicus (following Aristarchus of Samos) and then Kepler devised a better mathematical model for the system of stars and planets. Even now, we are often faced by the ugly or the arbitrary in the heavens: stars may appear and disappear, and matter falls together in whirls and clouds in unpredictable ways. The distant ideal is still a Platonic or Pythagorean one, to grasp the numbers that lie behind the phenomenal and also the physical world.

The story so far is still compatible with the modern, monistic assumption: that there is indeed one world, not two. The difference between the phenomenal, the material and the geometric stories is not a difference of worlds, as though there were several realities without any cross-connections. On the contrary, there is one world only, which we misperceive, because – precisely – we rely on our perceptions. That real world, even or especially by modern materialist standards, is radically unlike the world of common sense. We can then move on from the simple model, of bodies in relative motion through an empty space (the Democritean 'atoms and the void') to the counterintuitive world of modern physics, described in a higher mathematics intelligible only to the few. Plato's dialectic will then still apply: what sort of being do such numbers have, and what is it that 'breathes fire into the equations'?

> Even if there is only one possible unified theory, it is just a set of rules and equations. What is it that breathes fire into the equations and makes a universe for them to describe? The usual approach of science of constructing a mathematical model cannot answer the questions of why there should be a universe for the model to describe. Why does the universe go to all the bother of existing? Is the unified theory so compelling that it brings about its own existence? (Hawking 1988, p. 174)

It remains a sensible question, and one that Platonists would have answered aphoristically – that 'theory' was indeed enough, if we remember that 'theory' means contemplation (so Plotinus, *Ennead*, III.8 [30].8). Plato's own answer is to appeal to 'the Good', as the explanation both of existence and of order. This 'Good' or 'One' is not itself *an existent*: how should we explain existence in general by appealing to one of the things that exist? It lies, he said (or imagined Socrates saying), 'beyond being' (*Republic* 7.509b), and beyond our understanding. Later Platonists concluded that reality has never, as a whole, ever had to 'come into being', but that its being depends on its being focused on the One. The phenomenal and material realms in turn depend on their 'wishing' to be real, or on the soul's activity in experiencing that real, as it were, piecemeal and moment by moment. Whether this was what Plato himself intended is uncertain. In *Timaeus* he mythologized, explaining how the greatest Craftsman moulded the material world to mirror Forms, while leaving details to some lesser gods. Whether he meant to suggest that this world had a temporal beginning, or merely that we can imagine its structure more easily by seeing how it might be composed, we don't know. Pagan Platonists, by and large, believed the latter. Abrahamic Platonists – Jewish, Christian or Muslim – more often reckoned that the story was that of *Genesis*, and that Plato had learnt it there.

Heaven was the World of Forms: had the Creator made that too, or was it implicit, somehow, in His Divinity? Was the Word, the *Logos*, the Pattern of All Things, 'made' or was it 'begotten, being of one substance with the Creator'? That problem was addressed in early Christian speculation with particular force, but has its replicas in the other Abrahamic strands. Is there an eternal *Koran*, an eternal idea of Humanity, or were these also things that the Creator *made* and might have made quite otherwise?

Whatever the outcome of that dispute, there is at least some sign that – despite my earlier comments – Platonists did suppose that there were, in a way, two worlds, and that we were torn between them. As the Pythagoreans said, we are children of earth and heaven, imprisoned here for a while and hopeful of our release. Initiates of the mysteries may or must say to the gods: 'I too am a star, wandering around together with you, shining out of the depths' (Kingsley 1999, p. 130). Some may have intended this to be true for the literal lights in the sky, and that they would be visible gods. Most understood that the lights in the sky were shadows, and that it was the 'real world' of which they were to be citizens. So also in another of Plato's stories he describes how the world of human experience is no more than a puddle on the surface of the real and brighter world. We are sitting around the Inner Sea, like frogs around a pond (*Phaedo* 109a).

That image – illuminatingly – also features in the life and writings of a twentieth century author, the seminal science fiction writer Olaf Stapledon. When Stapledon's last men, our immensely remote descendants, peer into a pool on Neptune, admiring their distant cousin, Homunculus, they relive Stapledon's own visit to the pools of Anglesey: 'what a world this pond is! Like the world you are to plunge into so soon' (Stapledon 1972, p. 344; McCarthy 1982, p. 32), says one to her companion, who is about to immerse himself in the long-dead past of the early twentieth century. Similarly in a later work, Stapledon imagines how the greatest of galactic intelligences would watch the rise and fall of civilizations as 'might we ourselves look down into some rock-pool where lowly creatures repeat with naive zest dramas learned by their ancestors aeons ago' (Stapledon 1937, p. 204). The world of our present experience is no more nor less significant than those pools. How then shall we manage ourselves here-now, in what is no more than a side-show, or a moment in eternity?

> Man's life is a business which does not deserve to be taken too seriously; yet we cannot help being in earnest with it, and there's the pity. Still, as we are here in this world, no doubt, for us the becoming thing is to show this earnestness in a suitable way. . . . I mean we should keep our seriousness for serious things, and not waste it on trifles . . . while God is the real goal of all beneficent serious endeavour, man . . . has been constructed as a toy for God, and this is, in fact, the finest thing about him. All of us, men and women alike, must fall in with our role and spend life in making our play as perfect as possible. . . What, then, is our right course? We should pass our lives in the playing of games – certain games, that is, sacrifice, song, and dance. . . . [Mankind should] live out their lives as what they really are - puppets in the main, though with some touch of reality about them, too. (*Laws* 7.803–4)

In these words, Plato seems to evoke the story told in Mesopotamia, though with a more playful, hopeful moral. What happens here is of no lasting significance, though we are bound to feel it significant. And what is it like 'there'? That we do not know.

> It's enough that Plato perceived that there are two worlds: an intelligible world where truth itself resides, and this sensible world that we obviously sense by sight and touch. The former is the true world, the latter only truthlike and made in its image. (Augustine 1950, p. 144 [3.17.37])

Politics

Another way of reading the allegory of the cave may do more justice to Plato's own concerns, which were not only metaphysical but moral. Who or what are the puppeteers of his story? All that we experience and admire are shadows in the play that they are making, but why do they spend their time like this? The mundane answer is that they are poets, rhetoricians, politicians and seducers, all trading on our wish to be respectable. There are two stages in Socratic purification. In the first, we are merely shown that common notions of justice, virtue and success don't make any sense we can explain. The danger at that stage is that we shall assume that words like 'just' and 'unjust' are only ways of managing the people, that all they can 'really' mean is 'helpful to the rulers' and 'unhelpful'. Once disillusioned, we can take our place among the puppeteers, helped along by mercenary rhetoricians, all seeking our own 'advantage'. But the second stage is to see that the puppeteers are also ignorant, and that their own notions of advantage and success are similarly shadows. The images they deploy are images – of realities beyond the cave.

By this 'mundane' account, the only agents in the story are human: people immersed in their own social worlds; politicians and seducers who know enough about the roots of human action to manipulate their prey. Later Platonists suspected that the predators were not only human: we were living, they thought, under the eye of demons, and our escape was from the wheel of fortune.

The other and greater allegory that Plato presents, within which the Cave is only a passing story, is the City. Challenged to show that there are good reasons to be 'just' even when being unjust 'pays better', Plato's Socrates embarks on a strangely complex story. Why do people gather together in groups at all? What arrangements would they make together if they could? How would they cope with temptation when their own lands no longer served to provide them with all they wanted? How would they – or rather how would Socrates' acquaintances (and Plato's relatives) – defend themselves against aggressors, and police the effects of riches? The moral, eventually, is that what is needed is a caste or clan of smart and courageous people without any personal economic stake, who have shown themselves – through rigorous testing – to be immune to the temptations of power and pleasure. Only such carefully bred and educated officials can be trusted to maintain the impartial laws we need. And if ever unsuitable candidates get adopted into the caste or clan, we can expect a gradual collapse, as each generation slips further away from devotion to the City's good. By imagining how easily the City can decay, and how obviously evil the effects for everyone, we can be encouraged to believe that it is better if the City – and each citizen – has in mind the good of the whole City, and that this doesn't consist in military power, or wealth, or even 'liberty'. Actual cities, tribes and empires that take military power, or wealth, or liberty, as their criterion of good will visibly decay. So also will individual persons. That last conclusion is the real moral of the story. We have no hope of establishing the City as a political reality, and even if we did, we know it will soon decay. Instead of resting our hopes on politics, even politics of this high-minded sort, we'd better build the City in our hearts and minds. Instead of living to indulge our sensual desires, or gain a good reputation in the world, we had better attempt to live as 'reason' would have us live.

The City that Socrates describes was openly allegorical – but it had a political effect. Some critics suppose that Plato sketched an authoritarian, class society, in which all individual thought would be suppressed, to benefit an inbred aristocracy. Others, though acknowledging that Plato's aim was to preserve an official class uncorrupt and competent, have disliked the measures he suggested. The Guardians of his City must lie to convince the people that most people and the officials are really innately different, and must lie to the officials themselves about the breeding programme. That latter is indeed the crux: the official class (and by extension the mass of the people too) are to be treated as domestic animals, to be bred and reared for specific valued properties. That the Guardians themselves (the most senior and most heavily tested of the official class) are the product of just this programme ought to encourage humility, but more likely won't. By hypothesis, no-one is to be such a Guardian unless they have intuited the Good – but deception and self-deception on this issue is far too common in history. Giving such power to any human group is likely to be disastrous (as Plato himself acknowledges). Nor are they likely even to *like* each other: we cannot assume that 'family feeling' will apply in the form we now experience, as though being 'brothers and sisters' in this diluted sense will be just like our fraternity (Aristotle, *Politics*, 2.1261b). Not that being 'brotherly' has ever been the same as 'loving'.

If we *could* be ruled by incorruptible and competent officials, each dedicated to loving each other and the City (and by extension the citizens) impartially and enthusiastically, we might accept this as a welcome relief from strife and mutual murder. Unfortunately, we have no such class, and probably never could: as long as they are human, they will be very much like us, and even those who have been tested – intellectually, physically, morally – may succumb to pride or a fresh temptation. They may do so the more easily because they know – who could know better – exactly what buttons to press, what mechanisms to install, to get people to love their servitude (see Lewis 1947). In imagining and planning the City, might we hope instead that something radically non-human take control of it? This would be to go a step further even than Plato's imaginings: his Socrates may suggest that the basic laws of the City should be unchangeable, but all laws, however detailed, always need to be interpreted and applied by fallible human judgement (as Aristotle also saw: see *Nicomachean Ethics* 5.1137b27–1138a3). Science Fiction in the 1950s had frequent recourse to the notion: let us hand all public decisions over to the Great Computer, programmed only and always to act for 'the greater good' – whatever that may be. We may not find this fruitful.

There is a final, paradoxical, implication. If the only officials that we could trust to rule and police us are ones bred, reared and consciously selected to be servants of the City, and if there are no such officials, then there is no-one we can trust to rule and police us all. From which it follows that the best available rule is Anarchy. Actual cities and empires have always claimed to focus their subjects' loyalty and devotion: they have claimed, implicitly, to be or to house a god. Rulers will also claim to serve that god – and sometimes to *be* that god. Disobedience is sacrilege. But if there are no gods, then there is nothing to deserve devotion. If cities and empires show in their behaviour that at least *their* gods are empty or depraved, then they at least don't deserve it. What then shall we do?

There seem to have been two sorts of 'religious' answer in the centuries after Plato. The first, and perhaps the commonest, is to acknowledge that our gods have faults, and yet they are *our* gods: little enough, and silly enough, to have our mocking affection. By uniting around them, not too closely, we can have just enough fellow-feeling not to indulge too often in repression, riot and murder. Our devotion is vague at the edges: there are other worthy objects of affection and attention, and the principal gods of our cities don't demand exclusive devotion. Plato pictures democracy as 'the most gorgeous political system. . . . adorned with every species of human trait, as a cloak might be adorned with every species of flower' (*Republic* 8.557c): perhaps this isn't entirely a bad thing. 'Let a hundred flowers blossom, and a hundred schools of thought contend' (not forgetting what tyrant said this, to get his enemies to reveal themselves).

The second answer is the philosophical and the sectarian one alike: the Eternal Sky is our fatherland, and only the one true God deserves devotion.

CHAPTER SIX

The Aristotelian synthesis

'The master of them that know'

Aristotle of Stageira (384–322 BC) is another giant figure, and one much abused. Elementary histories of science identify a dreadful bogey, who could not even count his own wife's teeth correctly, and wished on medieval Europe a tale of stones that fell more quickly the heavier they were, and species that were created quite distinct and never to be lost or mingled. He also provided an appropriate rhetoric for slavery: some people, he supposed, were *properly* enslaved, because they were slaves 'by nature'. Worst of all, he conditioned people to believe that only what was written in the texts was true, and that observation and experiment alike were vain. Science rescued us from Aristotle by successive stages: light and heavy stones turned out to fall at the same – increasing – speed; the earth revolved around the sun; species lost their essential, hard-edged quality; and living things were no longer moved by '*pneuma*', but by lever and sinew mechanisms. It was vital for seventeenth century scientists and philosophers to disown the Aristotelian synthesis, and scientists since – with rare and praiseworthy exceptions – believe all that they read.

Almost all of this is false. Aristotle himself was the son of a medical household in a city on the edge of Thessaly, student in the Academy, tutor of Alexander and an indefatigable inquirer. Even the Aristotle of the later middle ages, embellished by pagan and Islamic commentaries and adapted by Aquinas to a Christian role, was also a greater figure than the Enlightenment pretended, but that shape lies outside my limits. By founding his own school when he returned from posts in Lesbos and in Macedon (while a native Athenian ruled Plato's Academy) Aristotle became the father of a different line of philosophers, the Peripatetic, which was – at least on Augustine's word (*Contra Academicos* 3.19.42) – one of the last three surviving pagan schools in the fifth century AD (the others being Cynics and Platonists). Platonists considered Aristotle himself a Platonist, who created formal logic and corrected, or sought to qualify, Plato's own divisions of language and the world (see Gerson 2005). That the best life, for Aristotle as for Plato, was to contemplate and serve the God of Intellect was undisputed. That our characters needed to be trained as well as our minds educated was also common doctrine. That something divine and beautiful could be discerned in even the most trivial of natural entities was implicit in Plato, explicit in Aristotle. In later ages, Aristotle provided an alternative to Platonism by emphasising personal being against what seemed a mystical extravagance. But even then no-one supposed that Aristotle was Plato's enemy. He held that, where both are friends, true piety prefers the Truth to Plato – but Plato had said just the same, and Aristotle really meant that Plato was indeed his friend (*Nicomachean Ethics* 1.1096a16; Plato, *Republic*, 10.595c). In the Renaissance, Plato became a rallying cry against Aristotle, insinuating that we had share enough of the divine to intuit real truths, when medieval Aristotelians had been content to save the phenomena by models and useful hypotheses. A little later the pair were seen as archetypes for the Rationalists and Empiricists.

It may be true that Aristotle had more natural sympathies than Plato with the staunch empiricism expressed by certain authors of the Hippocratic Corpus, a body of texts from various dates recording the thoughts and diagnostic notes of Hippocratic would-be healers. The author, for example, of *Ancient Medicine* (sometime in the fourth century BC) spoke scornfully of theorizing as a route to medical truth – though this is a rhetorical rather than a rational stance, and not always a helpful one. Aristotle and the Hippocratics are at any rate alike in rejecting, as it seems, a Platonic concentration upon such forms as Universal Humanity, as that can be conceived and analysed by merely intellectual effort. The realities, they both insist, are countable, discrete substances, not ideal types, and finding out what to do requires an account of those particulars: not what we imagine an Ideal Humanity requires, but what experience teaches us that this or that diseased or injured human being needs for his/her recovery. It is a necessary response to exaggerated hopes of modelling a complex universe by thought alone. It is also, unfortunately, a strategy that relies, uncritically, on anecdotal evidence, without attempting to test the hypotheses that experience might suggest: apparent successes are applauded, and repeated failures blamed on an intractable condition. Not knowing why any particular treatment works – or worse still, creating an imaginary mechanism that appeals by being familiar – we cannot distinguish chance recoveries from real cures. Aristotle was usually wiser.

It may be the effect of family tradition also that Aristotle was insistent that even the most trivial and vulgar creature could show something wonderful, something divine, if it were examined honestly. His fascinated attempts to find some order in the sprawling complexity of biological nature were constantly modified by observation, even though he also hung on tight to methodological aphorisms like 'nature does nothing in vain'. And what about women's teeth? The claim is made in passing in a compendium of observations known as *Historia Animalium* (2.501b19–21), and probably had an empirical basis. As the author – for it may not be Aristotle himself – goes on to note, in some women the wisdom teeth erupt very late. Women would most likely have lost teeth to a poor diet, and to childbearing. At least the claim could not have been rebutted, as Bertrand Russell sneeringly suggested, by inspecting his wife's teeth. His remarks about the relative speed with which heavy and light things fell are also not rebutted by observation but by the Galilean argument that a two pound weight cannot fall faster than two linked one-pound weights, though the medium through which they fall may partly retard weights falling with less force.

At the farthest remove, it seems, from natural history, Aristotle created formal logic, specifically the systematic study of syllogistic reasoning. He identified the valid forms of syllogism, by example and by argument. The first mode combines two premises with a shared middle term (functioning as predicate in the minor and subject in the major premise, which are claims about the smaller and the larger class, respectively): as it might be, 'all humans are mortal and all poets are human'), thence concluding, in what was later called 'Barbara', that 'all poets are mortal'). The second mode, with the shared term as the predicate in each premise, can only, in its valid forms, have a negative conclusion (e.g. 'If no philosophers mind about money and all professors do, then no professors are philosophers': which is in Cesare). The third, with the shared term as the subject in each premise, can never result in a universal conclusion (e.g. in Ferison: 'If no non-human animals have duties and some non-human animals have rights, then some things that have rights do not have duties'). The fourth mode, merely converting the conclusion of the first mode (so: 'some mortal things are poets'), was added later, for completeness' sake. These jolly transformations were the bread and butter of medieval logicians, and used then for much the same reasons as originally they were, in dialectical contests (see Kneale and Kneale 1962). Aristotle, in short, decided to regularıse and discipline the art of rhetoric as practised in courts and schools. And the chief point of the formal syllogistic is not to use such syllogisms to prove a point, but to show how often speakers will use *fallacious* arguments, and to have an easy response to them. Rhetoric can be good or bad, and is at least a legitimate subject of study.

Some have supposed that Aristotle intended 'science' to be reconstructed as a simple axiomatic system, rather as Euclid did with geometrical propositions (condensing centuries of Babylonian – and Indian – mathematics). If only we could find the proper premises we could deduce exactly how the world must work. But there are at least two problems with that proposal. First of all, and clearly, we do not have such premises: and yet 'a chain of reasoning, to be valid, should proceed from premises which are not doubtful to the conclusion which is in dispute' (Cicero, *De Divinatione*, 2.49.103). Premises such as 'the laws of logic' are, of necessity, compatible with every possible scenario, and hence cannot be used as the foundation of all knowledge: they make no distinction between one possible world and another. Premises, on the other hand, that have substantive implications can be meaningfully denied. Cicero's commonsensical examples of irrefutable premises, 'if she has born a child, she has slept with a man', and 'if he has been born, he will die', were at least thrown into doubt, as Marius Victorinus (fourth century AD) observed, by Christian stories (Cameron 2011, p. 219): 'for among them it is certain that someone was born without the intervention of a man and did not die' (or at least not forever). Nowadays, the first example is simply, materially, false, and there are even some who imagine that the second may also, one day, be false. Nor can we, in practice, identify strictly universal premises for any syllogistic argument: *most* green things may be plants, and *most* frogs green, without any frogs at all being plants. Even if there are universal, necessary and substantive truths, we are unlikely to know what they are. Even the Stoics, who believed that the world must be precisely what it is, did not claim to know exactly why. They could only, at best, insist that all truths make a difference: lies are usually uncovered, because we cannot make our lies consistent enough with all acknowledged truths.

The second reason for doubting that Aristotle was advancing the claims of a purely deductive science, and that all truths were *necessary* truths, is that he clearly denied this. He addressed the issue directly in a chapter of a short work *On Interpretation*, and later philosophers, including Stoics, had rather little to add to what he said (though some thought that he was wrong). Consider the truth or otherwise of some simple prediction about tomorrow: that there will, or else there won't, be a Mediterranean sea-battle then. One or the other claim is true, and in that case – so it seems – one or the other claim must already be firmly settled: if it is already true that there will be, then nothing we can do today will alter that event; if it is already true that there won't be, then nothing we can do today will bring such a battle about. Worse still, the truth or otherwise of this imagined event has always been firmly settled, from the beginning, or forever (if there never was a beginning). Stoic philosophers argued against the seemingly 'lazy' implication: if the thing is already settled, then we need do nothing to make it happen. They answered that what we do (or what we find ourselves doing) is part of the chain that brings about the event (Cicero, *On Fate*, 28–30: LS 1987, vol. 1, pp. 139–40 [55S]). Even though we cannot *alter* anything, we should still attempt to do whatever seems right (acknowledging that we may find tomorrow that something else entirely was what God and Nature required). Aristotle denied the argument: the truth or otherwise of tomorrow's battle is not yet settled. Whichever result turns out true tomorrow has *not* been settled forever: 'p or not-p' is indeed a necessary truth, but it does not, in this case, imply that either limb is necessary. So far from allowing the surface logic of an argument to dictate his conclusions, Aristotle invoked his extra-logical certainty that some things could turn out either way. Formally speaking this does not rebut the law of excluded middle ('necessarily p or not-p'): the claim that either there will be a battle or there won't are not true contradictories. The statements that really fit the formula are 'either it is settled that there will be or else it *isn't* settled'. And from that we cannot infer that either outcome is settled. Cicero used Aristotle's analysis in his attack on divination.

How can anything be foreseen that has no cause and no distinguishing mark of its coming? Eclipses of the sun and also of the moon are predicted for many years in advance by men who employ mathematics in studying the courses and movements of the heavenly bodies; and the unvarying laws of nature will bring their predictions to pass. Because of the perfectly regular movements of the moon the astronomers calculate when it will be opposite the sun and in the earth's shadow — which is 'the cone of night' — and when, necessarily, it will become invisible. For the same reason they know when the moon will be directly between the earth and the sun and thus will hide the light of the sun from our eyes. They know in what sign each planet will be at any given time and at what time each day any constellation will rise and set. You see the course of reasoning followed in arriving at these predictions. But what course of reasoning is followed by men who predict the finding of a treasure or the inheritance of an estate? On what law of nature do such prophecies depend? . . . Hence it seems to me that it is not in the power even of God himself to know what event is going to happen accidentally and by chance. For if He knows, then the event is certain to happen; but if it is certain to happen, chance does not exist. And yet chance does exist, therefore there is no foreknowledge of things that happen by chance. (Cicero, *De Divinatione*, 2.6–7)

This is not a purely 'logical' argument: it depends on a meta-physical judgement, that there is such a thing as 'chance' (or rather, since chance itself is not a thing nor a causal power at all, many processes have equally possible outcomes, and no single future is now predictable, even for an imagined omniscience). Not even an omniscient God can now 'know' whatever will one day be true: since the future is not yet settled there are no such truths to know.

Nor are all classifications exact. One of Aristotle's favourite terms is '*pos*', which means 'in a way'. And in considering the classes of living beings he insists that there are many hybrids and difficult cases to consider: nature is a continuum, and for that reason cannot be broken up into clearly exclusive classes. Between every two identifiable classes there will be intermediates; many kinds can most easily be understood as variations, deformations of a wider kind (as seals are 'deformed quadrupeds', or flatfish 'twisted' from the norm). There is even some suggestion that all animals there are can be explained as variations from an ancestral type to be identified with the 'least specialised, best balanced, most complete of kinds', the human (see Clark 1975, pp. 29, 38). Classes are conveniences of description, but such biological kinds are not mere mirrors of distinct, eternal forms. It is not the species-form that is transmitted in procreation, but the father's individual form, more or less well replicated in maternal matter (see Balme 1980). In brief, the later notion that distinct species leapt from the mind of God and never were (nor should be) mixed is not Aristotelian.

So, is there some truth in the conviction that Aristotle distrusted Plato's theories? His political theories, requiring that the statesman balance opposing interests in the hope of peace, are seamless developments from Plato's writings. His ethical theories, which identify the human good as one to be achieved within community, in the pursuit of what is good and beautiful, do little more than shift an emphasis. His epistemology does not overtly rest on any notion that we already 'know' or 'half remember' fundamental truths, but recognizes intellectual intuition as the source of vital principles, things that must be known already before any demonstration is possible. He relied much more than Plato did on what we ordinarily perceive, but was also confident that we 'perceived' more than we strictly saw or heard or touched. Colours are 'special' objects of sight, perceived – one might conceive – because our eyes could 'become' them. But shapes, sizes, times, relations and the like (the properties later called primary) are not special to any one sense: we perceive them, commonsensically, because our minds (not our eyes only) can become them: that is, the world in each of us unfolds into patterns that are the very same as the world that contains us all.

It is in his metaphysics that the difference lies – but it is in his metaphysics that Aristotle is least clear. He begins from individual substances, like people: these are the primary subjects of predication, things that endure through time and change, that cannot be taken apart and put together again, nor broken up into more of the same kind (as stones can be broken into stones). Such substances can be counted, as non-substances cannot (though the latter can be weighed). A person may be pale or tanned; weigh ten stone or eleven; be in the town or country, at morning or evening; be father and/or son; be cloaked or cloakless; lying down or standing; acting and being acted on (which concludes the list of ways that Aristotle thought something could be 'categorised'). In all those separate ways a person could change and yet be the same person. What that person was essentially, what it was for that person to exist at all, was not equivalently 'present in' the person (as if she could endure through losing it). To know the person properly is to know what it is for her to be. That nature, in turn, could – 'accidentally' – be predicated of the matter which constitutes the person: that lump over there, one might say, is Critias (but there is no definite lump at all except that Critias is there). This radical individualism turns Plato on his head. Aristotle insisted that it was the individuals that carried the shared properties. Without individual bodies to be red there could be no redness; whereas a red thing might turn blue or colourless without being destroyed (and red patches, even red afterimages, aren't substances but effects).

Unfortunately, a merely individual, unrepeated instance cannot be described. Individuals cannot be known in their own individuality: only a shared form is knowable (even if the form is only potentially shared). And individual substances are more than instants or punctiform particulars: if Critias can be present, being Critias, on more than one occasion it can only be because the 'what it is for Critias to be' (which is, what Critias *qua* Critias does) is possessed by successive moments of material nature (and maybe there are therefore 'forms of individuals', as Plotinus is sometimes supposed to have believed: but see Vassilopoulou 2006). Properties are predicated of real substances – but the essence of those substances belongs to an underlying stuff. That stuff, by successive arguments, begins to look like the primary matter that troubled later thinkers: it is the ultimate subject of all predication, and has all properties, but it actually *is* nothing. It is the receptacle, the Nothing, on which the form of life is cast. And because it is nothing, we cannot know it. Only the forms are knowable (which is where we began, with Plato, and perhaps with the Egyptians).

Slaves and citizens

What of the other main charge, that he defended slavery, and natural hierarchy in general?

On the one hand, each of us has her own life to live, and no-one else can do it. On the other, each of us needs companions. When Aristotle observed that 'man is a political animal' (*Politics* 1.1253a2ff), he did not mean that people were always 'politicking' in a modern sense (i.e. pursuing power), but that people were always likely to live, or prefer to live, in small, self-governing communities of the relatively like-minded, sharing a common language, history and largely unargued assumptions about what counted as good reasons. The pattern is not only Mediterranean, nor only ancient. Alexis de Tocqueville, in his study of the new American nation, remarked that 'wherever men gather together township automatically comes into being. Municipal society exists in all nations whatever their customs or laws. Man it is that makes monarchies and founds republics; the township seems a direct gift from the hand of God' (De Tocqueville 2003, p. 72). How much land such '*poleis*' managed to control, and whether they had to share it with less like-minded peoples, was historically contingent. There were also larger loyalties that transcended any particular *polis*, to earlier ancestry and to shifting alliances against still less like-minded peoples. Migrant craftsmen were always also welcome (see Burkert 1992, p. 23); Sophists and exorcists not quite so much. What was most valuable to such travellers were skills, not property. And that was a moral that even stay-at-homes might cherish.

Aristippus [of Cyrene], the Socratic philosopher, shipwrecked on the coast of Rhodes, perceiving some diagrams thereon, is reported to have exclaimed to his companions, 'Be of good courage, I see marks of civilization:' and straightaway making for the city of Rhodes, he arrived at the Gymnasium; where, disputing on philosophical subjects, he obtained such honours, that he not only provided for himself, but furnished clothing and food to his companions. When his companions had completed their arrangements for returning home, and asked what message he wished to send to his friends, he desired them to say: that the possessions and provision to be made for children should be those which can be preserved in case of shipwreck; inasmuch as those things are the real supports of life which the chances of fortune, the changes of public affairs, and the devastation of war, cannot injure. Thus, also, Theophrastus says, 'that the learned man is the only person who is not a stranger in foreign countries, nor friendless when he has lost his relations; but that in every state he is a citizen, and that he can look upon a change of fortune without fear'. (Vitruvius, *On Architecture,* 5 Introduction 1–2)

Some visitors were welcomed, even if they were not full citizens. Others were merely slaves, denied any share in 'politics' but vital to civilized life. Preferably, these were 'barbarians' (which is to say, non-Greeks). For the Greeks, there were two kinds of barbarian. Examples of the first were 'Scythians' and other 'uncivilized' peoples, whether they were nomadic or partly settled. It was widely assumed that they lived impulsively, or in pursuit of honour. The other kind were Easterners, and much more like ourselves: civilized, but slavish, in pursuit of material goods. The subjects of the Great King considered themselves his slaves, and had no other image of obedience. This was the 'evil empire' that the Athenians believed themselves to have opposed and defeated at Marathon and Salamis.

But despotism – rule modelled on that master-slave relationship – was not confined to the Orient. On the contrary, it was because so many Greek cities had accepted the rule of 'tyrants' that others feared what would happen when the Persian Empire could impose a similar rule throughout. Nor was 'the Orient', even as conceived by Greeks, without its protest movements. Conversely, many imagined that 'foreigners' were fair game – and Aristotle objected.

Those who wish to examine the matter closely might perhaps think it exceedingly strange that it should be the business of a statesman to be able to devise means of holding empire and mastery over the neighboring peoples whether they desire it or not. How can that be worthy of a statesman or lawgiver which is not even lawful? and government is not lawful when it is carried on not only justly but also unjustly—and superior strength may be unjustly exercised. . . . Yet most peoples seem to think that despotic rule is statesmanship, and are not ashamed to practise towards others treatment which they declare to be unjust and detrimental for themselves; for in their own internal affairs they demand just government, yet in their relations with other peoples they pay no attention to justice. Yet it is strange if there is not a natural distinction between peoples suited to be despotically ruled and those not suited; so that if this is so, it is not proper to attempt to exercise despotic government over all people, but only over those suited for it, just as it is not right to hunt human beings for food or sacrifice, but only the game suitable for this purpose, that is, such wild creatures as are good to eat. (Aristotle, *Politics*, 7.1324b20ff)

But is anyone fitted for slavery? Can we dismiss slave-taking as an aberration? Unfortunately, slavery is so far from being a 'peculiar' institution that 'it has existed from before the dawn of human history right down to the twentieth century, in the most primitive of human societies and in the most civilized' (Patterson 1982, p. vii). It is indeed, as Gaius' *Institutes* named it in the late second century AD, part of the common law of nations (Wiedemann 1988, p. 23). Chattel slavery (as distinct from serfdom or caste-inferiority) may have been more important in Greek and Roman society – once debt-slavery of fellow nationals had been abolished – than elsewhere, but slave-traders belong to one of the oldest professions, alongside hunters and fishers (Aristotle, *Politics*, 1.1256a35). Murray's odd claim that 'the Greeks are not characteristically slave-holders' (nor 'characteristically subjectors of women') had this much reason: that practically every society has kept slaves, and subjected women, and that some Greeks did wonder, briefly, if they should (Murray 1934, pp. 15, 19).

They wondered – but Aristotle articulated the claims of common sense in answer. 'The slave has no deliberative faculty at all; the woman has, but it is without authority, and the child has, but it is immature' (*Politics* 1.1260a12f). These three subordinate classes (women, children, slaves) need guidance, of different sorts. Women, he supposed, had their own sphere of authority, in the household, but needed male assistance to help control their passions. Children should be obedient to their parents, but would one day grow up. Slaves – or those who are slaves 'by nature' – will never themselves be able to act rightly.

But what exactly is a slave? The easy answer is 'a human being deprived of freedom at the pleasure of an individual master or the state'. Freedom in turn is just the opportunity to make and act upon our own life-choices. Hardly anyone since hunter-gatherer days has really had much freedom of that sort. How free we are depends upon how flexible our neighbours and our rulers are, and how costly our life-choices. No-one on these terms is wholly free – nor wholly slave, since even a chained slave will have some choices to make, of greater significance because they are so limited. Maybe, as Epictetus argued, the only choice that any of us has is how to think about our situation (*Discourses* 1.1.7). A more serious issue is that slaves lack protection against arbitrary force. But most slave-societies do give slaves some protection, by law or public opinion. There are limits beyond which owners forfeit their claim to own something, whether that thing is a slave, an animal, a wife, a child or a fresh spring. Owners are not protected absolutely in the enjoyment of what they claim; neither are slaves or any other dependents left wholly unprotected. It seems to follow that a slave who seeks to purchase 'freedom' only exchanges one role for another, and may prefer, after all, to stay a slave (almost a domestic animal). That option existed for slaves in Hebrew law, who should otherwise be freed after seven years service – though such a choice was widely considered contemptible (Maccoby 2002, p. 75).

Consider Patterson's judgement: 'slavery is the permanent, violent domination of natally alienated and generally dishonoured persons' (Patterson 1982, p. 13). What chattel slaves don't have is their own family: they are stripped of ancestry, of offspring and of honour – except what they may receive as household slaves from their master's connections. Serfs, though they may have a narrower compass than a rich man's slaves, at least have families, and land, and household gods. Cato the Elder, as an extreme, made sure his slaves weren't friendly even with each other (Plutarch, *Cato the Elder*, 21.4: Wiedemann 1988, p. 182), but even in a better household, a slave's ties to other slaves must always have been flimsy: they could always be sold on. There is, in a real sense, no social or economic class of slaves, and so no common social or economic interest. Cruel and stupid masters may goad slaves to rebellion, but those rebellions are not revolutions, unless the slaves discover some new faith to follow.

Perhaps the closest ancient analogy to the Mosaic revolution can be found in the story of Spartacus, who led a slave revolution against the Roman state in 73 BCE. According to one account, Spartacus intended to fight his way to the north where he planned to set up an independent state based on new principles of freedom, but he failed to persuade his army to leave Italy, where eventually he and they perished. Moses was a Spartacus who did leave the country of the oppressors behind and persuaded his fellow revolutionaries (though with many difficulties) to aim at a political future in a new land. (Maccoby 2002, p. 57)

Moses' people in turn did not quite 'enslave' the Canaanites they conquered, though they aimed to make them serfs (or at least the Hebrews later rewrote their history to show what they should have done). Neither were Helots, Penestai, Dorophoroi, Gymnetes, Karynephoroi and the rest of the oppressed peoples of the Greek world *slaves*, though they were permanent subjects. There are no *communities* of slaves, as Aristotle said (*Politics* 3.1280a32): no *poleis* at least. This is why the supply of slaves must always be replenished, by kidnapping, piracy and wars of conquest. Slaves, precisely, are captives: people whom we might have killed, but spared. Owing us their lives, they were bound to serve us, and served our reputation by accompanying us home. Conquered peoples are useful for tribute – but the best tribute is the visible presence of our captives, proof at once of our power and our magnanimity. The primary function of slaves is not productive – even if many were put to such productive work – but 'practical' (*Politics* 1.1254a8). They help us to act 'nobly'. In many slave societies slaves produced nothing (Patterson 1982, p. 11), or nothing that would be worth the price.

Such adjuncts increase our honour, and our capacity to perform 'noble deeds' – which are not what Socrates or Euthyphro considered '*kalon*'. 'We use other people's feet when we go out, we use other people's eyes to recognize things, we use another person's memory to greet people, we use someone else's help to stay alive - the only thing we keep for ourselves are our pleasures' (Pliny, *Natural History*, 28.14, cited by Patterson 1982, p. 339). Slaves are not the only people to suffer this indignity: that is how kings use their 'friends' (Aristotle, *Politics*, 3.1287b30ff), and lose them. But the case is particularly clear with slaves. Calvisius Sabinus, so Seneca tells us, had so bad a memory – and so great a wish for a good one – that he bought and trained a gang of slaves to cap quotations from Homer and the poets. 'The same number of book-cases would have been cheaper, but Sabinus' attitude was, that whatever anyone in his household knew, he knew' (Seneca, *Letters*, 27.5f: Wiedemann 1988, p. 126).

Slaves are part of their masters (Aristotle, *Politics*, 1.1255b11), as my limbs are part of me, because they make no *decisions*. Captives have no more honour to defend, since they have agreed to live as captives. No free man willingly endures tyrannical or despotic rule (*Politics* 4.1295a22) – so those who do endure it are of a slavish nature. There may sometimes be excuses: Helots and Thessalian serfs rebel, but Cretans don't, because the former have potential allies in neighbouring *poleis* (*Politics* 2.1269a40f). Aristotle is less inclined to excuse the subjects of empires for their subservience (*Politics* 3.1285a21). He acknowledges that the Persians have had to crush rebellions among those whose 'spirit has been stirred by recollection of their former greatness' (*Politics* 3.1284b2) – but most prefer peace to greatness. An obvious retort is that slaves, unlike serfs, are deliberately deprived of allies and familiar faces. If the entire household of slaves is punished for one slave's rebellion, every slave is a hostage for every other's 'good' behaviour. So present obedience is no proof of servility, but rather of good sense. Again: if natural slaves cannot deliberate because they cannot look ahead (*Politics* 1.1252a31), and Asiatic barbarians are just the sort of people who are natural slaves, how can those same barbarians be 'intelligent and inventive'? (*Politics* 7.1327b25f). How can it be right to think that household management (including the command of slaves) is best handed over to slaves? (*Politics* 1.1255b35). Some critics (e.g. Smith 1991) conclude that Aristotle is hopelessly confused, sometimes supposing that slaves lack *logos* entirely, but sometimes admitting that they can understand and act on their instructions.

Natural slaves, who are slaves everywhere, whatever their legal status (*Politics* 1.1255a31f), can be identified in two ways – the physical and the ethical. In the physical sense, they are able to labour, but not to look ahead (*Politics* 1.1252a31f). 'Nature would like to distinguish between the bodies of freemen and slaves, making the one strong for servile (*anankaion*) labour, the other upright and although useless for such services, useful for political life in the arts both of war and peace' (*Politics* 1.1254b26f). The point must not be merely that the slavish are strong and tough, but that they need instruction how to use their muscles. Is this just a lack of wit? That doesn't fit his other remarks about them. Slaves, in any case, aren't usually labourers. They're office boys, memory men, pedagogues, barbers, librarians, speech-writers, concubines and so on – in brief, the writer and most readers of this book: white collar workers. What of the 'ethical' discrimination? Natural slaves are not insensate, and neither are they solitary beasts (*Politics* 1.1253a29). They share enough in *logos* to perceive it, but not have it (*Politics*

1.1254b22). They cannot form a *polis* because they have no share in *eudaimonia*, nor in living *kata prohairesin* (*Politics* 3.1280a32). They do not – strictly – deliberate (*Politics* 1.1260a12), but it is spirit they lack (*Politics* 7.1327b27f), not wits. It is slavish to put up with insults (*Nicomachean Ethics* 4.1126a8; see *Politics* 4.1291a8), and slavish not to seek revenge (*Nicomachean Ethics* 5.1133a1); slavish to depend on anyone but a friend (*Nicomachean Ethics* 4.1124b31). A freeman, by contrast, is one who is 'for himself' (*Metaphysics* 1.982b25).

In brief: slaves, or the slavish, don't aim at doing what's right. In Aristotle's moral psychology, they don't strictly 'act' at all. Animals, children and slaves may all do things willingly, or unwillingly, but none act for the sake of beauty (*to kalon*), which is the goal of virtue. The prospect of pleasure or pain is all that moves them, since they can expect no honour for their acts. One further gloss: barbarians show their slavishness by treating women as slaves (*Politics* 1.1252b5f), and Persians in particular by treating their sons as slaves (*Nicomachean Ethics* 8.1160b28f). He could have added that Persian kings followed older Mesopotamian precedent in treating *all* their subjects as their property, and were outraged if ever the property spoke back, or recalled a favour to mind (see Herodotus 7.39). In brief, it is slavish not to recognize unslaves when we see them.

So are there any 'natural slaves', people who are indefinitely manipulable by fear or greed, without a conception of nobility, or any capacity for collaboration in the worthy ends for which a *polis* exists? (as *Politics* 3.1281a2). The first answer is 'minor crooks'. Psychopaths of the kind described as 'bestial' (*Nicomachean Ethics* 7.1148b19ff), or the obviously 'feeble-minded', might also be best served as slaves. But the second and more wide-ranging answer is 'ourselves'. It is a philosophical truism that we ourselves are slaves – to greed, fear, falsehood and the like. What are our goals? The virtuous aim to contemplate and to perform the beautiful. For this, they are willing to endure physical hardship, danger and social disapproval. Those others who would live on *any* terms, or judge the quality of life by the amount of pleasure, wealth, applause or trivial information it contains are at least not virtuous. To let oneself be treated as a slave is to become a slave, and almost to deserve it. Dignity, nobility, beauty are the central concepts of an Aristotelian ethic – but not of modern ethics. 'It is beautiful to die instead of being degraded as a slave' (Publilius Syrus: Wiedemann 1988, p. 76). But if nothing is worth dying for, and the value of a life is reckoned solely by its weight of pleasure, how can we avoid the threat of literal enslavement? If our ethic is that of stereotypical, 'natural', slaves, can we be surprised if more traditional people eventually seek to enslave us? What else could they do with servile populations that have forgotten honour, who will betray any bond and accept any degradation to preserve their lives and comforts?

Or is there a final transvaluation? After all, Aristotle himself was capable of irony. In elevating the contemplative life above the political, he affirmed the superiority of resident aliens, 'metics' (*Politics* 7.1324a16ff). The *polis* exists – and citizens much troubled with the management of that *polis* live and work – to enable 'aliens with no political ties' to contemplate the divine. He knew that this would seem absurd, and that most such resident aliens had other business (including such disreputable business as trade and money-lending). What he does, implicitly, is to show how a despised class may be truer servants of the beautiful. He himself makes no such explicit use of 'slavery' – but the option was there, and taken up thereafter. The Stoics, Cynics and Christians who thought us slaves to sin also held out the hope of being 'slaves of God' instead.

Aristotle denies that masters and slaves are friends – except that, qua human beings, they can be (*Nicomachean Ethics* 8.1161b5f). To see someone as a slave (or master) is to deny the possibility of common interest, or a common concern for beauty. But seeing and treating another as mere human is to acknowledge something that transcends all social ties. At least it is better to be a fellow freeman than a despot (*Politics* 7.1325a25) because such freemen see a greater beauty than their own reflection. Being 'free' within an unequal society always obscures the truth, by placing us simultaneously above and below our fellows. Slaves transcend the social order, and greet each other simply as fellow creatures. They have the chance to be those 'beasts or gods' whom Aristotle places outside the *polis*: paradoxically, they can be, because they have to be, more truly 'self-sufficient' than the more obvious heroes of his ethics. Stripped of any place in society, they can discover something better, the god in each of us. Slaves are the world's first individuals, cast back on their own resources, and the gods.

Post-Aristotelian centuries

Among the cities that Aristotle investigated was the Phoenician colony of Carthage, which he identified as having an oligarchic constitution much like other cities. Sicilians held that they had defeated the Carthaginians, at the battle of Himera, on the very same day as the Athenians won at Salamis, and so preserved Hellenic freedoms from an imagined two-pronged attack. In the centuries following Alexander, while his successors battled over the Middle East, Carthage, Syracuse and the northern Italian city of Rome disputed control of the Western Mediterranean. Among the many 'What Ifs' of history we can include these questions: what if Alexander or one of his successors had turned west (see Braudel, pp. 277–80), or what if Carthage, or if Syracuse had won their fights?

In the event, it was Rome that conquered Italy, the West and the Mediterranean world. The Romans' 'practicality' won out. The event was also significant for philosophy. When Cicero decided to educate his fellows, it was the Peripatetic School, the Aristotelian, that he preferred – though he also expounded Stoic and Epicurean doctrine. Virtue, he thought, was paramount, but pain and distress were evils. Some part of the soul (the intellect) must be immortal, but we need not be afraid of death, whether or not it was the end of living. We may not be able to demonstrate any particular account of life, the world and everything, but some stories are much more likely.

Still later, the scholastic movement created commentaries on Aristotle's works, and so began the tradition that philosophy consists in examining and criticizing particular canonical texts. The result has been that modern common sense is broadly Aristotelian. It is correspondingly hard to engage with Aristotle's own esoteric texts (which are mostly lecture notes) because he seems to be only saying what is – now – obvious (see Rubenstein 2003).

The power of persuasive speech, so Diodorus claimed (1.2.5), is what 'makes the Greeks superior to the barbarians, and the educated to the uneducated, and, furthermore, it is by means of speech alone that one man is able to gain ascendancy over the many'. Aristotle, among his many creations, also established the study of rhetoric, suggesting that the power of persuasion rested on *ethos*, *pathos* and *logos*: the perceived character of the speaker, the emotions aroused in the audience and the reasoned arguments for one conclusion or another. Without attention to rhetoric, even the most rational, most 'logical' of philosophers cannot hope to persuade opponents.

The Aristotelian Commentators concerned themselves with issues in the interpretation of Aristotelian texts: what exactly does he mean by motion, being, time and actuality? Is there any use for 'Primary Matter', the basic stuff of things, and how does 'the Unmoved Mover' move the world? Any close examination of Aristotle's philosophy rapidly grows as confused and as confusing as examining Heracleitos. But the general theme is clear, and has had a rhetorical influence. Aristotle suggested – though not consistently – that we should prefer 'rational' discourse to 'mythological', 'literal' to 'metaphorical', and that we should aim for clarity of expression and of thought. In this he seemed to repeat the forgotten message of the 'heretic Pharaoh' Akhenaten, who defied the metaphor-using, paradoxical mythologies of Egypt. 'Amun was replaced by Aten, mythical statement by rational statement, many-valued logic by two-valued logic, the gods by God' (Hornung 1982, p. 244). But Aristotle was not a prophet. Whereas it makes sense to summarize Akhenaten's revolution in the words 'There is no god but Aten, and Akhenaten is his prophet' (Hornung 1982, p. 248), Aristotle himself shared a bias against 'enthusiasm', and a soft spot for mythology, despite his conviction that the highest happiness was 'to love and serve the Lord' (*ton theon therapeuin kai theorein*: *Eudemian Ethics* 8. 1249b20), and to live the life of immortals (*Nicomachean Ethics* 10.1177b33).

Quite what that life should be were questions that the great philosophical Schools addressed, each in their own way. The ones we mostly remember from the 'Hellenistic Period', between the death of Alexander and the rise of the Roman Empire, were united in believing that our duties were to *this* life and *this* world. That there was another world, another age, to come was too un-Aristotelian, too un-Ciceronian, a thought. Would things have been different if Carthage or Syracuse or some heir to Alexander had been dominant instead?

CHAPTER SEVEN

Living the philosophical life

Stoics and Cynics

After his life and death, as it was portrayed by his indignant friends, the feeling that not being Socrates, one should still *wish* to be Socrates (Epictetus *Encheiridion* 51.3) was definitive of true philosophers until a century or two ago. Philosophy was intended as a way of life, not merely a scholarly discipline. The Greeks may not have learnt much from Indian Gymnosophists about Hindu or Buddhist thought, but they were not wrong to think that such 'Gymnosophists' were not unlike 'philosophers'. 'The road to the gods is bound with brass, and both steep and rough; the barbarians discovered many paths thereof but the Greeks went astray, and those who already held it even perverted it. The discovery was ascribed by the god [that is, Apollo] to the Egyptians, Phoenicians, Chaldaeans (for these were Assyrians), Lydians and Hebrews' (Eusebius *Praeparatio* 9.10.3). According to Lucian of Samosata (c125–80 AD: a Syrian or Assyrian by birth and culture), Philosophy was first sent to India (where Brahmins retained the tradition), Ethiopia, Egypt, Babylon (where there were Chaldaeans and Magi), Scythia and Thrace. After that general success, she sent Eumolpus and Orpheus to prepare the way in Greece. But after the Seven Sages the truth was obscured by Sophists, and only Cynics kept Philosophy alive (Lucian, *De Fugitivis*, 6.11, cited by Johnson 2006, p. 132). Only the Cynics, that is, were wandering ascetics, disrespectful of all local cults and customs. But was that really what Philosophy required? And who and what were the Cynics?

Diogenes, formerly of Sinope on the south coast of the Black Sea but long resident in Corinth (404–323 BC), is known through anecdotes: as that, asked by a momentarily respectful Alexander what he, Alexander, could do to help, he replied 'Get out of my light' (Diogenes, *Lives*, 6.38). Among his followers was Crates, who'd abandoned a rich inheritance to live the Cynic's life (accompanied by a similarly devoted wife, Hipparchia). He left his fortune in trust, with instructions that his sons, if ordinary men, should have the money, and if philosophers, it should be given to the people, as his sons would have no need of it. A merchant from Citium in Cyprus, another Zeno, happened on Xenophon's account of Socrates at an Athenian bookstall and asked where he could find a man like that: the bookseller pointed to Crates, and Zeno abandoned trade for good, eventually establishing himself in the Painted Portico, the Stoa. Citium was a partly Phoenician, partly Hellenic, city, and it is likely enough that Zeno was Phoenician. Unfortunately, we have no definite evidence of a Phoenician philosophical tradition or curriculum (Grainger 1991, p. 79), but it is not unreasonable to suspect at least that the conjunction of Phoenician and Hellenic thought and practice had an effect.

'Why be surprised I'm Syrian? We live in one fatherland, the world, my friend. One is the emptiness (*Chaos*) that bore all mortals' (Meleager of Gadara (first century BC): *Greek Anthology* 7.417).

The early Stoics were almost as shameless as Cynics, acknowledging no merit in traditional distinctions and taboos. Why not have sex in temples, eat one's dead parents and reckon other people's property one's own? The gods, after all, own everything; friends have everything in common, and only the wise are really friends of the gods: so the wise own what they please, though being wise they will not use it for escapable desires. Later theorists toned down the effect, and cultivated a more intellectual style. A Stoic philosopher was someone whose behaviour would not change from State to State, being governed by nature, not the spurious 'laws' decreed by foolish rulers: but the real laws were the ones demanded by traditional ideas of justice. Private property, in one sense, was absurd, since the whole world was available for all – but actual property rights must be respected, just as a seat in the theatre is in one way public and in another reserved for the one who first sits there. Stoicism requires one to remember what is really in one's power: I cannot always prevent tyrants' (or petty villains') robbing, torturing or killing me, but they in turn cannot prevent my doing what God-and-Nature means me to. My inescapable needs are few: if I ensure I want only what I can get, and remember that 'the door is always open' (i.e. I can always kill myself), I am immune to bribery and threat alike. Only so can I be 'free': only the wise are free, and only they are sane.

Stoic ethics are, they said, the albumen of philosophy, but they also engaged with logic (the shell) and natural philosophy (the yolk). Their logical analyses constitute one of the most creative periods in the history of logic, as they advanced from Aristotle's syllogistic (now mostly seen as a fragment of predicate calculus) to what is now known as propositional calculus, and the discussion of natural and conventional signs. Their natural philosophy, in turn, was a challenging exploration of a rigorously deterministic, naturalistic universe. Among the greatest names, now known to us only through fragments, are Cleanthes of Assos in the Troad (c330–c230 BC), Chrysippos of Soli, in Cilicia (279–206 BC) and Poseidonius of Apamea. The last seems to have adopted a more nearly Platonic realism, while the second established the monistic materialism that was mainstream Stoicism. Nothing had any causal powers, most Stoics said, except corporeal individuals, and those causes could not have any effects but those they actually did. What happens is determined by the principle that is their immanent God. God is not now quite obvious – at least to ordinary folk – but there will be a time when God is all in all, when everything is obviously full of God, the 'conflagration' at the end of the world age. Each following age, as God again withdraws from open view, will unfold exactly as the earlier did: wisdom lies in welcoming that repetition. Particular maverick Stoics (of whom Aristo of Chios, a third-century pupil of Zeno's, was the chief) denied that there would be any special conflagration (since God already ruled the whole), and that there was any value at all in the things we ordinarily desired (food, drink, sex and shelter). The majority preferred to agree that it was not now obvious that all was well, and that such morally indifferent things (as food, drink, sex and shelter: for after all, no one is a better person just because he has such things) were still what nature made us to pursue. Pain on the other hand is – by definition – distressing, but not therefore an evil. Good Stoics chose the 'preferable indifferent' while still reminding themselves that it really made no difference to what really mattered ('virtue').

Stoicism has had a bad press in more sentimental times: good people, we suppose, must mind about what happens to their friends, and especially to children. Detachment is no longer much admired, and we find it difficult to think that both pity and envy are to be abandoned as moral and intellectual errors (Cicero, *Tusculan Disputations*, III.10: 'a wise man is incapable of envy, and consequently incapable of pity'). But the Stoics' theory of moral consciousness (and the practice of their major sages) was kinder, and rested upon the love of children. The 'rights of future generations' were never in doubt in Stoic thought, even if they expressed the moral (more aptly) in terms of our duties. 'As we feel it wicked and inhuman for men to declare that they care not if when they themselves are dead, the universal conflagration ensues, it is undoubtedly true that we are bound to study the interest of posterity also for its own sake' (Cicero, *De Finibus*, 3.64). Sentimentalism, not sentiment, was their enemy: when Epictetus counselled a tearful father who was too upset to nurse his fevered son, he drew attention to the way the father's 'pathetic' nature was getting in the way of love. 'Apathy', detachment, is not apathetic in the modern sense, but simply not pathetic.

Some Stoic doctrine is assimilable to a modern 'scientific' outlook. Our beliefs and behaviour should be modified by holding on to a conception of the world as orderly and eternal. Any complaints we have about our particular fates are foolish: whatever it is we suffer is a necessary condition of our being at all, and to ask for things to be otherwise is to demand that the whole cosmos be upended to save our passing convenience. Even our current myopia, and the speed with which we forget our theories under the impact of pain or passion, are also necessary quirks. God Himself – which is only to say the Universe – can do no other. Named gods are only natural elements and forces, which can be understood or even, in some degree, employed to help us, but they no more care for us than the gods of the Epicureans. The Stoic gods do only and exactly what they must, and could not be expected to take any care for fools (and the wise don't ask them to).

On the other hand, practising Stoics appeal to God and to the gods, and seem to report an answer.

Marcus Aurelius thanks the gods 'that I had clear and frequent conceptions as to the true meaning of a life according to Nature, and that as far as the gods were concerned and their influence and assistance and intentions, there was nothing to prevent me from beginning to live in accordance with Nature'. He also refers to 'reminders and almost instructions'. (Liebeschuetz 1979, pp. 209–10, citing *Meditations* 1.17.5)

Aurelius was also prepared to practice an imaginative re-visioning of ordinary, bodily enjoyments that repels most moderns:

> How useful when roasted meats and other foods are before you to see them in your mind as here the dead body of a fish, there the dead body of a bird or pig. Or again to think of Falernian wine as the juice of a cluster of grapes, of a purple robe as sheep's wool dyed with the blood of a shellfish and of sexual intercourse as internal rubbing accompanied by a spasmodic ejection of mucus . . . you must do this throughout life; when things appear too enticing, strip them naked, destroy the myth which makes them proud. (Aurelius, *Meditations*, 6.13, as cited by Liebeschuetz 1979, p. 213; see also Palladas, *Greek Anthology* 10.45)

Other ascetical philosophers, including many Stoics, recoil from this contemptuous devaluation of our current world. It is one thing not to be trapped by our sensations, and quite another to despise the beauties on which our world depends. Aurelius's attitude could as easily encourage a nihilistic approach to pleasurable sensation as an ascent to higher beauties. Diogenes of Sinope masturbated openly, and wished it was as easy to satisfy hunger (Diogenes, *Lives*, 6.46).

Hebrews and Zoroastrians

The Seleucid Empire, which governed the Middle East for nearly a hundred years after Alexander's death, was pushed aside in 247 BC by a Parthian dynasty, the Arsacids, who allowed the doctrines of Zoroaster, though the empire was heterogeneous, and its rulers often philhellene. They were replaced in turn, in 224 AD, by a Persian dynasty, the Sassanids, who were more firmly Zoroastrian. The renewed Persian Empire lasted until the Arab conquests of the seventh century. Some Mediterranean philosophers appear to have accepted a brief exile in Damascus in 529 AD: the legend that the Emperor Justinian had ordered that the School of Athens be closed appears to have no substance, but at least a few philosophers thought it wise to leave for a while (they returned, it seems, quite quickly, and continued to teach in Athens). The legend is a reminder that both people and ideas could travel between the Roman and the Persian Empires, and more generally between the Mediterranean and Middle East.

> Transplanted Greek communities mingled [in the Hellenistic period] with ancient Phoenician traditions on the Levantine coast, with powerful Egyptian traditions in Alexandria, with enduring Mesopotamian institutions in Babylon, and with a complex of societies in Asia Minor. (Gruen 1998, p. xiv)

The God of the Hebrews demanded justice, specifically for the poor and otherwise excluded: what does the Lord require of thee but to do justice, and love mercy, and walk humbly with your god? (*Micah* 6.8). This is not to say that no other god before Him demanded justice of a kind: on the contrary, many gods, as they were imagined in Mesopotamia and the Mediterranean lands, insisted that we keep our oaths, give hospitality to strangers and especially to suppliants, and that we never go 'too far' in seeking what we wish. We are biologically equipped to feel compassion as well as passion. Maybe this was the origin of all humane society, as Lucretius thought (though he erred in imagining that our ancestors were solitary predators):

> Then neighbours began to form friendships, eager not to harm one another and not to be harmed; and they gained protection for children and for the female sex, when with babyish noises and gestures they indicated that it is right for everyone to pity the weak. (Lucretius, *On the Nature of Things*, 5.1015: Gaskin 1995, pp. 256–7)

Unfortunately, pity is not a wholly humane solution, nor one that all philosophers endorsed: what we pity we may also learn to despise, or value only for its use to us. 'Pity would be no more, if we did not make somebody poor' (Blake 'The Human Abstract': 1966, p. 217). The problem that all human societies face is that 'justice' often means what Plato's Thrasymachus declared it in *The Republic*: namely, the interest of the stronger, those who are in charge. The God of the Hebrews explicitly required that the strong must serve the weak out of respect, and not just pity, and in the Christian variant of that tradition God Himself accepted the obligation. According to the Mishnah 'Scripture regards one who destroys a single soul as if he has destroyed a whole world': meaning that 'each person is himself/ herself a world' (Maccoby 2002, p. 13).

The temple in Jerusalem was demolished in 70 AD, and – in the aftermath of Bar Kochba's revolt, in 135 AD – the Jews were forbidden to live in Jerusalem, and mostly ferried away to other parts of the Empire. Many Jews had lived outside Palestine for generations, from Spain to Babylon, but the experience of apparently permanent exile, and the end of the temple cult, led many to adopt Rabbinic scholarship, the reading and interpretation of the Torah, as their central religious activity. The Mishnah are brief Rabbinic debates, initially compiled by Judah ha-Nasi of Galilee ('Prince Judah'; second century AD) and incorporated into both the Palestinian and Babylonian Talmud over the next few centuries. The Babylonian version in the end had greater authority, despite – or perhaps because – it left most issues undecided (see Solomon 2009, p. xxi).

Is there any evidence that the Jewish scholars adopted Parthian or Persian doctrines? Zoroaster was often mentioned by Greek writers on philosophy, as a possible source of Greek doctrine. Conversely, one of the Nag Hammadi documents retells Plato's 'Myth of Er', from *Republic* bk.10, as being about Zoroaster. But most of the doctrines and texts mentioned as Zoroastrian are simply astrological, not clearly much like the *Zend Avesta*, a fragmented collection of laws, liturgies, stories about demons and warnings of the dangers of polluting earth, fire or water by contact with human or canine corpses, or menstruating women. One significant feature of the text which had no influence on Mediterranean thought is its concern for dogs: allowing a pregnant bitch to perish from neglect amounts to wilful murder, and great care is taken to specify who is responsible (Darmesteter 1880, pp. 176–80). This is only one of the ways in which the Magi differed from what they once had in common with the Aryan tribes of India: the most obvious being that they reversed the value of the supernatural entities they shared. In India, '*asura*' names an anti-god, and '*daeva*' a friendly spirit. For the Magi, 'Ahura Mazda' is the Spirit who is our friend, and 'devils' (an etymological coincidence) are our enemies (Russell 1977, pp. 103–4).

This is one theme of Magian religion which may have had an influence: that there is a distinct principle of evil, Angra Mainyu, the peacock angel. There are traces of this idea in older mythologies: the Olympians battled Titans, Typhoeus and the Giants, and may sometimes have been almost worsted. Despite Zeus's efforts, in person or through his heroic offspring, there are monsters and villains yet to fear. Chthonic divinities like Hecate are associated with a malevolent witchcraft at odds with civil peace, but with no common purpose. Order always needs to be imposed and is always under threat from human selfishness, the recalcitrance of things or the jealousy of Hera – notions given more abstract sense in the conflict of Form and Matter. But 'Matter' as such is almost nothing, and has no will or purpose of its own: conflict is between individuals, or between different conceptions of the good, and no-one chooses evil just as such. Hebrew prophets might denounce the worshippers of Baal or Molech, but they did not usually suppose that there really were such gods at work against us, or that we should fear them. 'Shall there be evil in the city and I the Lord have not done it?' (*Amos* 3.6; see *Isaiah* 45.7).

The point is not that He acts wickedly but that there is no other power than His to create monsters, plagues, catastrophes for His own purposes, and to make them stop. But later developments in the monotheistic tradition do seem to suggest after all that there is an Enemy, a source of natural and moral evil, which has more in mind than passing satisfactions, and is not merely mistaken about what – in the long run – satisfies. 'Some enemy has done this' (*Matthew* 13.28). Maybe the figure of the Devil, as that has emerged in the last two millennia, has its origin in Zoroastrian stories (see also Segal 1977 on Jewish and Christian developments). The sense that there is war in heaven, and that there are real powers which wish us ill, provides us with a reason to expect that there are also traitors, 'enemies of all the human race' (Christians, Witches, Communists or Bankers). Even though Zoroastrians expected the Truth to defeat the Lie through the actions of their expected Saviour, this could be no more than a wish. And we are not always sure which is the correct, or the winning, side. Maybe the God of this world is indeed the Devil in disguise, and some of our piety goes to feed his agents.

Epicureans and Buddhists

Stoic and Epicurean philosophers shared many social and moral ideals, but differed in their account of nature in at least three ways: Stoics believed that everything happened according to immutable causal laws, that there was no 'void', no gap, within the cosmos, and that what happened always served some good. Epicureans believed neither that everything happened of necessity, nor that there was a good reason for whatever happened; they also supposed that the fundamental, abiding entities were kept apart by the void. The Stoic cosmos is a single unbreakable whole. The Epicurean is an infinite array of separate unbreakable wholes. Both sects accepted the reality of the traditional gods, but neither thought them likely to help us out: the Stoics, because the gods were bound, like Homer's Zeus, by Destiny; the Epicureans, because their gods neither wished to intervene, nor could. In both cases, we might encourage ourselves by thinking of the gods and their felicity. In neither could we expect, like Zoroastrians or Jews, any 'supernatural' aid or eschatological vindication.

High minded moralists were more usually attracted to the Stoic school, whether or not they understood the doctrine. So Lucian's Hermotimus 'heard everyone saying that the Epicureans were self-indulgent and pleasure-loving; the Peripatetics were avaricious and argumentative; and the Platonists arrogant and vainglorious. But many said that the Stoics were manly and understood everything, and that the man who followed their path was the only king, the only rich man, the only wise man, and the only everything' (Lucian 2006, p. 95). In fact, the pleasures that Epicurus (341–270 BC) advocated are those that bring no pain, and are chiefly those of friendship and a quiet life. Pleasures can be guaranteed if we restrict desire, and pains endured until they are unendurable, when 'the door is open'. Epicurus was born in Samos, but by 306 BC he was established in a garden outside Athens, and his disciples called the Friends. 'Epicurus says you should be more concerned at inspecting whom you eat and drink with than what you eat and drink. For feeding without a friend is the life of a lion and a wolf'. (Seneca, *Letters*, 19.10: LS 1987, p. 127 [22I]). He thought that Pleasure was what counted (where the Stoics mentioned Virtue), but there was little difference in practice. Roman administrators could feel that Stoic insistence on our duty to family, friends and country was more useful than an Epicurean readiness to cultivate one's garden, but radical Stoics were no irritating as radical Epicureans could be agreeable. Radical Stoics after all (even if they no longer suggested that we could legitimately eat our parents) might urge us to abuse the Emperor, while Epicureans would prefer to leave the court alone. Once again, we have little but excerpts and fragments to rely upon – and the greatest single work of philosophical poetry, Lucretius' *On the Nature of Things*. That poem, written in the last days of the Roman Republic, opens with an appeal to Venus to calm down the god of war, but the only agency with any power to do so must be human (see Sedley 1998). Let us make love, not war.

The Epicurean vision is usually considered atheistical, and it is true that they denounced 'religion' – that is, the assumption that the gods demanded sacrifice, and that we would suffer after death for our offences. But they still thought there were gods: as Epicurus said, 'the knowledge of them is self-evident' (Epicurus 'Letter to Menoeceus' 123: LS 1987, p. 140 [23B]). Whatever we perceive is real – though we may make mistakes about its meaning. Epicurus 'used to say that all sensibles were true. . . . .Orestes, when he seemed to see the Furies, his sensation, being moved by the images, was true, in that the images objectively existed; but his mind, in thinking that the Furies were solid bodies, held a false opinion' (Sextus Empiricus *Against the Mathematicians* 8.63: LS 1987, pp. 81–2 [16F]). The Stoics thought that such figments were only in our minds, the Epicureans that the world was full of sensibilia spawned far away. An infinite reality may contain all possibilities: our mistake is to suppose that these visions have any other effect on us. Visions of the gods represent the kind of life we might hope for, and we might, if we choose, admire them – but they will not help or harm us. This world will one day dissolve, and though something like this world is already forming somewhere, there is no continuing self. Indeed, there is no 'self' at all. There are sufficient similarities of Epicurean doctrine and Buddhist to suggest that there was some contact: in particular, both doctrines deny the existence of a 'self' distinct from the elementary parts that animate our body. Enlightenment lies in realizing that there are no destinations, and no travelers, but only the fall of atoms through an unending void. Epicureans, like Buddhists, sought refuge in their Saviour, in his doctrine, and in the community of friends: *Buddha*, *Dharma* and *Sangha*. The fourfold remedy: 'God presents no fears, death no worries. And while good is readily attainable, evil is readily endurable' (LS 1987, p. 156 [25J]).

Buddhists of another sort were ready to suggest that there were hell-worlds waiting for us if we were self-indulgent, though we could also expect eventually to escape them. Lucretius (and other Epicureans) supposed that stories like that simply created or reinforced our fear of dying, and that it was better by far to accept annihilation: the eternity of our post-mortem non-existence was no different in kind from the prenatal eternity before we began to exist, and need be feared as little. It is possible that Lucretius felt the need to argue against the pains of hell even though most educated pagans thought they were old wives' tales (as Cicero *Tusculan Disputations* I.6) because there was still an Etruscan influence in Roman thought to give them strength (Liebeschuetz 1979, p. 48). Maybe his target is Pythagoras. It is also possible that he was detaching himself from variants of the Buddhist creed that he thought had gone astray from its founder's helpful enlightenment.

The centre of Epicurus' creed was ethical, but he made natural philosophy his base. In his account, the Democritean vision reasserts itself: reality is 'atoms and the void', and the seeming substances of everyday (and the visionary forms of deities) were only aggregates of atoms, having no enduring substance. Atoms are unbreakable because there is no internal void in them. Logically, they cannot even 'touch' each other (as there would then be no void *between* them, and the resulting union could not thereafter be broken). The Stoic view that human individuals are only parts of the one substance and the atomistic that they are only aggregates of lesser bits, both urge us to discount our felt identities. Enlightenment is the discovery that I don't exist.

Lest that conclusion seem abrupt: the *Questions of King Milinda* (Menander, ruling in the second century BC in north-west India) will usually feature only in histories of Indian or Buddhist thought, but they have as much right here. The Buddhist Nagasena explains to Menander that no complex entity is anything but the confluence of its parts: better still, such words as seem to name that complex entity are only convenient designations for what has no substantial being. 'Nagasena' itself is 'but a way of counting, term, appellation, convenient designation, mere name for the hair of the head, hair of the body. ... brain of the head, form, sensation, perception, the predispositions and consciousness. But in the absolute sense there is no ego to be found' (Radhakrishan and Moore 1957, pp. 281–4). Later Buddhists dissolved even the elements to which the complex entities had been reduced, at the same time as they identified desire as the sole cause of everything. Buddhists, like the Hellenistic sages, wished to save 'us' from distress, and do so, in their various ways, by creating the conviction that there is no-one to be saved, and that it is only desire that keeps the illusion going.

Epicureans were conscious, it seems, of the suggestion that sentience cannot arise from merely insentient elements. If all atoms were insentient, how could their combination – their being briefly alongside each other – produce subjective experience? Lucretius's solution was to suppose that there were 'soul-atoms', especially subtle bits that were equivalently the bits that make up that experience. They are joined together in us with atoms of another subtle sort: fear, rage and indolence may predominate in one kind and one person or another according as those atoms mix together (*On the Nature of Things* 3.231–307: Gaskin 1995, pp. 163–5). This is a further Buddhist trope, though the more usual trio of forces that govern our behaviour are lust, rage and ignorance.

Buddhists are also generally known – as inconsistently as Pythagoreans – for their sympathy with the non-human worlds. Being human is a rare achievement, and the one form of life that permits us to 'escape', to break out of the world of constant sorrow. But we are all akin, and the Buddha himself, again like Pythagoreans such as Empedocles, remembered his animal lives. Unfortunately, the Epicurean school adopted the same reasoning as Stoics, namely that since we could make no enforceable contract with the non-human we could not owe them justice (nor could they have duties to us). But there are at least some signs that there were also more animal-friendly elements, especially in Lucretius (Campbell 2008).

Most of the Hellenistic Schools offered a way of life, not just a systematized cosmology nor even a training in argument. Most hoped only to achieve a *tranquil* life, though none had any strong reason to suppose that such tranquillity was possible. How easy is it to be 'tranquil' when there is no escape? Does it matter whether the world is so interconnected as to leave no wiggle room (as it were) or so disconnected as to allow atomic bits to swerve aside at random? In either case we can't control even our own brains and bodies, and 'enlightenment' demands that we give up any hope of a 'better' world than this. There were those, however, who held to a better hope.

> Why, in the name of Truth, do you show those who have put their trust in you that they are under the dominion of flux, and motion and fortuitous vortices? Why, pray, do you infect life with idols, imagining winds, air, fire, earth, stocks, stones, iron, this world itself to be gods? Why babble in high-flown language about the divinity of wandering stars to those men who have become real wanderers though this much-vaunted - I will not call it astronomy, but - astrology? I long for the Lord of the winds, the Lord of fire, the Creator of the World, He who gives light to the sun. I seek for God himself, not for the works of God. (Clement of Alexandria, *Protrepticus,* ch. 6: 1919, p. 153)

CHAPTER EIGHT

Ordinary and supernatural lives

Abstract virtues and the Romans

One of the oddest features of Roman civic religion is its devotion to abstract deities such as Liberty, Faith and Peace, and the proliferation of little gods to micromanage every moment of daily life. Carneades employed an argument against the divinity of major rivers and major virtues that fell flat in Rome. If any 'abstracts' were gods, he said, all would be (see Liebeschuetz 1979, p. 37 after Varro), and if Ocean is a god so is every little stream (Sextus, *Against the Mathematicians*, 9.186f; see Augustine *City of God* 4.21: 1998, pp. 167–8).

And why not? One point of deifying abstractions, and each element of the natural and human world, is simply to name what matters. Filling our world with images and reminders is a way of keeping ourselves on track. Those imaginings, even if they have no 'objective' reality, have an influence on our minds and hearts.

To dedicate a temple to an abstract deity was of course to make a public affirmation of the importance of that particular quality. But if cult has any meaning the worship implied that a supernatural power was interested in a particular kind of behaviour, and would help to make it prevail among its worshippers. Moreover, worship of moral abstractions could not logically limit itself to ritual: respect for the deity had to be shown in behaviour also. A man who wished to honour *Libertas* ought to uphold the republican constitution. A statue of *Concordia* in the senate house could be expected to restrain the aggressiveness of the speakers. (Liebeschuetz 1979, p. 52)

In addition to the corporeal images they scattered around their cities, the Romans also marked out Time (using a lunar calendar, and identifying years mostly by contemporary events or annual officials). In Plato's *Laws*, 'it is the divine gift of the liturgical cycle with all the concomitant sustenance which the deities bring to these festivals, which distinguishes human beings from the wild animals which have no such gifts of order, rhythm or harmony' (Pickstock 1998, p. 40, commenting on Plato *Laws* 2.653dff). That is why, in Hesiod's *Theogony*, the Hours are born to Zeus and Themis, alongside Good Order, Justice, Peace and also the three Fates (*Theogony* 901–6), all part of the human order. The revolving passage of Time does not exist until there are creatures like us, who divide and organize the days.

There are two distinctive features of the Roman experiment. The first, that these 'abstractions' inspired a genuine passion, a focused loyalty and pride. *Fides*, faith and the keeping of faith, was something Romans felt they should mind about, and sometimes did. Or so Silius tells us, in his *Punica* (2.515; see Liebeschuetz 1979, pp. 175–8). The second is that the stories built up around them were not, as in other traditions, about the deities themselves. Jupiter, Mars and Quirinus, 'the Archaic Triad', were hardly more than abstractions. Even Jupiter, Juno and Minerva, the later 'Capitoline Triad', were no richer. The Romans borrowed stories from the Greeks and the Etruscans about the gods they shared (or the gods they chose to recognize as theirs: Jupiter and Zeus, Mars and Ares are actually quite different, and Quirinus baffled the syncretists entirely), but the stories that they made themselves were mainly human histories. In Hesiod's account, abstractions give way to gods and monsters with particular characters, supernatural powers and stories. In the Roman story, it is human beings that act. The story of the early kings is likelier to be myth than history, like the Euhemerist versions found in Philo of Byblus or Snorri Sturlusson. Faith was expounded, for example, in the story of Regulus: captured by the Carthaginians, and sent back to Rome under oath to propose a treaty of peace, he took the occasion to persuade the Senate not to make peace at all – and then went back to Carthage to suffer death by torture (250 BC: Horace, *Odes*, 3.5). The Carthaginians' lack of faith, in turn, was exemplified in Hannibal's breach of a later treaty, when he invaded Italy. Both stories, probably, are false or at least misleading, but they gave substance to the merely abstract and indefinite ideal. Faith is to keep one's word, even to one's own destruction. In this the Romans and the Hebrews were agreed: 'Lord, who shall abide in thy tabernacle? Who shall dwell in thy holy hill? . . . He that sweareth to his own hurt, and changeth not' (*Psalm* 15.1, 4).

Did the Romans expect disaster if they broke their word? And did they break their word less often because they idealized *Fides*? Neither question is easily answered. Later moralists suspected that the Romans did *not* keep their word, and suffered for it, by finding themselves, increasingly, under the rule of tyrants. Did they believe that the Virtues, and the little household gods, were 'real'? Or were they merely internal to the human heart?

And why were so many Virtues female? Virtues were depicted on their public monuments as clothed female figures: the four statues ornamenting the Library of Celsus in Ephesus, for example, are of *arete*, *ennoia*, *episteme* and *sophia*. Roman coins carry similar figures to represent equity, good faith, modesty and the like. Whether those who admired the statues or glanced at the coins ever sought to invoke these virtues, constructing moving images of them in the way advised by esotericists, is unknown. It is also not altogether easy to understand what any of these virtues actually are (see Cicero, *Tusculan Disputations*, X.8): *sophrosune*, for example, has been variously translated as moderation, self-control, chastity and integrity. Possibly, 'self-possession' would be the fittest version.

Plotinus, teaching in Rome in the late third century AD, suggested that we needed to polish our internal statues – a theme which suggests that at least some Romans consciously internalized the images, and hoped to invoke a helpful presence, who would come to inhabit and move them. This is the substance of a practice often thought 'magical': the animation of statues by Egyptian sages. It may be that engineers in Egypt did create literal moving statues to excite the faithful (see *Asclepius* 23–4: Copenhaver 1992, pp. 80–1). But this was perhaps unnecessary: 'The Egyptian Heraiscus [late fifth century AD] . . . . had the natural gift of distinguishing between animate and inanimate sacred statues. He had but to look at one of them and immediately his heart was afflicted by divine frenzy while both his body and soul leapt up as if possessed by the god'! (Damascius 1999, p. 195).

Whatever the truth behind these stories, we should wonder whether, as stories, they are ones that we wish to govern us: many of them, after all, appeal to our own conceit. Stereotypical, civil virtues, even if they preserve a peace, are not respected by most saints or sages. We need, Plotinus said, to go beyond the statues, into the innermost shrine, where there are no images a probable reference to the Holy of Holies in the temple at Jerusalem. We must even, tradition says, go naked. The association of nakedness and the sacred goes back at least to Philo of Alexandria (fl. 40 AD): the High Priest must strip off the soul's tunic of opinion and imagery to enter the Holy of Holies. And 'enter naked with no coloured borders or sound of bells, to pour out as a libation the blood of the soul and to offer as incense the whole mind to God our Saviour and Benefactor' (Philo *Legum Allegoriarum* 2.56: 1929–62, vol. 1, p. 259). So also Plotinus:

> The attainment [of the good] is for those who go up to that higher world and are converted and strip off what we put on in our descent; (just as for those who go up to the celebrations of sacred rites there are purifications and strippings off of the clothes they wore before, and going up naked) until passing in the ascent all that is alien to the God, one sees with one's self alone. (*Ennead* I.6 [1].7)

But these strippings and deliberate unsayings are another story. As far as common Roman civic virtue was concerned the images were what we needed. Pompey found it ridiculous that the Holy of Holies was empty. In a later century, the pagan Senator Symmachus (c340–402 AD) protested when a Christian emperor removed the altar of Peace from the Roman Senate:

> The divine Mind has distributed different guardians and different cults to different cities. As souls are separately given to infants as they are born, so to peoples the genius of their destiny. We ask, then, for peace for the gods of our fathers and of our country. It is just that all worship should be considered as one. We look on the same stars, the sky is common, the same world surrounds us.

What difference does it make by what pains each seeks the truth? We cannot attain to so great a secret by one road. (Symmachus, *Relation*, 3, ch. 10)

This was one of the chief complaints of Romans against the Christians, that they seduced people away from their ancestral gods, and so rewrote the stories that should guide the peace. Pagan philosophers had done almost as much to deconstruct the stories, and point away from the images, but they were an elite group, unlikely to have much influence on the masses. Christians were more dangerous, not because they were likely to mount armed rebellions, but because any rewriting of the human story has no foreseeable ending. Christians were the atheists of their day, despite the efforts of their evangelists to suggest that they would go on honouring 'the powers that be', as having authority from God. They did not need to appease the little gods of household and urban settlement. In place of the fabulous history (Aeneas, Romulus, Horatius, Regulus and the rest) that animated Roman sensibility, they told stories of a crucified and risen Jew, and a God who promised the overthrow of tyrants. But they were not the only people to speak of such a God.

Sons of God

There was once a reputed Son of God, born of a mortal mother, required to labour in the service of humanity despite – or because of – being the rightful king. He was tempted, and resisted the temptation, to take the easier, pleasanter path. He perished through the treachery or folly of a trusted friend, but was raised up to Heaven and thereafter served as an ideal, an inspiration, even a supernatural aid. His double nature led some to suppose that there were two of him – one in Heaven, and the other (a mere shadow) in the land of the mortal dead (so Plotinus, *Ennead*, IV.3 [27].32, 24–8; I.1 [53].12, 32–5). The hero in question was Heracles, one of the mortal sons of Zeus, adopted into the Olympian hierarchy, and identified with the Tyrian god Melqart (see Teixidor 1977, pp. 34–5). Worshippers – for example, on Thasos – distinguished the Olympian, to whom they gave the sacrifices due an immortal, from the other to whom 'they delivered funerary honours as with a hero' (Herodotus 2.44; see also Miles 2010, p. 103), but the two were also one. Heracles did more than excuse colonial conquest: he had chosen the path of Virtue (Xenophon, *Memorabilia*, 2.1.21–34). The Cynics especially took him as their patron, as one who showed it was possible to live entirely by one's wits and courage, even in the face of celestial – that is, Hera's – malice (see Galinsky 1972).

It is generally agreed that during the whole time which Heracles spent among men he submitted to great and continuous labours and perils willingly, in order that he might confer benefits upon the race of men and thereby gain immortality. (Diodorus 1.2.4)

The figure of Heracles united many strands of Mediterranean and Mesopotamian custom. His techniques of water management – in cleaning out the filthy Augean stables – were learnt from Mesopotamia, and he was associated with a Mesopotamian god, Nergal, as well as with the Tyrian Melqart (see Kingsley 1995, pp. 274–5). Socrates swore by him, and Xenophon's band of mercenaries regularly prayed to 'Zeus the Saviour and Heracles the guide' (*Anabasis* 4.8; 6.5). He was honoured in Carthage as well as in Rome, and by emperors as well as by wandering Cynics.

The imperial theology of the greatest of the persecutors [that is, Diocletian] had important features in common with the religion which they persecuted. Jupiter is the supreme god. His son, Hercules, acts as his executive representative, and is a benefactor of man. The resemblance to Christian theology is obvious. (Liebeschuetz 1979, pp. 242–3)

None of this is to say that the early Christians had Heracles as their model, despite the formal congruencies and their shared worship of an ambiguous Saviour: ambiguous in that he was both mortal and immortal, and worshipped – in the end – by both establishment figures and the dispossessed. But the resemblance is a reminder that the early Christians could have been considered a sort of Cynic philosopher (see Downing 1987), and that the metaphysical and moral choices they made were not the obvious ones. They did not merely themselves abandon the luxuries of settled, city life (as many pagan philosophers did), but also sought to establish networks of support for the poor and dispossessed, so successfully indeed that when the Emperor Julian attempted to revive the older Olympian religion he had to suggest that pagans should imitate the Christian Churches in looking after the poor. In reasoning about the paradox of a mortal god, Christians mostly insisted that Jesus was a single being (not two) and that he did not have a muddled, middling nature, but was both God and Human, each perfectly and entirely: one person with two natures. There were easier options: many philosophers, especially of the Stoic sort, could have agreed that any wise man 'had the Mind of God', and was equal as far as his virtue goes with Zeus Himself (according at least to Chrysippus: LS 1987, p. 380 [61J]). Others could have acknowledged a miracle worker or a prophet in the old philosophical style. Apollonius of Tyana (c15–c100 AD) was recognizably a philosopher, as even Jerome – no friend of pagans – was to agree (Jerome, *Epistle*, 53.1: Cameron 2011, p. 557): he had visited Persia and Ethiopia 'to see the Gymnosophists and the famous table of the sun spread in the sands of the desert'. As Cameron has argued (2011, pp. 554–8), Apollonius was rarely seen as a rival to Christian doctrine, but much that he said and did was what Christians might approve. 'Wherever he goes Apollonius criticizes local cult practices. He attacks gladiatorial games, chariot-racing, public baths, luxury in every form and, above all, blood sacrifice' (Cameron 2011, p. 555). It would have been easy to find a comparable role for Jesus and his followers. Nor was it any surprise that such philosophers would sometimes be treated badly: Socrates was executed by the Athenians, and Zeno of Elea tortured to death by a tyrant. Plato had made it clear – in *The Republic* and elsewhere – that the fate of the 'just man' might be very painful, and yet that his life was better than his killer's. Even a god might find himself cast down into mortal troubles, or come down of his own accord to help us out.

> The doctrine that Jesus at his birth was but a 'mere man' and that the spirit of God only descended on Him much later [which was judged the Adoptionist heresy] avoided the very substantial objections which a Greek philosopher was almost bound to raise to any incarnation of God. (Walzer 1949, p. 86)

All of these options were possible, and could have been acknowledged – if not as exactly 'true', still as acceptable stories.

> An old saying is still current that the deity goes the round of the cities, in the likeness now of this man, now of that man, taking

note of wrongs and transgressions. The current story may not be a true one, but it is at all events good and profitable for us that it should be current. (Philo, *De Somniis*, 1.232f: 1929–62, vol. 5, p. 421; see *Hebrews* 13.2)

The Christian Churches chose a more paradoxical and dangerous road, not simply to be difficult but to stay true to their experience. Nor did they take another, pagan, road: maybe Zeus had miscalculated after all, and he was to be deposed – as was traditional – by a heroic son! The Hermetic Corpus came close to this, in suggesting that 'the one who is really human is above [the gods of heaven] or at least they are wholly equal in power to one another' (*Corpus Hermeticum* 10.24: Copenhaver 1992, p. 36; see Fowden 1986, p. 111), but not above God Himself. The idea surfaced among Christians – that the God of the Old Covenant was in truth the devil, as Marcion of Sinope (85–160 AD) proposed – but this idea too was rejected. They placed Jesus at the centre of their cult and ethics, but insisted still that He was the Creator's Word.

Heracles was a myth, whether or not there was a historical hero behind the story. Jesus of Nazareth was a Jewish *hasid*, from Galilee (see Vermes 2001). Like Pythagoras, Socrates and Ammonius Saccas, he left no writings of his own, and yet was the most influential of philosophers, whether among believers or opponents. Apocryphal stories, not endorsed in the Christian canon, suggested that – like other philosophers – he had visited Egypt, Chaldaea and even India before his brief public life. Maybe he was associated with an ascetic Hebrew sect, the Essenes, and learnt both mystical and moral lessons there – but maybe, just as easily, he learnt all this (if He needed to) from neighbourly conversations in a Galilee populated by Hebrews, Syrians and Greeks.[1] His moral advice was familiar: treat others as you would wish to be treated; don't hold grudges; don't worry about the future; don't imagine that money matters; heal what evils you can, but remember that the kingdom of Heaven – doing justly and loving mercy – will grow by slow degrees, and little acts of kindness. 'It is like', he said, 'a mustard seed that grows into a bush – and all the birds of the air (he adds, with the confident exaggeration that was his trademark) will come and make their nests there' (*Matthew* 13.31–2). His claims could also be heard – were often heard – as dangerous. One thesis is now often misheard completely: to give Caesar what is his, and give God His own (*Matthew* 22.21).

This is not the pallid suggestion that politics and religion, business and faith, be disjoined, and that we should give time and cash to each. On the contrary, no man can serve two masters (*Matthew* 6.24). The thesis is that just as the coin he was shown carries the image of Caesar, and is his, so every human being is stamped with the image of God, and therefore belongs to Him. And every one is also different from every other, and so not substitutable for any other.

> A man stamps many coins with one seal, and they are all identical, but the King of the kings of kings stamped every man with the seal of the first man, and none is identical with his fellow. Therefore it is the duty of every one to say: For my sake the world was created. (*Mishnah: Sanhedrin* 4.5: Urbach 1979, p. 217)

As long as all that Caesar asks of us is money, there is no problem: the money was his before. If he asks our active obedience, in opposition to the Word and Will of God, we cannot give it, any more than Socrates could obey the courts of Athens rather than the god Apollo (Plato, *Apology,* 37e).

More was made of Jesus by his followers than pagans would have expected. It was not unusual to think that sages might have been, or someday would be, gods.

> Even before this coming to be we were There, men who were different, and some of us even gods, pure souls and intellect united with the whole of reality; we were parts of the intelligible, not marked off or cut off but belonging to the whole; and we are not cut off even now. (Plotinus, *Ennead,* VI.4 [22].14, 18ff)

A little less metaphysically, anyone could think and speak, in principle, as God or the Truth would have her speak. And anyone could refrain. Jesus could have ended his days as a jobbing carpenter, and Pontius Pilate instead have embodied God's Word and Wisdom (see Clark 1991, pp. 122–35). Nor would there be any problem if there were more than one such sage, identical in their manners, thoughts and purposes but not the same individuals. The Christian Church insisted rather that there could be only one: there was a strict identity between Jesus of Nazareth and the Word of God, not simply as Socrates has become identified, in a way, with 'true philosophy'. Once again, that would have been a much easier way of expressing part of the doctrine: just as no later would-be philosopher can avoid the challenge of Socrates, so also (it could be said) we are challenged by that homeless, crucified *hasid*. In accepting crucifixion (which is death by torture), Jesus did what Socrates also did: he compelled his fellows to act out their vision of justice, and by doing so destroyed that vision, and released us all from the guilty conviction that we *should* obey Nobodaddy. When any just man is condemned according to law, and by the will of the rulers, it is that law, those rulers, whose authority is diminished. This is what Roman peace and Hebrew purity have come to.

Is there anything else to be said about Jesus himself, all later dogma aside? One issue has been a little neglected. The Rabbi Eliezer, when he appealed to Heaven, was asking for confirmation that his interpretation of the law was right. He was a traditionalist, who claimed never to have been original (rather as Plotinus insisted that he was only repeating Plato), whereas his opponents hoped to amplify and develop the tradition. A story told, most likely, by opponents of one such Rabbi, Akiva (c50–c137 AD), has it that Moses himself was miraculously carried ahead to one of that Rabbi's classes, and found himself confused by the Rabbi's exposition of the Mosaic Law (Maccoby 2002, pp. 181–4) – a story, incidentally, that assumes that all times and places are equally present to God. Anti-traditionalists believed that the Law had hidden implications, or could at least be applied outside its original form. It is an interpretative device that has often been used 'progressively', or in a 'liberal' spirit: even in more recent times the claim that 'all men are created equal' has had more effect than its writers really expected (since they weren't thinking of slaves, or even of women, or natives). But in some Rabbinic circles the hermeneutic might also be a device for imposing new burdens on the faithful, teaching as doctrine the commands of men (*Matthew* 15.9). No part of the Law is to be abandoned (*Matthew* 5.17) – and for that very reason nothing is to be added to it (though Jesus's own practice may suggest that he thought it possible to uncover the law behind the overt commandment, and offer that instead: see *Matthew* 5.21–2, 27–8). Eliezer was excommunicated by his colleagues, and was even brought before a civil court to be judged for apostasy (and acquitted). Jesus at any rate was thought to be holding to the original Law: to love God, and to love our neighbour as we do ourselves (*Matthew* 22.35–40; after *Deuteronomy* 6.4; *Leviticus* 19.18). Anything else – as Rabbi Hillel of Babylon (110 BC – 10 AD) also taught – was gloss, and of less weight (*Babylonian Talmud, Shabbat* 31a).

Can we know anything of Jesus's metaphysics? What did he think of God, and of reality? Did he think of himself as a messenger, as many before him had done? Did he have a message explicitly about the world to come? Like other Hebraic theorists, his attention was given to a future, rather than a mystical other. The Kingdom of God was to come, rather than being in Heaven, or an alongside world. Nothing that happens here and now is 'God's judgment on the wicked' (see *John* 9.1–5; *Luke* 13.1–5), but the 'Day of the Lord' is coming. Justice will one day be done, and we had better be ready for it – by being compassionate now (*Luke* 6.35–8).

> Love your enemies and pray for your persecutors; only so can you be children of your heavenly Father, who makes his sun rise on good and bad alike, and sends the rain on the honest and the dishonest. If you love only those who love you, what reward can you expect? . . . There must be no limit to your goodness, as your heavenly Father's goodness knows no bounds. (*Matthew* 5.44–8)

And what is 'God'? No one has seen God at any time, not even Moses (*John* 1.18; see also *I John* 4.12): He is revealed only in what is done by the Man: to heal the sick, the blind and the lame, and preach good news to the poor (*Matthew* 11.4–5). The Gospels, on their own, seem still to privilege 'the lost sheep of the house of Israel', but the wider world is also to be considered. 'It is from the Jews that salvation comes. But the time approaches, indeed it is already here, when those who are real worshippers will worship the Father in spirit and in truth' (*John* 4.22–3), not simply in Jerusalem and on Mount Gerizim where the Samaritans then worshipped. On the one hand, 'God' refers to something wholly unlike any creature; on the other, it is always here. Or rather, in Jesus's vocabulary, He is here. Notoriously, it is as 'Father' that Jesus routinely addresses and speaks of God. Both he and his disciples make a distinction: only those who are loving can claim God as their Father, while the 'judgmental' have a different, diabolical father. Non-Christian commentators may find this hard to square with Jesus's own extremely judgemental attitude to 'scribes and Pharisees, hypocrites'! (e.g. *Matthew* 23.13–36).

Other metaphysicians have held that 'it is impossible even for the gods either to make the diagonal commensurable with the side [of a square], or twice two five, or any of the things that have happened not to have happened' (Alexander of Aphrodisias 1983, p. 80 [*De Fato* 200.21–3]; see Walzer 1949, pp. 29–30). This is no weakness in the Omnipotent: merely a recognition that these challenges are gibberish (can God make doodleglims warpsome?). The Omnipotent can do everything – but 'making twice two five' means nothing (unless we've missed its meaning). According to Jesus, although it is easier for a camel to pass through the eye of a needle than for a rich man to achieve the kingdom, 'with God all things are possible' (*Matthew* 19.24–6).[2] John the Baptist had agreed: 'God can make children for Abraham out of these stones' (*Matthew* 3.9). We may not ourselves be able to imagine what success in this would be like (any more than we can conceive round squares or warpsome doodleglims): it need not follow that the Creator is similarly limited, or that we can work out what is the case by eliminating what (we think) is impossible. Many centuries later the Bishop of Paris insisted that we had no right to limit God by supposing that, for example, He cannot create a vacuum (a something that is essentially nothing). 'If we must assign a date for the birth of modern science, we would, without doubt, choose the year 1277 when the bishop of Paris solemnly proclaimed that several worlds could exist, and that the whole of the heavens could, without contradiction, be moved with a rectilinear motion' (Pierre Duhem, quoted by Grant 1962, p. 200). As Descartes also realized, we cannot assume that our logic rules the Omnipotent, nor be entirely sure, before the event, what really is or isn't impossible. We cannot, in short, work out what the world is like merely by examining our own ideas of it, as philosophers often hoped.

Is there any chance of locating *God*'s idea of it? Later writers conceived that Jesus himself was the very Word of God, the thing that the Omnipresent has been saying, is saying, from the beginning, and through whom all things were made. Rabbinic speculative poetry or metaphysics proposed that Zion, which is Jerusalem, was the very first thing to be made: Jerusalem the City was the centre of history, even if – in human history – it came late. Muslims similarly were to suggest that the heavenly *Koran* was written 'before' all worlds. Christians concluded instead that Jesus was the centre, the very first bit of the story as it is conceived in God. In all these cases, there were some features of the story, the place, the text as it was enacted in human history that really could have been otherwise, and other features that really could not have been different, since they were what God always is and says. Is this a story that Jesus himself could have told, as the gospel writers suggest he did? It is at least not clear that he couldn't have: either the story is true (and clearly He could have told it) or it is at least a story that Hellenized Jews could tell (as Philo of Alexandria almost did).

Divination and technology

Matthew's Gospel declares that 'wise men from the East' had seen a star that signified, to them, that the King of the Jews was born, and followed it, via Herod's court, to Bethlehem (*Matthew* 2.2–12). Later tradition had it that there were three of them to match the gifts they brought (gold, frankincense and myrrh), and that they represented the three lines descended from Noah's sons (Shem, Ham and Japhet). The other gospels make no mention of the star, nor of astrological prophecies. Possibly, the astrologers had a conjunction of Saturn and Jupiter in mind; possibly there was a literal nova, or perhaps a comet (see Humphreys 1991); and possibly the story was made up afterwards. Whatever the truth of it, no Christian could suppose that the stars compelled Messiah's birth: at most, they might have signalled it. The stars weren't gods, and neither was the world so closely knit that whatever happened aloft must be linked to what happened below in ways that could allow us to predict any future but the stars' own motions.

But that theory did have followers, armed with the force of astronomical observations and well-made machines. The Antikythera Mechanism – a careful assembly of cogged wheels that work together to represent the motion of the planetary stars, and even predict eclipses – is so elegant, and so complex, that there must have been other such devices. This sort of prediction or retrodiction was both exact and reliable, and so lent weight to other prophecies. The reasoning behind other forms of divination, from entrails or the flight of birds, was more easily mocked by sceptics. Did the gods interfere when a sacrificial beast was chosen, or alter the state of its liver after it was killed? Did the gods signal to us through the lightning by making the clouds clash? (as, apparently, the Etruscans thought: Seneca, *Questiones Naturales* II.32). At least those forms of divination were more open to clever interpretation to fit the circumstances and the wishes of officials. Astrology had the air of destiny, and this fitted well with Stoic philosophy.

So Cicero summarized the thesis (before demolishing it):

> Reason compels us to admit that all things happen by Fate. Now by Fate I mean the same that the Greeks call *heimarmene*, that is, an orderly succession of causes wherein cause is linked to cause and each cause of itself produces an effect. That is an immortal truth having its source in all eternity. Therefore nothing has happened which was not bound to happen, and, likewise, nothing is going to happen which will not find in nature every efficient cause of its happening. (*De Divinatione* 1.55.125)

Everything is so firmly connected to everything else that not even the slightest difference in the course of things could be imagined without amending the whole. What does not happen, cannot happen – a thesis logically equivalent to the converse Epicurean notion: everything that can happen, does (so logical equivalence is not all that matters). An ideal intelligence, on the Stoic theory, could deduce all past and future events from a single falling leaf, how much more from the motion of stars. The obstacle in our way is that we are not ideally intelligent. We can't trust ourselves to make accurate deductions, and the information from which we begin is always incomplete, and always inexact. The most we can hope is that there are some particular, noticeable signs of what is yet to come – the more confidently if the gods are friendly.

> If there are gods and they do not make clear to man in advance what the future will be, then they do not love man; or, they themselves do not know what the future will be; or, they think that it is of no advantage to man to know what it will be; or, they think it inconsistent with their dignity to give man forewarnings of the future; or, finally, they, though gods, cannot give intelligible signs of coming events. But it is not true that the gods do not love us, for they are the friends and benefactors of the human race; nor is it true that they do not know their own decrees and their own plans; nor is it true that it is of no advantage to us to know what is going to happen, since we should be more prudent if we

knew; nor is it true that the gods think it inconsistent with their dignity to give forecasts, since there is no more excellent quality than kindness; nor is it true that they have not the power to know the future; therefore it is not true that there are gods and yet that they do not give us signs of the future; but there are gods, therefore they give us such signs; and if they give us such signs, it is not true that they give us no means to understand those signs — otherwise their signs would be useless; and if they give us the means, it is not true that there is no divination; therefore there is divination. (Cicero, *De Divinatione*, 1.38.82–3)

Cicero went on, in the second part of his treatise, to deconstruct, to dismember this and related arguments. We may agree with him, except to note that the Stoics at least had an argument for the optimistic thesis at the heart of our modern science: that the universe is comprehensible. They were undoubtedly wrong in detail and execution: there is nothing to be learnt, by us at least, about the future of empire from a diseased cow's liver. But they could have learnt something about local conditions: the ancients, said Vitruvius,

> after sacrifice, carefully inspected the livers of those animals fed on that spot whereon the city was to be built, or whereon a stative encampment was intended. If the livers were diseased and livid, they tried others, in order to ascertain whether accident or disease was the cause of the imperfection; but if the greater part of the experiments proved, by the sound and healthy appearance of the livers, that the water and food of the spot were wholesome, they selected it for the garrison. If the reverse, they inferred, as in the case of cattle, so in that of the human body, the water and food of such a place would become pestiferous; and they therefore abandoned it, in search of another, valuing health above all other considerations. (Vitruvius, *On Architecture*, 1.2.9)

We can at least hope to grasp the signs of the times, if we listen and look with the proper attitude. 'If prophecies, based on erroneous deductions and interpretations, turn out to be false, the fault is not chargeable to the signs but to the lack of skill in the interpreters' (Cicero, *De Divinatione*, 1.52.118). Experience can teach us something, and if we can keep records of past observations we may guess right in the future. But there are necessary limits to what we can possibly guess.

Can there, then, be any foreknowledge of things for whose happening no reason exists? For we do not apply the words 'chance', 'luck', 'accident', or 'casualty' except to an event which has so occurred or happened that it either might not have occurred at all, or might have occurred in any other way. How, then, is it possible to foresee and to predict an event that happens at random, as the result of blind accident, or of unstable chance? By the use of reason the physician foresees the progress of a disease, the general anticipates the enemy's plans and the pilot forecasts the approach of bad weather. And yet even those who base their conclusions on accurate reasoning are often mistaken: for example, when the farmer sees his olive-tree in bloom he expects also, and not unreasonably, to see it bear fruit, but occasionally he is disappointed. If then mistakes are made by those who make no forecasts not based upon some reasonable and probable conjecture, what must we think of the conjectures of men who foretell the future by means of entrails, birds, portents, oracles, or dreams? (*De Divinatione* 2.6ff, after Carneades)

Was he unduly sceptical of the ideas he didn't share, and credulous of his own? Egyptian priests 'not infrequently foretell destructions of the crops or, on the other hand, abundant yields, and pestilences that are to attack men or beasts, and as a result of their long observations they have prior knowledge of earthquakes and floods, of the risings of the comets, and of all things which the ordinary man looks upon as beyond all finding out' (Diodorus 1.81.5). Maybe Thales did predict a bumper olive crop, and Pherecydes an earthquake, even if they did not know why they succeeded.

Everything is interconnected. On the Stoic account, only bodies have any causal power, since only bodies can push against each other. But why should they always push in the same way? We may speak loosely of 'the laws of nature', but since those laws themselves aren't bodies, they can have no effects. We may remark that different bodies have identical 'natures', but the Stoics denied that such universals were anything more than words. Why then is there any identity to govern what different bodies do? We might as well say that Sirius, the star, will bark as loudly as Sirius, the dog, merely because we call them 'Sirius'. Philosophers with Platonic leanings might believe in eternal natures that even constrain the Creator (as Galen suggested in an attack on the Hebrew theory of creation: Walzer 1949, p. 27). The Stoic answer was superficially more like the Hebrew in appealing simply to the will of God, the divine spirit (*pneuma*):

> [A] something far more deeply interfused,
> Whose dwelling is the light of setting suns,
> And the round ocean and the living air,
> And the blue sky, and in the mind of man;
> A motion and a spirit, that impels
> All thinking things, all objects of all thought,
> And rolls through all things
>
> (William Wordsworth, 'Tintern Abbey';
> see Sharples 1996, pp. 44–5)

But if this God is also bodily, the metaphysical problem remains unsolved. What guarantees that the different parts of that one, corporeal, spirit will act in the same way? If the universe is to be recognizably law-abiding, we need to suppose that there is something that remains the same through all distinctions of place and date and scale. How can that something be one body like any other? And how, if bodies are causal agents because they can push against each other, can we suppose that a body which *permeates* all others, without facing any obstacle, can push at all? The Hebrews were wiser in agreeing that there was a Wisdom interfused with all things, but that this was not corporeal. Neither was It in any place. Rather, it was their God Himself who was the Place where all things happen. Perhaps the Stoics, if they borrowed from Hebrew or Phoenician sources, mistook the point of a metaphor: God's spirit may be like the wind, but it wouldn't be able to do the work for which it was invoked if it were merely 'a portion of breath'. The merely corporeal universe, defined as an array of bodies, depends on something that is not corporeal. Pagan Platonists agreed:

> Let us apprehend in our thought this visible universe, with each of its parts remaining what it is without confusion, gathering all of them together into one as far as we can, so that when any one part appears first, for instance the outside heavenly

sphere, the imagination of the sun and with it the other heavenly bodies follows immediately, and the earth and the sea and all the living creatures are seen, as they could in fact all be seen inside a transparent sphere. Let there be, then, in the soul a shining imagination of a sphere, having everything within it, either moving or still, or some things moving and others standing still. Keep this, and apprehend in your mind another, taking away the mass: take away also the places, and the mental picture of matter in yourself, and do not try to apprehend another sphere smaller in mass than the original one, but calling on the god who made that of which you have the mental picture, pray him to come. And may he come, bringing his own universe with him, and all the gods within him, he who is one and all, and each god is all the gods coming together into one; they are different in all their powers, but by that one manifold power they are all one; or rather the one god is all. (Plotinus, *Ennead*, 5.8 [31].9, 1–18; see Dillon 1986)

Neither pagan Platonists nor the Hebrews approved of divination: their sacrifices were for other causes. But like the Stoics they were 'cosmic optimists'. There were some clues on how to cope in a world that seemed arbitrary and unmeaning. Virtue, too often, did not seem to be rewarded, and even worthy purposes, even imperial purposes, might suffer a catastrophic end. Imperial purposes especially: Scipio Aemilianus, who led the last campaign against Carthage, and presided over its obliteration, is said to have wept at the sight, and expressed the fear that the same would someday be done to Rome (Polybius 38.21.1, cited by Momigliano 1975, p. 22). The gods cut down the successful, and nothing lasts forever: that prophecy at least was regularly fulfilled.

Could we delay the event? As Plotinus reminded his disciples, 'the law says those who fight bravely [and – we might add – skilfully], not those who pray, are to come safe out of the wars' (*Ennead* III.2 [47].32, 36–7). The gods may possibly warn us, but they probably won't help. Technological innovation has often been guided and motivated by military or economic need: catapults, siege engines, rams. Archimedes of Syracuse (287–212 BC), for example, was responsible for better ways of sinking ships (including, possibly, the use of mirrored surfaces to start fires), as well as detecting financial fraud. The Roman soldier who killed him in accidental defiance of his general's order did not please the Roman establishment, which had hoped for the benefit of his particular genius. Engineers like Archytas of Tarentum were wiser – *pace* Plato– in spending their talents on making toys instead: like the mechanical flying bird he is said to have constructed, powered by steam (Aulus Gellius *Attic Nights* 10.12.9, after Favorinus of Arles [c80–c160 AD]). We have some idea of what Roman engineers were doing: they managed aqueducts and arches, built ships from borrowed plans and sometimes improved them. We know, from example, that there were craftsmen who worked with bronze, iron, pottery and glass, without bothering to write down how and why. It is sad, from our perspective, that astrologers and augurs devoted so much intelligence and effort to a dead-ending system of prophecy, and that they got more honour for it – save from Sceptics – than the humbler variety of hands-on engineers.

Poseidonius did not share the disdain the literati felt for technology. He even suggested that crafts (including baking, pottery, metal-working, carpentry) were invented by 'philosophers' (Seneca, *Letters*, 90: Kidd 1999, pp. 359–66). Seneca insisted that proper philosophers couldn't care about such things: '[the philosopher] would never have judged anything worth inventing, which he would later have judged not worth lasting use; he would not have picked up what had to be laid aside'. But maybe Seneca was wrong.

The Roman military engineer and architect, Vitruvius Pollio (c80–c10 BC), is almost our only source for understanding how hands-on engineers reasoned about their work. They applied mathematical theorems to the material world, as Archimedes did: did they worry about *why* mathematics worked? (see Wigner 1960). Did they rely on a Pythagorean sense that numbers were the foundation of the world? Or were they merely 'practical'? Vitruvius thought otherwise, insisting that practice and theory are both essential. Indeed, an architect, it seems, should be a master of many crafts and sciences.

An architect should be a good writer, a skilful draftsman, versed in geometry and optics, expert at figures, acquainted with history, informed on the principles of natural and moral philosophy, somewhat of a musician, not ignorant of the sciences both of law and physic, nor of the motions, laws, and relations to each other, of the heavenly bodies. . . . . Moral philosophy will teach the architect to be above meanness in his dealings, and to avoid arrogance: it will make him just, compliant and faithful to his employer; and what is of the highest importance, it will prevent avarice gaining an ascendancy over him: for he should not be occupied with the thoughts of filling his coffers, nor with the desire of grasping every thing in the shape of gain, but, by the gravity of his manners, and a good character, should be careful to preserve his dignity. In these respects we see the importance of moral philosophy; for such are her precepts. That branch of philosophy which the Greeks call *physiologia*, or the doctrine of physics, is necessary to him in the solution of various problems; as for instance, in the conduct of water, whose natural force, in its meandering and expansion over flat countries, is often such as to require restraints, which none know how to apply, but those who are acquainted with the laws of nature: nor, indeed, unless grounded in the first principles of physic, can he study with profit the works of Ctesibius, Archimedes, and many other authors who have written on the subject. (*On Architecture* 1.1.3; 1.1.7)

That philosophy, music and astronomy should be reckoned useful for their 'practical' importance may be only what Vitruvius (and others) felt that they had to say to their Roman masters. But even in saying this they subverted more obvious, public, values: 'such as possess the gifts of fortune are easily deprived of them: but when learning is once fixed in the mind, no age removes it, nor is its stability affected during the whole course of life' (Vitruvius *On Architecture* 5: Introduction, 3). Wealth and the favour of princes may not last: learning may at least last longer. There was a higher object too: 'Man himself has come to be in order to contemplate and imitate the world, being by no means perfect, but a tiny constituent of that which is perfect' (Cicero, *On the Nature of the Gods*, 2.38: LS, vol. 1, p. 326 [54H]). We begin to understand those things in the world that we can imitate, not merely by intuiting a theory of how they work, but by actually building things. What began from necessity, as our ancestors built houses in imitation of swallows' nests (*On Architecture* 2.1.2), has become a mode of understanding.

The voice arises from flowing breath, sensible to the hearing through its percussion on the air. It is propelled by an infinite number of circles similar to those generated in standing water when a stone is cast therein, which, increasing as they recede from the centre, extend to a great distance, if the narrowness of the place or some obstruction do not prevent their spreading to the extremity; for when impeded by obstructions, the first recoil affects all that follow. In the same manner the voice spreads in a circular direction. But, whereas the circles in water only spread horizontally, the voice, on the contrary, extends vertically as well as horizontally. Wherefore, as is the case with the motion of water, so with the voice, if no obstacle disturb the first undulation, not only the second and following one, but all of them will, without reverberation, reach the ears of those at bottom and those at top. On this account the antient architects, *following nature as their guide*, and reflecting on the properties of the voice, regulated the true ascent of steps in a theatre, and contrived, by musical proportions and mathematical rules, whatever its effect might be on the stage (*scena*), to make it fall on the ears of the audience in a clear and agreeable manner. Since in brazen or horn wind instruments, by a regulation of the genus, their tones are rendered as clear as those of stringed instruments, so by the application of the laws of harmony, the antients discovered a method of increasing the power of the voice in a theatre. (*On Architecture* 5.3.6–8)

Philosophy and foolosophies

Cicero's reasoned attacks on divination depended on the assumption that we should seek evidence for our beliefs. Indeed, we should go further, and seek out counter-evidence: let us attempt, at least, the purificatory practices that Socrates advised. Notoriously, these practices are painful. It is easy to fall in love with our own ideas and notions, and easy to forget their sources. Once we acquire a notion, it is ours, and we'll continue to use it as a reliable premise, or a helpful model, even when we also know it's false, or at least that the evidence we had is poor. The deeply ascetic challenge is to believe only what can be proven true, and that challenge is rarely met.

Strictly, indeed, it cannot be. Sceptics, as a distinct school of Hellenistic philosophy, argued that, on Stoic principles, 'wise men' wouldn't believe what was not infallibly supported, and therefore should not believe anything. Stoics rested their science on the notion of '*kataleptike phantasia*', a cognitive impression: I can only rightly believe my impression that Jemima is eating oranges if nothing else but the fact that she is could explain the impression (which may itself be compounded of several distinct impressions, of sight, smell, texture, conversational enrichment). But it is easy to show that everything in our experience could *in principle* be caused by something else. Heracles was confronted, with complete conviction, by the appearance of sworn, deadly enemies, and killed them (though they were his wife and children). Can any of us, at any one time, be properly convinced we're sane, and so 'in touch with reality'? Stoic philosophers themselves said that all those who aren't wise are indeed insane, and that our usual world is a dream and a delirium (Aurelius, *Meditations,* 2.17.1).

The Sceptical response to the failure, as it seems, of demonstration, was to balance each unprovable belief against its opposite, and so give in to neither. Even their own argument against the Stoics was not one they endorsed as certain. Might we still hold fast, for the moment, to the Rational Rule, to believe only on 'good evidence', even if no evidence is absolutely good? That, after all, has been the slogan with which pagans often berated Christians, who were supposed themselves to believe that we should rely on 'Faith', not 'Reason'. Tertullian's aphorism, that he believed the Christian story because it was incredible (Tertullian, *De carne Christi,* 5.4), has been taken to be just such a rejection of 'reason'. Actually, it was a standard rhetorical trope much used in court. If a witness's story is bizarre when he could have made up a plausible story instead we have a reason at least to suspect that the story may be true (Aristotle, *Rhetoric,* 2.23; see Moffat 1916; Sider 1980).

The Stoics correctly argued that it is difficult to mount a convincing argument against the possibility of ever rightly being convinced: that very argument, it seems, must have a convincing conclusion! And they were right in what they said we should avoid. We need to be careful in presenting cases: appealing to jurors to convict the accused by showing them pictures of victims, or asking them to consider the victims' friends, is very improper behaviour. Such details might be relevant when deciding what to do with someone who has been convicted, or when deciding how much time and effort should be spent in investigating the alleged offence; they don't help determine whether the accused *is* guilty. The Stoic principle is also sound, that the weight of evidence depends on how easy or hard it might be to produce such seeming evidence on any other hypothesis. This creates problems, as the Sceptics saw, and itself depends on assumptions, about the effort that hoaxers might deploy or their skills in doing so. But we can agree that it is 'better' to be thus 'rational' than simply to choose a belief, without any evidence, and maintain it against all comers.

This is not to say that such reason will always be right: Augustine argued well against the idea of Antipodeans, pointing out that there could be no way of meeting them, as they lay beyond the oceans that, by hypothesis, divided us from them and made it impossible that they should be descendants of Adam (*City of God* 16.9: 1998, p. 710). As it happens, he was mistaken, and so also were the Pythagoreans who thought that the equatorial regions were too hot to pass. That the earth was a sphere, and that it orbited the Sun, were both unlikely doctrines (though the former at least was well known, maybe even to Homer: see Strabo 1.1.20)[3]. All too often, we mean by 'reasonable' only that the thought is congenial to our received opinions. But 'truth must of necessity be stranger than fiction, for fiction is the creation of the human mind, and therefore is congenial to it' (Chesterton 1960, p. 82). It follows, so it seems, that the truth will sometimes seem unlike what we expected, and that there will be no other evidence for it than its own force. Once having seen it, as Plotinus said, we may easily fall asleep again:

> It is as if people who slept through their life thought the things in their dreams were reliable and obvious, but, if someone woke them up, disbelieved in what they saw with their eyes open and went to sleep again. (*Ennead* V.5 [32].11)

Such dreams may be created behind our backs, as it were, but also by ourselves, when we trust 'private reasonings' and so 'construct and build the city of the mind that destroys the truth' (Philo, *Legum Allegoriarum*, 3.228f: 1981, p. 151). Truth breaks in, like a thief, and steals from us our little dreams and fancies.

But we still need to check. When Eusebius of Caesarea was faced by the charge that Christians depended on 'uncritical and untested faith' (*Praeparatio*, Prologue 1.1.11; see also Walzer 1949, pp. 48–56), he replied that there were good reasons for thinking the gospel true, but also reasons to think it better to believe it: 'from [Jesus's] utterances and from his teaching diffused throughout the whole world, the customs of all nations are now set aright, even those customs which before were savage and barbarous; so that Persians who have become his disciples no longer marry their mothers, nor Scythians feed on human flesh' (Eusebius, *Praeparatio*, 1.4.6: Johnson 2006, p. 206). The charges against barbarians (and others) are familiar ones, and may be lies, but the overall claim may stand. At any rate, anyone supposing that the Christian Churches have made life *worse* than it was in heathen times and places should read more history! The notions that we should be kind to each other, and that rulers will be accountable to God for what they do, have had some good effects. But the point of interest is not that Eusebius was right (or wrong) to think that the world was kinder than it had been, but that he was prepared to consider reasons for 'belief' and for spreading 'beliefs' that were more like Protagoras's than like Plato's. Granted that we cannot uncover the truth of things, and be sure of them, may we not at least discover a better way of living? Even this, as Plato argued, must depend on our believing that this at least is true: we can't be forever saying that we believe things only for their good effects, unless we can be properly persuaded that they really have these effects, and that the effects are good. We can't in the end escape the need to hang on at least to the notion of truth, even when we can't be sure of it. We must somehow have faith!

So, how to live in uncertainty? The answer for some is simple: to fall back into the easy world, where nothing is ever questioned and no-one confronts an uncongenial truth. We cannot be sure they are wrong. Others may seek to pursue a philosophic path to truth – but as Lucian of Samosata argued, their first steps on the path are taken without proof. In the dialogue, *Hermotimus,* a long-term student of the Stoic school is shown that he has not achieved the calm and purity of mind the Stoics offered, and that his teacher hasn't either! Why exactly did he pick the Stoics, and spend twenty years of his life, and money, on that path?

> There have been a lot of philosophers, Plato, Aristotle, Antisthenes, your own school founders, Chrysippus and Zeno, and all the others. So, what persuaded you to ignore the others and to decide to choose the creed you did to guide your studies? Did Pythian Apollo treat you like Chaerephon, and send you to the Stoics as the best of all? His practice is to direct different people to different philosophies, as he knows each individual's requirements. (Lucian 2006, p. 94)

Every School, in short (including the modern School, of Science), requires its students to dedicate themselves before they have adequate evidence, or a right judgement, about the truth of its teachings. It was easy for pagan rationalists like Celsus, Lucian's contemporary, to insist that Christians 'were like quacks who warn men against the doctor' (Origen, *Contra Celsum*, 3.75: cited by Walzer 1949, p. 53), but even quacks may sometimes be correct (and the doctors often weren't)! Why we pick one School rather than any other will depend on personal and historical circumstances beyond our control or knowledge, and once we have embarked on it, we'll tend to ignore the problems. Lucian's own answer, so it seems, is to follow the common way, without any claim that this – the guddle of inherited ideas and customs – has a stronger claim to truth. It is only cheaper and easier.

Must we choose, in the end, between Plato and Protagoras, or Plato and the Sceptics? Clement's assault on the 'inherited conglomerate' of civic custom and philosophy in his *Protrepticus* invoked Plato as an ally, and it was Platonism that shaped the serious thought of the early centuries AD. However important their disagreements, Philo of Alexandria (Jewish), John Evangelist and Clement (Christian), and Plotinus (Pagan) shared a world. The grand deductive structure created by the pagan Platonist Proclus was mirrored in the work of the Christian ps-Dionysius a few years later, and in later Christian and Islamic texts (as well as being imitated in its structure at least by Spinoza). Renaissance Europe rediscovered Plato, and was inspired to scientific as to literary effort. Nor was that an accident: Platonic tools remain of vital importance to the rationalist and realist endeavour, as they do to an honest piety. According to the Hermetic Corpus, the philosophy of the Greeks is 'an inane foolosophy of speeches' (16.2: Copenhaver 1992, p. 58; see also Fowden 1986, p. 37). But there was more to be said on its behalf, and theirs.

So what line connects Athens, Alexandria, Jerusalem and Rome? Plato's immediate successors as heads and leaders of 'the Academy' were more recognizably 'academics' than any previous philosophers. They might make contributions to political life, and were expected to set good examples. It was expected that they might have been *converted* to philosophy: Polemo, for example, the fourth head of the Academy till 276 BC, had in his youth secreted cash around the city so that he could always have the wherewithal to buy himself a pleasure, but was transformed by a meeting with the great Xenocrates (the third head, who died in 314 BC). Their ways of life, and death, were scrutinized for signs that their philosophical pretensions were hypocritical. But they were for the most part settled and secure, retiring scholars seeing no need to go the Cynic way or lead their audience to the light eternal. As one head succeeded another, the connection with Plato grew fainter: Arcesilaus directed the Academy in more eristical directions, setting himself and his successors to subvert the dogmatists', especially the Stoics', certainties (he was head from 273 to 242 BC). Such 'Academic Scepticism' could find inspiration in the memory of Socrates, knowing only that he knew nothing, and the contest between Stoic and Academic Sceptic served to keep their minds alive. Carneades (retired 137, died 129 BC), especially, contributed to the discussion of Stoic ethics, but, like Socrates and other sages both before and since, wrote nothing down. When he visited Rome in 156 BC, he gave a public lecture in defence of justice, to general applause. On the next day, he gave a public lecture in defence, instead, of injustice: Cato the Elder (who was to demonstrate his own commitment to 'justice', of a sort, by procuring Carthage's destruction) objected to such philosophers because they upset the young. *Pyrrhonian* Sceptics were, in a way, less challenging.

Attending to what is apparent, we live in accordance with everyday observances, without holding opinions – for we are not able to be utterly inactive. These everyday observances seem to be fourfold, and to consist in guidance by nature, necessitation by feelings, handing down of laws and customs, and teaching of kinds of expertise. By nature's guidance we are naturally capable of perceiving and thinking. By the necessitation of feelings, hunger conducts us to food and thirst to drink. By the handing down of customs and laws, we accept, from an everyday point of view, that piety is good and impiety bad. By teaching of kinds of expertise we are not inactive in those which we accept. (Sextus Empiricus 1994, p. 9: *Outlines of Pyrrhonism* 1.23–4)

The Pyrrhonian seeks to behave in ordinary life as an academic philosopher behaves in seminars! After all, our task as philosophers, seeking to induct our students into the philosophical tradition, is to present opposing cases, not to persuade our students of any particular dogma. Sometimes the seminar argument may be resolved: no-one has anything else to say, at the moment, against some synthesis. But we may still be aware that in some other seminar the argument will continue. Even if we cannot ourselves think of an argument against some current thesis, we may remember occasions in the past when the argument has been settled, only to be subverted by the dawn of a new idea (Sextus 1994, p. 12: 1.34). Is it so difficult to imagine that we retain this attitude even outside the academy? Favorinus, in the Emperor Hadrian's day, reckoned that the Pyrrhonian habit was an advantage in the courts – and maybe also in the court. Those not enamoured of any particular doctrine can adapt themselves more easily to power, and to its loss.

It is one thing to have no settled or strong opinion about most matters of fact or fancy. It is harder to agree that we need no settled opinions in the 'moral' sphere. It is already easy to be persuaded that it's quite alright, for us, today, to do what others (and ourselves on other occasions) think is wicked. But can we really live 'in balance' on such issues? Or is the point that genuine Sceptics will remember *not* to be persuaded by those eminently convincing reasons? Montaigne made a good case for them, especially against the libel that they were bound to do nothing at all:

> [Pyrrho] did not want to make himself a stone or a stump. He wanted to make himself a living, discoursing, thinking man, depending on and making use of all those bodily and spiritual parts in the prescribed and proper way. The fantastic, imaginary and false privileges of governing, ordering, and establishing truth that man has usurped, he has renounced and abandoned in good faith. Indeed, there is no sect that is not constrained to allow its wise man to go along with a number of things neither understood, nor perceived, nor assented to, if he wants to live. (Montaigne 2003, p. 67)

But perhaps Pyrrhonism is still an evasion, a way of making oneself content to abandon knowledge, a way of concealing from oneself the helplessness, the *aporia*, that Socratic questioning was once meant to induce – with a view to opening our hearts to inspiration. Modern philosophers do often deserve Kingsley's magisterial rebuke (which is also Epictetus's).

> There is no secret about the fact that originally the word 'philosophy' meant love of wisdom. Now it has just come to mean the love of endlessly talking and arguing about the love

of wisdom - which is a complete waste of time. Philosophy is a travesty of what it once was, no longer a path to wisdom but a defence against it. There is only one way to wisdom: by facing the fact that we know nothing and letting our reasoning be torn apart. Then reality is what is left behind. (Kingsley 2003, p. 156)

Antiochus of Ascalon (fl. 87 BC) returned the Academy to Platonism, though in a shape that cannot be identified in Plato's published works. There were truths that we could count upon, despite the Sceptical challenge. Socrates had turned his back (for a while) on truths that nature veiled in mystery, but Plato had established a single enterprise conducted in two cooperating schools, the Academic and Peripatetic, under Xenocrates and Aristotle. That in turn was in agreement with the most important doctrines of the Stoa. It seems that Antiochus conceded more to the Stoics in denying the intelligibility of 'immaterial substance' than any genuine Platonist could stomach (and Augustine reckoned this was a poison that Cicero dispelled: *Contra Academicos* 3.18.41), but his chief endeavour was to identify the criterion of truth and the proper end of action. We discover truth by following the lure of beauty: the forms and norms that are in the mind of God.

The central theses of the 'perennial philosophy' (the belief that there is a truth that we can partly grasp if we reform our souls), as it developed in the hands of Poseidonius, Antiochus, Philo of Alexandria, Plotinus, Proclus and others, are these. Although we do not always see things straight, we can, in good health and our wits about us, take hold of some immediate realities. By constantly recalling ourselves (being recalled) to the Mind and Word of God, we are saved from all the mistakes and vices symbolized as beasts (by Epictetus, Clement and Spinoza among many). That Word is not an 'arbitrary' creation, as though the One could have had some other image: it is, metaphorically, 'begotten' rather than 'made', and 'of one substance with the Father'. In short, recognizable notions of the Divine Trinity (the One, the Word, the Spirit) and of the Divine Humanity pervaded the early centuries of our era. Disputes about the details of those doctrines became, within the Christian churches, occasions for denouncing heresy – a term itself derived from the Greek for 'philosophical school' (*hairesis*) – but they were familiar questions, at least as familiar as disputes about the details of evolutionary theory in our day.

CHAPTER NINE

Late antiquity

Fixed stars and planets, and an escape from Fate

Divination and technology both give some hope that we can improve our lives, and give employment to the learned. But there is another side to a belief in Fate. Armstrong's account of the late Roman atmosphere is exaggerated:

> It was a period in which the sense of individual isolation in a vast and terrifying universe was perhaps more intensely felt than even immediately after the breakdown of the city-state into the Hellenistic world. For in the Roman Empire, under Babylonian influence, the view of the ruling power of the universe as a cruel, inaccessible Fate, embodied in the stars, worship of which was useless, had come to its full development. The individual exposed to the crushing power of this Fate, and the citizen also of an earthly state which seemed almost as vast, cruel and indifferent as the universe, felt to the full the agony of his isolation and limitation. (Armstrong 1936, p. 28)

The 'city-state' had not in fact broken down, though such townships were submerged in wider empires. Almost everyone continued to live as they always have, in cheerful or at least contented ignorance. If there was no escape, at least our jailers were not as a rule so powerful and so malevolent as to exclude all chance of sometime happiness. 'A shadow's dream is man, but when a god sheds a brightness, shining light is on earth and life is as sweet as honey'.

But some did indeed believe that, for better or maybe worse, we lived beneath the eye of visible gods in the heavens.

> Since [the Chaldaeans] have observed the stars over a long period of time and have noted both the movements and the influences of each of them with greater precision than any other men, they foretell to mankind many things that will take place in the future. But above all in importance, they say, is the study of the influence of the five stars known as planets. (Diodorus 2.30.2–3)

This 'Chaldaean' or 'Sabian' religious doctrine – as Maimonides was to call it (Maimonides 1995, pp. 175–80: 3.29) – may have been a back-formation from monotheistic denunciation of idolatry rather than any real religious practice. The stars, planetary or fixed, weren't worshipped in many Mediterranean cities, even by astrologers. The Olympian gods may give their names to the wandering stars, the 'planets' (including Sun and Moon, but not – of course – the Earth), and persons mentioned in Greek or other fables may be pictured in the constellations (irrespective of any merit), but this does not *prove* their importance. Even in Egypt, only the Sun is identified as a god. But maybe there was more to the doctrine.

> Because of those Sabian ideas they put up statues for the stars: golden statues for the sun and silver statues for the moon. . . . . They built temples and placed images in them. They claimed that the powers of the planets were emanated onto these images, and those images spoke, understood what was spoken to them, reasoned, [and] gave revelations to people. (Maimonides 1995, p. 177)

Those images may really have been, as I suggested earlier, those of the worshippers' imaginations, not magical automata. But perhaps they were not images to be admired, but demons to be controlled – our would-be puppeteers. Numenius (whom Plotinus was said by some to have copied) and Amelius (one of Plotinus's friends and followers) both suggested that the soul was corrupted in its descent through the planetary spheres (Scott 1991, pp. 5ff; see also Couliano 1991, pp. 188–211). The planets, so called because they did not keep the steady onward march of the 'fixed stars', could easily be thought perverse, and so responsible for any unwelcome features of our terrestrial souls. Conversely, according to the Hermetic text, *Poimandres*, in its ascent 'the soul gives back the power of increase and decrease in the first sphere (i.e. the Moon), evil plotting in the second (Mercury), lust in the third (Venus), the proud desire to rule in the fourth (the Sun), impiety and audacity in the fifth (Mars), greed for wealth in the sixth (Jupiter) and malevolent falsehood in the seventh (Saturn), and escapes the rule of Fate' (Copenhaver 1992, p. 6: 1.25). These are the faults we acquired in our descent. According to Macrobius (fl.400 AD), more optimistically, we pick up 'reason and understanding' in the sphere of Saturn, 'in Jupiter's sphere, the power to act, called *praktikon;* in Mars' sphere, a bold spirit or *thymikon*; in the sun's sphere, sense-perception and imagination, *aisthetikon* and *phantastikon*; in Venus' sphere, the impulse of passion, *epithymetikon*; in Mercury's sphere, the ability to speak and interpret, *hermeneutikon;* and in the lunar sphere, the function of moulding and increasing bodies, *phytikon*' (Macrobius 1952, p. 136: I.13). These powers may not be needed while we are among the stars, but they aren't actively maleficent.

Plotinus gave a less detailed story than either – and one that he immediately qualifies:

> In the *Timaeus* the God who makes the world gives 'the first principle of soul,' but the gods who are borne through the heavens 'the terrible and inevitable passions', 'angers', and desires and 'pleasures and pains,' and the 'other kind of soul', from which comes passions of this kind. These statements bind us to the stars, from which we get our souls, and subject us to necessity when we come down here; from them we get our moral characters, our characteristic actions, and our emotions, coming from a disposition which is liable to emotion. So what is left which is 'we'? Surely, just that which we really are, we to whom nature gave power to master our passions. (Plotinus, *Ennead,* II.3 [52].9, 7ff, after Plato, *Timaeus,* 69c5ff)

Each of us is double, he goes on to say, and our liberty lies in rising to a higher world. That progress upwards can be conceived as a successive stripping away of the garments donned in the earlier descent from heaven. Plotinus insists that 'the sun and other

heavenly bodies. . . communicate no evil to the other pure soul',
unless such evil comes from the mixed, double souls of those stars –
or rather, of those planets.

> If it is a loving disposition it becomes weak in the recipient and
> produces a rather unpleasant kind of loving; and manly spirit . . .
> produces violent temper or spiritlessness; and that which belongs
> to honour in love and is concerned with beauty produces desire
> of what only seems to be beautiful, and the efflux of intellect
> produces knavery (*panourgia*); for knavery wants to be intellect,
> only it is unable to attain what it aims at. So all these things
> become evil in us, though they are not so up in heaven.

Plotinus's objection to the astrology of his day was not founded
on empirical observations but on his refusal to agree that even the
planetary stars could intend any evil, or that we were ourselves
bound by astral necessity to do or to be evil. But his account remains,
by modern standards, weird. The heavens, or the fixed stars, move
in a circle 'because it imitates intellect' (*Ennead* II.2 [14].1), and
the soul that animates them conveys a literally or spatially circular
motion to them because she is herself 'in orbit' around God (*Ennead*
II.2 [14].2, 13ff; 3, 20ff), as also are our 'real selves'. We are to
look toward the example of the heavens to get some sense of what
our real lives should be. Plato suggested – or at least his imagined
Timaeus suggested – that we 'must correct the orbits in the head
which were corrupted at our birth' (*Timaeus* 90d), and so bring
our selves into line with the astrological pattern. Plotinus supposed
rather that our real selves were already thus 'in orbit', and that only
our lower selves needed the reminder – but what exactly all this
means remains obscure. What does 'circular motion' mean, in this
spiritual sense? Why should we regret that our bodies do not 'go
round', or that 'our spherical parts', our heads, don't 'run easily,
being earthy'? How are we to 'imitate the soul of the universe and
of the stars'? (*Ennead* II.9 [33].18, 32).

The motion that Plotinus has in mind isn't spatial: 'one must
use "centre" analogically' (*Ennead* II.2 [14].2, 10) 'Circular motion'
is – in principle – unending, and never nearer or further from its
goal. It is therefore more 'perfect' than 'linear motion', since its end
and its beginning are the same: it has nowhere else to get to, but
is not static. 'Linear motion' is a process, culminating in arrival

or completion (after which, it ceases). 'Circular motion' is always already there, and because it needs nothing else to complete it, can be forever. According to ps-Dionysius it is in self-awareness that a 'circular motion' is found (*On the Divine Names* 4.9: 1987, p. 78), supporting itself, potentially, forever. A similar distinction had been drawn by Aristotle, between 'motions' (*kineseis*) and 'activities' (*energeiai*) – a distinction which is not exactly mapped by the grammatical or semantic distinctions he offered, but which had important ethical implications (see Ackrill 1965). Nothing qualifies as the essential element of *eudaimonia*, the good life, if it must, of its nature, end, and cannot, of its nature, be complete until that end. *Eudaimonia* is an activity, not a motion, and its highest form is God's life, *noesis noeseos* (*Metaphysics* XII, 1072b18ff).

> One must think that there is a universe in our soul, not only an intelligible one but an arrangement like in form to that of the soul of the world: so, as that, too, is distributed according to its diverse powers into the sphere of the fixed stars and those of the moving stars, the powers in our soul also are of like form to these powers, and there is an activity proceeding from each power, and when the souls are set free they come there to the star which is in harmony with the character and power which lived and worked in them. (*Ennead* III.4 [15].6, 22–8)

One possible descant on these notions is that the planets or the planetary spheres represent lesser values, each with their own devotees. 'They are there precisely for the sake of the whole living thing, as, for instance, the gall is to serve the whole and in relation to the part next to it; for it has to stir up the manly spirit and keep the whole and the part next to it from excess' (*Ennead* II.3 [52].12, 27ff). Plotinus does not clearly or explicitly give voice to this suggestion, but it may represent something familiar to his first audience. One moral might then be that it is through contemplating the fixed stars and their eternal recurrence that we begin to pass beyond the transient values of our present life. Simone Weil may have caught the intended moral in suggesting that 'by contemplating the equivalence of the future and the past [in the revolutions of the fixed stars] we pierce through time right to eternity' (Weil 1957, p. 96).

Plotinus might insist that neither the fixed nor the planetary stars intended us any evil, and that we could instead invoke them, or the idea of them, in our progression from too great an attachment to this world here. But others felt a greater malevolence or at least a greater harm in them, and hoped to appease or escape them. There was some hope of freedom, either by serving our term, or by attempting a prison break. Philosophizing in the proper Platonic style might help, but a more popular salvation came directly through the mysteries that Platonists used as metaphors. Apuleius of Madaura (125–180 AD) borrowed the plot of a popular pornographic novel (perhaps by Lucian of Samosata) in his *Metamorphoses* (or *The Golden Ass*). His hero, Lucius, entranced by a lust for magical power and knowledge, as well as sex, is transformed into an ass, and endures many deeply humiliating adventures until at last he appeals, despairingly, to the goddess Isis, who reveals herself as the very same goddess as many nations worship, under many names.

> I, mother of the universe, mistress of all the elements, first born of the ages, highest of the gods, queen of the shades, first of those who dwell in heaven, representing in one shape all gods and goddesses. My will controls the shining heights of heaven, the health-giving sea-winds, and the mournful silences of hell; the entire world worships my single godhead in a thousand shapes, with diverse rites, and under many names. The Phrygians, first born of mankind, call me the Pessinuntian Mother of the gods; the native Athenians the Cecropian Minerva; the island-dwelling Cypriots Paphian Venus; the archer Cretans Dictynnan Diana; the triple-tongued Sicilians Stygian Proserpine; the ancient Eleusinians Actaean Ceres; some call me Juno, some Bellona, others Hecate, others Rhamnusia; but both races of Ethiopians, those on whom the rising and those on whom the setting sun shines, and the Egyptians who excell in ancient learning, honour me with the worship which is truly mine and call me by my true name: Queen Isis. (Apuleius 1998, pp. 197–8 [11.5])

This extraordinary guddle of names may indicate some confusion. Lucius, however, recovers his human shape and is progressively initiated, at considerable expense, into the different grades of the Isis and Osiris cults. It is not altogether clear that he is no longer an ass: Isis may be real, and really kind, but perhaps her priests and officials still recognize a sucker. Nonetheless, and sympathetically, we can read the story as being about redemption:

> Secure under the patronage of Isis, and no longer subject to fate, [the initiate] became the real master of his life and could make a new start. [He] might hope for prosperity, the postponement of death, and, perhaps, at the discretion of the goddess, immortality. (Liebeschuetz 1979, p. 182, after Apuleius, *Metamorphoses*, 11.6, 15, 21; see also Teixidor 1977, pp. 36–40)

Classical and Magian culture

Oswald Spengler's insight was that there was another culture alive in the Mediterranean milieu, mingled with 'the Classical', though it never achieved a complete and undistorted political expression. The focus of Classical life and thought was the ideal human body in the here-and-now, and our duties were mostly civil duties. By contrast, the 'Magian', a title chosen without any reference to any historical Magi, had as its focus a transcendent One, for which all things were possible, including transmutation. For the Classical mind, the tangible was the real; for the Magian the imaginable. For the Classical mind, our hopes and fears are only for this life; for the Magian, we have eternal life to consider – a life we will share with non-humans. For the Classical mind, irrational affection is 'groundless superstition and womanish compassion'.[1] For the Magian, God is love (*I John* 4.16; see also Plotinus *Ennead* VI.8 [39].15[2]). For the Classical mind, humanity, expressed in the free adult individual (and his natural associates), was what mattered most; for the Magian, the community of faith (Spengler 1926, vol. 2, p. 235).

> Whereas the Faustian man [that is, the Western] is an 'I' that in the last resort draws its own conclusions about the Infinite; whereas the Apollonian man [the Classical], as one *soma* among many, represents only himself; the Magian man, with his spiritual kind of being, is only a *part of an pneumatic* 'We' that, descending from above, is one and the same in all believers.

This characterization of differing styles of humanity obscures the fact that 'Classical, Apollonian man' also conceived himself a member of a whole – but in his case, of the city rather than the sect, and by biological descent. Both might agree that we are the gods' toys, but this for the Classical mind is simply something to endure; for the Magian, a boast. For the Classical mind Law governed all, for the Magian someone's Will, a will not confined by 'Nature'. 'Classical' and 'Magian' are no more than two roughly delineated aspects of the real Mediterranean, reified into opposition. Both strands, and many others, went to make up reality, and neither is the essence of a distinct, organic culture with a normal course of life from which we might learn to predict the dying years of our own 'Western' culture (as Spengler suggested). Nor can we distribute individual writers and actors unambiguously to the different cultures. Even though, for example, most Stoics were mostly 'Classical', some were sometimes 'Magian'. The Hebrews (and other, related peoples) supposed that we were bodily beings, but also believed that individual human beings were of a piece with their lineage (so that 'Esau' may stand for the whole tribe of Edom, and 'Adam' for humankind), and that there was a non-corporeal creator. And Epicureans were something else entirely.

Even those philosophers who typify the 'Classical' had something of the 'Magian' in them: 'Mind is the god in us – whether it was Hermotimus or Anaxagoras who said so – and mortal life contains a portion of some god' (Aristotle *Protrepticus*: Ross 1952, p. 42 [fr.10c]; Betegh 2004, p. 284). Just occasionally, here-now, we may glimpse that possibility, when the world we see grows shadowy. 'Often I have woken up out of the body to my self', Plotinus says, 'and have entered into myself, going out from all other things; I have seen a beauty wonderfully great and felt assurance that then most of all I belonged to the better part' (*Ennead* IV.8 [6].1). These moments of truth are not to be dismissed for being rare or idiosyncratic: that is, if they are veridical, exactly what we should expect. Common opinion has some authority, but Plotinus himself suggested that 'all men are naturally and spontaneously moved to speak of the god who is in each one of us one and the same' (*Ennead* VI.5 [23].1).

On the one hand, the corporeal individual, a member of some earthly city; on the other, a spiritual being, whose fatherland is the sky. 'Humankind is the only living thing that is twofold', according to Asclepius (Copenhaver 1992, p. 70), and our remit is to care for earthly beings in the light of eternity. We are to consider ourselves spiritual amphibia, native both to the world of competing animals and atoms, and to the world of comprehensive beauty. 'Reason' is not only the social intelligence we need to live together in kindness (for a while), but also a direct insight, call it a revelation, into the real world of which this is a partial copy. Here, so far as our senses go, we live among figments, in a fever-dream. There, in the original real world we are, as it were, theorems of a universal science, aspects of a single beauty, bound by universal sympathies. That beauty is visible, for those who care to look, even in the smallest and the vilest of creatures (Aristotle, *De Partibus Animalium*, 1.645a15f). Every visible creature is, in a way, an image of the divine.

Biological and mythological hybrids, in turn, reveal a truth, not a danger: that Soul stretches without a break from the seemingly inanimate all the way up to the star-gods and beyond. Those of us born human may have a special opportunity, a special responsibility: we have the chance to glance aside from immediate, parochial and sensual concerns, and can care for every animate creature. Christian and pagan philosophers alike very often insisted that only human beings could be 'friends of God', and only the human could be a proper image of divinity. Pagan, Hebrew and Christian alike were offended by the Egyptians. But there was another option. Precisely because we are equipped to love and serve the Father, we must care for all His children: 'for anyone who feels affection for anything at all shows kindness to all that is akin to the object of his affection, and to the children of the father that he loves. But every soul is a child of That Father' (*Ennead* II.9 [33].15, 33–16.10).

Is such a life worth living?

Socrates, remember, suggested to his son that he owed his parents gratitude for bringing him into existence, 'to view so many beautiful objects, and to share in so many blessings, as the gods grant to men' (*Memorabilia* 2.2.2–3). Others have doubted this. The story was often told that King Midas, encountering the god Silenus, and asking what was the best of lives for us, was mocked:

> Best of all for mortal beings is never to have been born at all
> Nor ever to have set eyes on the bright light of the sun

But, since he is born, a man should make utmost haste through
   the gates of Death
And then repose, the earth piled into a mound round himself.
                    (Theognis 425–8: Gerber 1999, p. 234)

The tag was repeated, by Sophocles (*Oedipus at Colonus* 1225)
and Euripides in several plays, though the latter also allows, in
The Suppliants, that the good things of life outweigh the bad, or
else we'd all be dead (see Haigh 1896, pp. 261–73). Herodotus
records that Solon likewise told King Croesus that the best the
gods could offer in answer to a mother's prayer was the prompt
death of her sons (1.29–33) – though he also acknowledged that
the unassuming life of a peasant farmer (in good times) was good
(or at least was better than the life that Croesus lived). Similarly, in
Plato's Myth of Er, where he imagines how discarnate souls select
the earthly life they will be living next, Odysseus shows his wisdom
by searching out an 'ordinary' life, unnoticed by all others during
the Choice, and destined to be unnoticed during life (*Republic*
10.620cd). The very worst life is one in which we do everything
that we momentarily wish, seduced by sense. But even the best
seems pointless.

So is *any* life worth living? The author of *Ecclesiastes* –
traditionally Solomon, king in Jerusalem in the ninth century BC,
but more probably some later author – also had doubts.

Whatever my eyes coveted, I refused them nothing, nor did I
deny myself any pleasure. Yes indeed, I got pleasure from all my
labour, and for all my labour this was my reward. Then I turned
and reviewed all my handiwork, all my labour and toil, and I saw
that everything was emptiness and chasing the wind, of no profit
under the sun. (*Ecclesiastes* 2.10–11)

And 'the day of death is better than the day of birth' (*Ecclesiastes*
7.1).

The Speaker, Ecclesiastes, found what little answer he had in
enjoying simple pleasures, getting on with his work, and obeying
his God's commands: 'remember your Creator in the days of your
youth, before the time of trouble comes and the years draw near
when you will say "I see no purpose in them"' (*Ecclesiastes* 12.1).
This too is 'emptiness'. Some Hellenistic philosophers managed the

same solution, recalling the aphorisms attributed to the Seven Sages. Others merely endured. The God of This World, so some thought, is Fortune, and she makes no sense. So Palladas of Alexandria, a Greek epigrammatist of the early fifth century, proposes – when not abusing the rich, the poor, scholars, politicians, women – that we treat it as a joke, consoled by knowing that once dead we're safe from Fortune: 'all life's a stage, a plaything; either learn to play, unseriously, or else put up with troubles' (Palladas, *Greek Anthology* 10.72), and 'once you're dead there's nothing else can happen' (Palladas, *Greek Anthology* 10.59).

These epigrams (for livelier versions see Harrison 1992) have some affinity with Latin epitaphs, where the dead have also escaped from Hope and Fortune (see Bowra 1960). It's likely that the late nineteenth century pessimist A.G.Swinburne had something like this in mind as well.

> From too much love of living, from hope and fear set free,
> We thank with brief thanksgiving whatever gods there be
> That no life lives for ever, that dead men rise up never,
> That even the weariest river winds somewhere safe to sea
> ('The Garden of Proserpine': Swinburne 1924, vol. 1, p. 172)

But there were other ways to endure or to escape. Apuleius had found a harbour, safe from the deceits of Fortune, or at least he imagined how his hero, Lucius, might. The Delphic Oracle and Porphyry conclude their account of Plotinus's life with the expectation that he had joined 'the dance of immortal love' (Porphyry, *Life of Plotinus*, 23.36f, after 22.54ff): 'There the most blessed spirits have their birth and live a life filled full of festivity and joy; and this life lasts for ever, made blessed by the gods'. So pagan and Christian writers agree that the grace of the gods could help us into heaven, and that there were better hopes than simply to endure, or to wish we had never been. Some pagan Platonists might think that we made a mistake in accepting a life down here, and Christians might insist that the error came rather later: there was nothing in principle wrong with material life, but only with disobedience. At least in principle, Christian writers might reasonably expect that the prophecies of such as Isaiah would one day be fulfilled.

So Lactantius, quoting approvingly from Virgil's *Eclogue* 4 and from what he says is Virgil's source, the Sibylline Oracles, prophesies a future golden age after the day of judgement rather than in the past (*Divine Institutes* 7.24.8–9; see Campbell 2008):

> Wild beasts will not feed on blood in this period, nor birds on prey; everything will instead be peaceful and quiet. Lions and calves will stand together at the stall, wolf will not seize lamb, dog will not hunt, hawk and eagle will do no harm, and children will play with snakes. This will be the time for all those things to happen that the poets claimed for the golden age when Saturn was king. The mistake about them arises from the fact that prophets foretelling the future keep putting plenty of things forward like that, delivering it as if it had taken place. Visions were put before their eyes by the divine spirit, and they saw things in their sight as if in process and completion.

That was the moral of *Job*, and of other Biblical writings. It may also be an implication even of pagan myths:

> In the midst of praise of the established power, there remains the message that this has not always been so and hence does not need to remain so forever; 'fettered gods' may be approached and used for certain goals; and it is imaginable that they could rise again. (Burkert 1999, p. 104; see López-Ruiz 2010, p. 185)

The way we didn't take

What *might* have happened if one of the last – and probably the greatest – of firmly Hellenic sages had had the last word? This was Plotinus, whose friend and disciple Porphyry coaxed into writing (without notes and without revision) his considered views on almost everything. Plotinus was born in Lycopolis in Upper Egypt. Whether he was a Greek, a Roman or a native Egyptian, we don't know, as he wouldn't speak of his childhood. He was taught in Alexandria by Ammonius Saccas, who also taught an Origen, perhaps identical with one of the more philosophical of Church Fathers (eventually judged to have been close to heresy). After an abortive attempt to visit India by accompanying (or serving in) the Emperor Gordian's army, Plotinus went instead to Rome. There he ran seminars in a friend's house on the texts and thought of Plato, showing always 'his benevolence to any questioner, and his intellectual vigour' (Porphyry, *Life of Plotinus*, 13.10–11). He showed, so Porphyry tells us, great insight and great sympathy. When Porphyry thought of suicide, Plotinus turned up unannounced to say that this sprang from melancholy, not from reason. The Delphic Oracle, consulted about Plotinus, is said to have said that the gods often set him on the right track again, that he was granted a vision transcending 'the bitter waves of this blood-drenched life'. In brief, he seemed to his friends to have lived out the project defined by Epictetus: 'the affair is momentous, it is full of mystery, not a chance gift, nor given to all comers'. Plotinus managed it, but once he'd 'gone aloft', how could his followers cope?

How different would the future have been if a pagan Plotinism had won? Would we – as fantasists imagine – have had a scientific enlightenment, a technological revolution, if only the wicked Christians hadn't held back inquiry? Almost certainly, not. The likelier alternative was not even Neo-Pythagorean, but a return to ancient custom, to the gods of an older world. Epicureans said all impressions were true, as being what they were; Stoics said that all of us who weren't wise were mad, and therefore had no escape – except in fantasy – from our convictions; Sceptics of whatever school agreed to follow appearances. The conclusion, so far from being, as Whiggish writers think, a triumph for materialistic, common sense, released all manner of seemings in the intellectual world. Memories of triumph and heartbreak, ancient stories, seemingly (and therefore inescapably) meaningful occurrences are all 'obvious'. In the absence of provable truth, people had better stick to their ancestral creeds, and certainly not proselytize. That was, to the Emperor Julian's eye (331–63 AD), the Christians' greatest crime, that they abandoned 'the gods of their fathers'. Eusebius acknowledged the argument (though he also sought to rebut it):

> How can men fail to be in every way impious and atheistical, who have apostatized from those ancestral gods by whom every nation and every state is sustained? Or what good can they reasonably hope for, who have set themselves at enmity and at war against their preservers, and have thrust away their benefactors? For what else are they doing than fighting against the gods? (Eusebius, *Praeparatio*, 1.2: 1903, pp. 2–3)

Similarly, in the absence of any deep conviction that there was a 'real self', our multiple obsessions and emotions became as real as any. Fractured memories, discordant motives and concealed causes are not anomalies: they are the human condition, and only the saint, hero or philosopher has tamed and transformed the squalling horde of impulses so far as to 'know herself' as single. The rest of us do not know why we do things, are not 'the same' from one foolish moment to the next and constantly misidentify even our most 'present' and 'immediate' feelings. It is an important step in self-knowledge to be made to realize just how fluid and uncontrolled our ordinary thinking is.

> Whence came the soul, whither will it go, how long will it be our mate and comrade? Can we tell its essential nature? . . . Even now in this life, we are the ruled rather than the rulers, known rather than knowing. . . . Is my mind my own possession? That parent of false conjectures, that purveyor of delusion, the delirious, the fatuous, and in frenzy or senility proved to be the very negation of mind. (Philo, *On Cherubim*, 114f: 1929, vol. II, p. 77)[3]

In brief, the state of intellectual affairs in Julian's day was much like ours. Some serious thinkers, including the ones that Julian esteemed, devoted themselves to the control of 'demons' (which is, the memories, 'projections' and fragmentary selves I have described) by ritual and imagination. Reason, they said, was not enough: there must also be 'god-working' (theurgy) in open view – precisely because we could not reason our way to truth, nor keep our balance in the sea of blood merely by moral effort. They sought to recreate, in a wider world, the Olympian tour-de-force, to tame the demons, the mad impulses, the hideous memories, within a dramatic representation of what they took to be real relationships, as told them by the prophets. The rites that brought God's Word into the living imagination of believing Christians were not so unlike those that pagan enthusiasts employed for the sake of peace, except that the Christians – and some pagans – abjured blood-sacrifice.

Plotinus did not approve: we should not trouble ourselves with demons, but only with the '*daimon*' that was our better self, the voice of the divine intellect whom Christians identified with Christ. It would be one thing to agree that there *were* demons, and that they must be bound by Zeus's chain or swallowed up in Kronos (depending on what myth was allegorized); it is quite another to imagine that they are at one's beck and call, that the powers that rule the world are ours to command at will. Just so, it was one thing to agree, as Plotinus did, that the world of sense-experience was not ideal, and another to despise it. Plotinus probably thought of 'Christians' as included among the 'Gnostics' that he scorned: people who claimed so peculiar a grasp of the divine as to be relieved of any normal duties, including those of intellectual coherence (see *Ennead* II.9 [33]). Although popular religion has always found it easier to speak as if there were *two* worlds (this inferior version, and the heavenly other), no Platonist could quite agree to that. It is not that there are two real worlds, any more than there are two real things (the soul and the body). The body, so a later Platonist declared, is that part of the soul that is visible to the five senses (Blake 'Marriage of Heaven and Hell' $4: 1966, p. 149). The 'flight of the alone to the Alone', the purified to the pure, of which Plotinus spoke (*Ennead* VI.9 [9].11, 51; see also Porphyry, *Life of Plotinus*, 2.26) was, as he said, 'no journey for the feet'! (*Ennead* I.6 [1].8, 23) We shall not see things straight, so Platonists supposed, until we see their glory. Porphyry, who wrote more fiercely and more directly against Christians, would also have found himself agreeing with them, rather than with an emperor who took blood sacrifice to be a literal duty.

Julian tried to recreate a civil society that would do what the Christian churches did: to provide both meaning and a living to the struggling peoples of his day. Christians were not the only ones to care for the defenceless. Plotinus himself was trusted as the guardian of many orphaned children: like Crates the Cynic he kept their possessions safe in case they were not philosophers. But the Christian churches offered the only organized and ecumenical charity. Julian hoped to emulate this virtue, but could not shake free from the other features of pagan tradition. In seeking to reverse the Constantinian adoption of Christianity as the imperial religion, he combined a high philosophical Platonism with multiple sacrifices to appease the abandoned gods, even though he recognized that 'the eating of meat involves the sacrifice and slaughter of animals who naturally suffer pain and torment' (*Hymn to the Mother of Gods* 174a-b: cited by Gilhus 2006, p. 147). His attempt to reinstate, for example, oracles and blood sacrifice at Daphne (near Antioch in Syria, by the Castalian spring) in 362 AD, was attacked by Christians in terms that any Enlightenment thinker might deploy – except that the Christians gave most credit for the oracle's failure to the bones of the martyred Babylas.

Suppose that instead of following the 'theurgic school' that sprang from Iamblichus's teachings, and seeking to resurrect Olympian religion, Julian had been content with Porphyry or Plotinus. Could there have been a 'pagan' Platonic or Hermetic empire? In such a world, the Divine would have been known as Three Hypostases: the One, the Intellect, the Soul, in descending order, allegorized as Ouranos, Kronos, Zeus. The many gods of Mediterranean tradition could all have been aspects of the divine, and each sometimes addressed as the Creator: an Egyptian or Hermetic compromise. The human being embodying Intellect would not have been a mythical Ptahhotep, Pythagoras, Hermes or Heracles, but either a Platonic Socrates, or Plotinus himself. Our saints would have been sages. Matter would have been sacramental, and the sun would have been at once 'a red-hot mass of metal' and the visible image of the divine. There would have been no more blood sacrifices, not only because such sacrifices fed inferior spirits but because the creatures would have been our friends. A Plotinian empire might have been kinder – Julian's was not.

Might it also have been more tolerant, either than the pre-Christian empire or the Christian? Maximus of Tyre, at any rate, suggested in the second century AD that it hardly mattered where we got our inspiration, as long as we were inspired to love:

> Let them know the divine race, only let them know. If Pheidias' art rouses the Greeks towards memory of God, and the honour of animals rouses Egyptians, and a river some, and fire others, I do not denigrate their disharmony. Only let them know, only them love, only let them remember. (Maximus of Tyre, *Dissertationes*, 2.10, cited by Johnson 2006, p. 214)

Possibly so, but there must at least be some debate about *what* to love, and how. Plotinus would himself have denounced all those philosophers and teachers who claimed a right of private judgement, in the name of their own superiority. Symmachus may have been right to say that there could not be one single route to discover 'so great a mystery'. But it does not follow that we can never recognize some roads as ending badly. Nor does it follow that we should never put up road signs and even barriers against those who would head off to their own destruction. The practical question remains, as it did for Plato, who decides? And who can we plausibly trust to decide on our behalf? A more strictly Plotinian Empire would have made a division between (a more civilised) Custom, for the masses, and an ascetic Wisdom for the few (which is how things happened in the Buddhist world). Julian's Empire would have lost all sense that ancient Custom could be criticised at all. He suggested, in fact, that Christians should not teach the classic texts, because they did not think them true. For all its faults the notionally Christian Empire that succeeded Julian insisted that there were 'ordinary' saints as well as sages, and that the classic texts could be interpreted and enjoyed even by those who thought them largely false. It was the Christian Church that popularized the more manageable (and cheaper) books instead of scrolls, and also had more respect for the work of human hands.

CHAPTER TEN

An end and a beginning

It would be neater if the Ancient Mediterranean ended as it began, with catastrophic changes. Climatic change set tribes wandering across the borders roughly maintained by Rome and Persia. There were volcanic eruptions or the like to explain some of the changes, though even 'the event' of 536 AD (meteor, comet or volcanic eruption) was not as devastating as some have imagined.[1] Times changed, as Times do. But there wasn't really any end, or even any abrupt division. The Roman Empire did not fall when Rome was captured by Alaric the Hun in 410 AD, nor did Mediterranean civilization collapse, even in the West. Greek texts were translated into Latin for western European readers by scholars such as Boethius (480–524 AD) and John Scotus Eriugena (815–77 AD). Visigoths, Vandals and Ostrogoths were usually *Christian* barbarians, with a Mediterranean culture. In the eastern Empire, Justinian did not close the schools of pagan philosophy in 529 AD, and neither did Christians seek to destroy all ancient learning. John Philoponus of Alexandria (490–570 AD) studied and criticized both pagan and Christian thought, rebutting Aristotle on falling weights and on the world's eternity (see Sorabji 2010). Byzantine scholars, theologians and philosophers continued to probe the movements of the human heart, the nature of substance, and the rights and duties of imperial subjects: for example, should the Emperor be obeyed when he sought to silence argument? Maximus the Confessor (580–662 AD) refused, at risk of his life and health, to be silent. '*Parrhesia*, "outspokenness", was the hallmark and privilege of the awkward holy man in all periods of Byzantium'! (Cameron 2010, p. 111) On the southern shores, Muslim artists and thinkers remembered and reworked the older texts: the *Theology of Aristotle*, for example, is a translation and expansion of some *Enneads* of Plotinus (see Adamson 2002).

Even in the North-West, far from the Inner Sea, the little tribal kings were often literate and even liberal. Witness Bede of Northumbria (672–735 AD) on King Ethelbert, who had learnt from his Papal instructors that no one should or even could be forcibly converted (Bede 1990, 1.26): conversion was a movement of the heart, and no-one who aped it out of fear of worldly or bodily consequences could have understood the gospel – which was that there was nothing worldly left to fear. Even when the North-West was wracked by rival kingdoms and marauding Norsemen, Boethius's *Consolation* was being read: Alfred of Wessex (848–899 AD), indeed, translated it into Anglo-Saxon, making the Lady Philosophy male.

The chief abstract argument remembered from that text in modern times is a demonstration that God's omniscience, His knowledge of human history, is compatible with our freedom. God does not know what we will do and suffer because He sees what causes us, ineluctably, to act: He knows what we do and suffer, by our own decisions, because He sees all history from Outside. The less abstract conclusion is that Fortune rules this world, and that her gifts of riches, power or glory (or poverty, weakness and public shame) should have no force to beguile us. All fortune is, in a way, good fortune: 'since every fortune, welcome and unwelcome alike, has for its object the reward or trial of the good, and the punishing or amending of the bad, every fortune must be good, since it is either just or useful' (Boethius 1969, p. 143: 4.7). The happiness we seek is God: not that God is happy, but that He is happiness (Boethius 1969, p. 101: 3.10), as earlier philosophers had said that He was *theoria*, or success, or love, or luck.

The *Consolation* also emphasized the smallness of this world, following in this the *Dream of Scipio*, a section of Cicero's *De Re Publica* and one of the most influential texts of medieval Europe. The eponymous hero of that work, on his ascent through the planetary spheres, saw 'stars which we never see from here below, and all the stars were vast far beyond what we have ever imagined. The least of them was that which, farthest from heaven, nearest to the earth, shone with a borrowed light. But the starry globes very far surpassed the earth in magnitude. The earth itself indeed looked to me so small as to make me ashamed of our empire, which was a mere point on its surface' (*Republic* Bk 6, ch. 3). So also Boethius:

> It is well known, and you have seen it demonstrated by astronomers, that beside the extent of the heavens, the circumference of the earth has the size of a point; that is to say, compared with the magnitude of the celestial sphere, it may be thought as having no extent at all. (Boethius 1969, p. 73: II.7)

The story of our world is of even less significance when compared with 'unending eternity' (Boethius 1969, p. 74). As Plotinus also asked, 'if you are wronged, what is there dreadful in that to an immortal?'. (*Ennead* II.9 [33].9, 15–16)

These were familiar thoughts. But there was, in a way, a beginning, which is most easily seen by comparing another self-styled beginning, centuries later. Thomas Sprat, in writing his proleptic *History of the Royal Society*, wrote vehemently of the Real Philosophy:

> The poets of old to make all things look more venerable than they were devised a thousand false Chimaeras; on every Field, River, Grove and Cave they bestowed a Fantasm of their own making: With these they amazed the world. . . . And in the modern Ages these Fantastical Forms were reviv'd and possessed Christendom. . . . All which abuses if those acute Philosophers did not promote, yet they were never able to overcome; nay, not even so much as King Oberon and his invisible Army. But from the time in which the Real Philosophy has appear'd there is scarce any whisper remaining of such horrors. . . . The cours of things goes quietly along, in its own true channel of Natural Causes and Effects. For this we are beholden to Experiments; which though they have not yet completed the discovery of the true world, yet they have already vanquished those wild inhabitants of the false world, that us'd to astonish the minds of men. (Thomas Sprat 1722, p. 340: cited by Wiley 1934, p. 213)

He was imitating Athanasius of Alexandria (c296–373 AD):

> In former times every place was full of the fraud of oracles, and the utterances of those at Delphi and Dodona and in Boeotia

and Lycia and Libya and Egypt and those of the Kabiri and the Pythoness were considered marvellous by the minds of men. But now since Christ has been proclaimed everywhere, their madness too has ceased, and there is no one left among them to give oracles at all. Then, too, demons used to deceive men's minds by taking up their abode in springs or rivers or trees or stones and imposing upon simple people by their frauds. But now, since the Divine appearing of the Word, all this fantasy has ceased, for by the sign of the cross, if a man will but use it, he drives out their deceits. (*On the Incarnation* (written c318 AD), ch. 8, para.47)

The Christian Gospel – and in this it did not differ greatly from other Abrahamic faiths – determined that the spirits of groves and streams were phantoms, to be dispersed by the 'divine appearing of the Word'. The Faithful were not the first to think of dispersing phantoms with a word – Empedocles, remember, vanquished rage by uttering a verse of Homer. But the phantoms to be banished now included dryads and naiads, spirits of wood and water. Earlier in Mediterranean history, it had been reckoned sacrilege, of a sort, to try to dig through a spit of land to make an island (Herodotus 1.174), or attempt to bridge the Hellespont (7.22–5, 34–7), or to cut down a grove. Even Mesopotamian and Egyptian water engineers might think of themselves as dealing with dangerous powers, who needed to be placated. And Aeschylus reckoned Xerxes' insult to the Hellespont was one reason for his expedition's failure (*The Persians* 64–71, 722–6). Hebrews – and other Semitic peoples – chose to empty nature of ceremonial meanings and concentrate instead on moral choice. So also Elijah, fleeing from the northern Hebrew kingdom in fear of his life, discovered that the Lord was not in the whirlwind, fire or earthquake, but in 'a still, small voice': 'What are you doing here, Elijah?' (*1 Kings* 19.13).

This secularizing process might also have its disadvantages. It was not only, not even very much, the Christian Churches that fostered the world-hating spirit that the author of *Asclepius* deplored, but perhaps they did too little to control it.

In their weariness the people of that time will find the world nothing to wonder at or to worship. This All – a good thing that never had nor has nor will have its better – will be endangered. People will find it oppressive and scorn it. They will not cherish this entire world, a work of god beyond compare, a glorious construction, a bounty composed of images in multiform variety, a mechanism for god's will ungrudgingly supporting his work, making a unity of everything that can be honoured, praised and finally loved by those who see it, a multiform accumulation taken as a single thing. They will prefer shadows to light, and they will find death more expedient than life. No one will look up to heaven. The reverent will be thought mad, the irreverent wise; the lunatic will be thought brave, and the scoundrel will be taken for a decent person. (*Asclepius* 25: Copenhaver 1992, p. 82)

There need have been no common themes, no common beliefs, in all the populations of whatever ethnic or religious background who lived around the Inner Sea. But it is possible to detect a certain widespread melancholy. Everything is always getting worse. Has the world existed literally forever? Is it also infinite in its extent? Do all things happen entirely as they must, or is there any degree of 'freedom' in their making? What exactly are we: individual mortal bodies or eternal souls? Is death an evil, or a release from evils? Are there reasons, or final causes, active in the world? Is the world revealed in its entirety through our senses, or is it available only to a non-sensual reason? Are 'natural' entities also 'supernatural'? Is the world good or bad or something inbetween? Is there another world than this? Are human beings especially favoured by the gods, or by 'right reason'? And what is 'reason'? What indeed is 'wisdom'? And must we expect the moral and physical disaster that so many writers described? Is there a reset button?

Spengler, for all his errors, was correct to see that there were different traditions, different ways of seeing, all struggling to express themselves around the Mediterranean coast. He may even have been right to suggest that they were likely to pass through similar stages, moving from an initial inspiration and creative efflorescence on towards a scholastic integration and a cynical decline. He was wrong to suppose that 'Egyptian' or 'Chaldaean' experiments were intellectually and imaginatively dead in the period I have been discussing, and wrong to characterize 'the other' strand of Mediterranean thought as 'Magian' (though in this he was only following, and elaborating, a familiar Classical theme). The point that has often been missed is that his was an optimistic vision: even if particular cultures were bound in the end to run out of fresh ideas, there would be others, now unimagined, rising to take their place. Neither 'Classical' nor 'Magian' cultures lasted, but there were new shoots growing from their decaying hulks.

Are we faced by similar changes? The long experiment of Christendom is, maybe, failing (though it has failed many times before, and somehow risen again), as may that other inheritor of Hebraic Platonism, Islam. If they fail, our descendants may find themselves once more in a world our forefathers knew well: the world of hopeless custom, caste and confusion, where we must make our choice between two sorts of barbarism – subjection to the Empire or a chaos of warring tribes. At the same time we can expect climatic changes, whether or not accompanied by meteor strikes and volcanic eruptions (several such events are, on precedent, long overdue). On the other hand, we have been here before. The very fact of being brought up among the ruins may yet impress some people with the thought that they at least are young. Whatever has been achieved before, and lost, there is a moment when the world is new and can reinvent or rediscover glory.

NOTES

Chapter 1

1 Aristotle even suggests that everything has already been discovered, and forgotten, an infinite – or at least an indefinite – number of times: *De Caelo* 270b19–20, *Meteorologica* 339b27–8, *Politics* 7.1329b25–6. So also *Ecclesiastes* 1.10: 'Is there anything of which one can say, "Look this is new"? No, it has already existed, long ago before our time. The men of old are not remembered, and those who follow will not be remembered, by those who follow them'.

2 Blake 'Vision of the Last Judgment' (1810), p. 95: in Blake 1966, p. 617.

3 See Ulansey 1989, pp. 76–81 for evidence that the precession was indeed Hipparchus's reasoned conclusion, and for the religious uses made of the idea thereafter.

4 See Virgil *Eclogues* 4.6–7: iam redit et Virgo, redeunt Saturnia regna; iam nova progenies caelo demittitur alto. Virgil's poem was long taken to be an unconscious prophecy of the birth of Christ.

5 Clement of Alexandria (c150–c215 AD) *Stromata* 1.15: *http://www. sacred-texts.com/chr/ecf/002/0020308.htm* (accessed 20th August 2011).

6 'As they are currently formulated, general relativity and quantum mechanics *cannot both be right*. The two theories underlying the tremendous progress of physics during the last hundred years – progress that has explained the expansion of the heavens and the fundamental structure of matter – are mutually incompatible' (Greene 1999, p. 3).

7 'You might accuse your opponents – according to genre – of mere story-telling, or mumbo-jumbo, or superstition (*deisidaimonia*). But the counter-charge, the come-uppance, that you yourself were doing no better, could also often be made, and often was, if not in your own generation, then in subsequent ones' (Lloyd 1990, p. 55; see Betegh 2004, pp. 352–3).

8 Though there does now seem to be evidence that rocks under tension release particles that interfere with the chemistry of groundwater in ways that creatures with a good sense of smell can notice: see Rachel Grant et al. 'Ground Water Chemistry Changes before Major Earthquakes and Possible Effects on Animals': *Int. J. Environ. Res. Public Health* 2011.8, 1936–56; doi:10.3390/ijerph8061936.

9 López-Ruiz 2010, p. 157 points out that these noises repeat a familiar theme: a monster with many heads – in this case: man, bull, lion, dog and serpent. Greene 1992 suggests that the noises mentioned are a realistic attempt to describe the eruption of Etna.

10 'The Watchers' also appear in the Hebrew *Book of Enoch* (1.5; 12.4) as fallen angels: a mark that Phoenicians and Hebrews shared, at least at first, a Canaanite mythology (see Baumgarten 1981, pp. 114–15).

11 Plutarch in 'On the Face in the Moon': *Moralia* 923A (1936, vol. 12, p. 55). Braudel (2001), p. 300 exaggerates the scorn that Aristarchus had to endure: nothing in Plutarch shows that there were constant insults, or that he narrowly escaped prosecution.

12 See also Wootton 2006, p. 35: 'the Hippocratics were good at setting bones and lancing boils, at hands-on manipulation. But none of their therapies directed at internal conditions worked.' Lloyd's mention of torture would also be relevant to the work of the Ptolemaic biologists Herophilus and Erasistratus who 'according to our chief source, Celsus (*On Medicine* I Proem 23f, 21 15ff.) . . . practised not just human dissection but also human vivisection (on criminals obtained from the kings, i.e. the Ptolemies)' (Lloyd 1990, p. 56).

13 Women were sometimes acknowledged as philosophers: the list includes Theano and Damo of Croton, Diotima of Mantinea, Lastheneia of Mantinea and Axiothea of Phlius (who both attended Plato's Academy), Hipparchia wife of Crates the Cynic, and Hypatia of Alexandria. Some fragmentary writings by women are collected in Plant 2004, including work attributed to Perictione of Athens, *possibly* Plato's mother (pp. 76–8).

Chapter 2

1 A text known as 'the Standard List of Professions' appeared first in the late fourth millennium in Uruk on the southern Euphrates and was copied faithfully for fifteen hundred years: see Van De Mieroop 2004, p. 27. The list ranges from priestly ruler down to agricultural labourer. Each rank is given rations of barley, oil and cloth.

2   The herb, and its loss, also occur in the work of Ibycus (sixth
    century BC: see Burkert 1992, pp. 123–4). Gaius Julius Hyginus,
    a superintendent of the Palatine library in Rome (64 BC–17 AD)
    records a Cretan fable that snakes had access to a herb that could
    raise the dead (*Fabulae* 136: Apollodorus 2007, pp. 144–5).

3   Gilgamesh to Enkidu, Old Babylonian Version: cited by West 1997,
    p. 121. Shamash is a Sumerian sun-god in origin, also serving
    as Hammurabi's god of justice in Babylon of the early second
    millennium BC.

4   According to Diodorus Siculus 1.94 Mneves [of Egypt] 'claimed
    that Hermes had given the laws to him, with the assurance that they
    would be the cause of great blessings, just as among the Greeks, they
    say, Minos did in Crete and Lycurgus among the Lacedaemonians,
    the former saying that he received his laws from Zeus and the latter
    his from Apollo. Also among several other peoples tradition says
    that this kind of a device was used and was the cause of much good
    to such as believed it. Thus it is recorded that among the Arians
    Zathraustes claimed that the Good Spirit gave him his laws, among
    the people known as the Getae who represent themselves to be
    immortal Zalmoxis asserted the same of their common goddess
    Hestia, and among the Jews Moyses referred his laws to the god who
    is invoked as Iao. They all did this either because they believed that a
    conception which would help humanity was marvellous and wholly
    divine, or because they held that the common crowd would be more
    likely to obey the laws if their gaze were directed towards the majesty
    and power of those to whom their laws were ascribed.'

5   Heracleitos, according to Clement of Alexandria, said that Dionysus
    and Hades were the same, which suggests that he too accepted the
    identity of Dionysus and Osiris (22B15DK: Waterfield 2000, p. 46).

6   The Roman poet Ennius translated Euhemerus's text into Latin in the
    second century BC, and the view that the gods were originally human
    was widely accepted – 'without in the least invalidating the worship
    of the deity thus given a human origin'! (Liebeschuetz 1979, p. 33).

7   This may be, as Osborne 1997 has argued, what Heracleitos intended
    in his remarks on the apparent folly of using blood to purify those
    defiled by murder (22B5: Waterfield 2000, p. 45).

8   See also *Ennead* IV.3 [27].11, and *Asclepius* 37: Copenhaver 1992,
    p. 90. All passages from Plotinus are as translated by Armstrong
    (1966–88), unless otherwise stated.

9   This was, the author said, to make a particular point, since the God
    who 'created the world out of formless matter . . . could have let loose

upon them a horde of bears or ravening lions or unknown ferocious monsters newly created, either breathing out blasts of fire, or roaring and belching smoke, or flashing terrible sparks like lightning from their eyes, with power not only to exterminate them by the wounds they inflicted, but by their mere appearance to kill them with fright' (*Wisdom of Solomon* 11.17–18).

10 This was also the home of Hermotimus, a legendary figure – according at least to Pliny *Natural History* 7.174 – whose soul went roaming round the world while his body lay seemingly lifeless (till his treacherous wife, bored with his long silence, had the body cremated). He was, it was said, an earlier incarnation of the soul that was also Pythagoras. Another philosopher from Clazomenae was Anaxagoras: Aristotle suggests that Anaxagoras picked up the cosmic significance of Mind, exactly, from Hermotimus (*Metaphysics* 1.984b15–22, *Protrepticus* fr.61 Rose: see Betegh 2004, pp. 283–5, who refers to Hermotimus as a 'frantic eccentric' despite acknowledging that he is a significant figure not only for Pythagoreans but for the development of a 'rational' cosmology).

11 This, coincidentally, was where Hermotimus showed that he had the same soul as a hero of the Trojan War, Euphorbus, by identifying Menelaus's shield: Diogenes *Lives* 8.4.

12 The pattern is not only Hellenic: *Ezekiel* 34.25–6 suggests that God gave the rebellious Israel 'statutes that were not good, and ordinances whereby they should not live . . . that I might destroy them.' So also *1 Kings* 22.19–23, where He is said to have sent a lying spirit to speak through the mouths of prophets urging King Ahab on to war.

13 A different reading of the story might be that Isaac was subjected to a near-death experience as part of his initiation into adulthood: a common enough custom, but not one that is mentioned in Hebrew history.

Chapter 3

1 David Hume *Dialogues concerning Natural Religion* (1779), part 2.

2 Blake misinterpreted Ezekiel's gesture: he was not *eating* dung, but using cattle-dung to cook his very limited diet, adopted as a signal about the austerity to come.

3 Alternatively: 'it must be that what can be spoken and thought is' (Waterfield 2000, p. 58).

4 See Ps-Dionysius *The Divine Names* 697A (1987, p. 73): 'Its nature, unconfined by form, is the creator of all form. In it is nonbeing really

an excess of being. It is not *a* life, but is, rather, superabundant Life. It is not *a* mind, but is superabundant Wisdom. . . . And one might even say that nonbeing itself longs for the Good which is above all being'.

5　A later thinker, Ibn al-ʿArabi (1165–1240 AD), contended both that Reality is eternal and unknowable, and that all beliefs are true (in that every one discloses some aspect of reality): see Chittick 1994, pp. 137–41. This may not be far from the Parmenidean paradox.

6　When KRS (1983, p. 279) suggest that 'of all the pre-socratics Zeno has most life in him today' they mean only that his 'paradoxes' can fascinate the few: that he – and other 'Pre-socratics' – had a more serious aim seems not to be worth considering.

7　The notion first appears in the record in that form in the twelfth century *Book of 24 Philosophers* and in Alain de Lille (c1128–1202). It quickly became a Platonic commonplace, and was variously attributed to Augustine and Empedocles. It remains a powerful epigram, used even by secular theorists, not always to good effect (see Small 1983).

8　See also Xenophon *Memorabilia* 1.2.9: '"But assuredly," said the accuser, "[Socrates] caused those who conversed with him to despise the established laws, by saying how foolish it was to elect the magistrates of a state by beans, when nobody would be willing to take a pilot elected by beans, or an architect, or a flute-player, or a person in any other profession, which, if erroneously exercised, would cause far less harm than errors in the administration of a state;" and declared that "such remarks excited the young to contemn the established form of government, and disposed them to acts of violence"'.

9　This is not to deny that Empedocles, Democritus, Lucretius and others (on whom see Sedley 2007) did variously anticipate the idea that the appearance of 'design' could be produced by the 'natural selection' of accidental mutations. But Aristotle was right to find the idea incredible, in the absence of any clear account of how the original organisms appeared – without any reason – in sufficient quantities to allow for viable combinations. Empedocles would have thought there was a supernatural reason.

10　Armstrong's version reads 'escape in solitude to the solitary', and Stephen MacKenna's, 'the flight of the alone to the alone': but '*monos*' here probably means 'pure' rather than 'alone'.

11　Samaritans reckoned that the split between the North and the South dated from the removal of the cultic centre from Mt Gerizim to Shiloh, long before the kings. The usual Jewish version was that the northern lands were lost to the true line of Israel, but both sides drew on the Pentateuch. See Broadie 1981 for discussion of Samaritan

philosophy. Marinus of Nablus (450–500AD), head of the Athenian
Academy after Proclus, was a Samaritan by birth, but a Hellene by
conviction: Damascius 1999, p. 237.

12 I am neglecting here those aspects of reformist Hebrew piety that
involved suppressing Canaanite hill-shrines (and the male prostitutes
attached to them), hacking down sacred pillars, and even depriving
the king's grandmother of her rank because she possessed 'an obscene
object made for the worship of Asherah' (*1 Kings* 15.13–15). We might,
at a distance, be able to summon up some sympathy for Canaanite
religion – but perhaps that is because we don't know much about it.

13 Some Rabbis concluded instead that Job was 'in the wrong' – and his
later apparent good fortune was only to ensure that he had 'had his
reward' in this life (Urbach 1979, p. 412).

Chapter 4

1 For most commentators this is enough to 'prove' that Aristoxenus
can't be trusted: Socrates just *can't* have practised usury! Huffman
2012 has made a strong case for a more positive interpretation:
Aristoxenus was actually praising Socrates for his good business
sense, and investing in a business is not what loan sharks do!

2 The contrast that Bloch makes between *Aletheia* and *Emeth* (see also
Miskotte 1967, p. 267) is overdrawn, as Barr 1961 has argued: most
of the time '*emeth*' is the same truth-of-correspondence that Aristotle
identifies, and the notion that God is indeed 'He who Is' is too solidly
embedded in the Abrahamic tradition to be easily overlooked, even if
it is not the only influential interpretation.

3 According to *Judges* 20.28, it was Phinehas who in later life
encouraged the general assault on the tribe of Benjamin for the
atrocious rape and murder of the Levite's concubine (*Judges* 19.16–30).

4 When Alexander's army encountered a bilingual people, in Bactria
in 329 BC, and discovered that they were descendants of the
Branchidae, hereditary priests of Apollo at the temple outside
Miletus, Alexander's response was to slaughter them, and obliterate
the city. The excuse offered was that their ancestors had committed
sacrilege when siding with the Persians; the real reason may have
been a wish to avoid having them back in control of the oracle at
Didyma (see Parke 1985).

5 Compare *James* 2.15ff: 'What use is it for a man to say he has faith when
he does nothing to show it? Can that faith save him? Suppose a brother

or a sister is in rags with not enough food for the day, and one of you says, "Good luck to you, keep yourselves warm, and have plenty to eat", but does nothing to supply their bodily needs, what is the good of that? So with faith; if it does not lead to action it is in itself a lifeless thing'.

Chapter 5

1   In *Cratylus* 396d Euthyphro is, by implication, said to have offered the same sort of allegorized interpretation of these stories as were later endorsed by Plotinus and others: Kronos is the pure mind, created by 'looking up' to the heavens (see also the Derveni Papyrus: Betegh 2004, pp. 185–7).

2   Zhu 2002 accurately summarizes Plato's judgement by saying that 'if his filial piety clashes with his religious piety, the latter should always be given the upper hand. Doing otherwise is not only wrong but also useless, for justice always wins against a crime by a mortal. For this reason, the Confucian idea of covering up for a family member is categorically ruled out by both morals and wisdom'.

3   This is not to excuse the practice of insisting on hidden motives for Plato's characters, as (e.g.) Howland does in suggesting that Euthyphro hates and resents his father (Howland 2011, pp. 141, 209). This is to miss the real difficulty in which Euthyphro finds himself, that his father is actually guilty at least of manslaughter, and that no effort has been made to pay for the wrong done.

4   See Julius Tomin *http://www.juliustomin.org/lostplatovolume1.html*, for an engaging and scholarly assault on the consensus about the dating and intention of the dialogues.

5   I have taken this and other passages of Vitruvius from Bill Thayer's valuable site: *http://penelope.uchicago.edu/Thayer/E/Roman/Texts/Vitruvius/home.html* (accessed 3 November 2011). The most recent translation and edition of Vitruvius's text is Vitruvius 2009.

Chapter 8

1   There is some dispute about how 'hellenized' the region was in total: the larger cities, Sepphoris or Capernaum, were perhaps not typical of rural Galilee, and the different communities may have had little intercourse (see Chancey 2002). But we do not have to suppose that Palestine was 'hellenized' to acknowledge that people of different

traditions can still talk! East of the Jordan, in Gerasa or in Gadara, lived the Pythagorean mathematician Nicomachus (60–120 AD), and the Cynic philosophers Menippus (third century BC), Meleager and Oenomaus (second century AD): see Navia 1996, p. 166.

2   The Babylonian Talmud uses the fantasy of an *elephant*'s passing through a needle's eye as an example of the (naturally) impossible (*Berakoth* 55b), but also suggests that with God all things, including this, are possible: 'The Holy One said, open for me a door as big as a needle's eye and I will open for you a door through which may enter tents and [camels?]' (*Midrash Rabbah*, *The Song of Songs*, 5.3). My thanks to the author of the Biblical Hebrew pages for these references: *www.biblicalhebrew.com/nt/camelneedle.htm* (accessed 2nd February 2012).

3   The idea was rejected by Lucretius, Lactantius and Cosmas Indicopleustes, all apparently persuaded that the direction 'down' was everywhere the same.

Chapter 9

1   So also Benedict Spinoza *Ethics* 4p37s1 (1982, p. 175), blaming this for 'the [supposed] requirement to refrain from slaughtering beasts'.

2   The two texts use different terms (*agape* and *eros*, respectively), but too much can be made of the supposed distinction between different sorts of 'love' (see D'Arcy 1946).

3   'The heart is deceitful above all things, and desperately corrupt; who can understand it?' (*Jeremiah* 17.9).

Chapter 10

1   See Keys 1999, who opts for a volcanic eruption in Java to explain the event identified by dendrochronology. Baillie 1999 preferred to blame a comet. Both greatly exaggerate the effect. 'There nothing in our evidence to suggest that the year 536 was a watershed moment between antiquity and the Middle Ages' (Arjava 2005, p. 92).

RECOMMENDED READING

Any serious student of ancient thought will read Plato's Dialogues (especially such classics as *The Symposium*, *The Republic*, *Phaedo*, *Phaedrus* and *Theaetetus*), and as much of Aristotle's drier texts as s/he can endure: most to be recommended for beginners must be *Nicomachean Ethics*, *Politics*, *Metaphysics I*, *On the Parts of Animals I*, and *Categories*. Complete works by other great philosophers include Plotinus's *Enneads*, Porphyry *On Abstinence from Killing Animals*, Proclus's *Elements of Theology* and Boethius's *Consolation*. The *Discourses* and *Handbook* of Epictetus, the *Meditations* of Marcus Aurelius, and the Letters of Epicurus, while containing little philosophical argument, are important evocations of the attitude once thought proper for philosophers. Lucretius *On the Nature of Things* is the greatest single work of philosophical poetry. The Hermetic Corpus had significant influence on later thought, especially during the Renaissance: see Copenhaver (1992). The Biblical texts which read most like 'philosophy' as that has been understood in early and late modern times are *Ecclesiastes*, *Job* and the epistles of Paul (but all need to be read in their historical and prophetic context). Selections from the (Babylonian) *Talmud* can be found, for example, in Solomon (2009): for an outsider to attempt the whole, without appropriate guidance, is impossible! Secondary, but still ancient, literature includes Cicero's *Academica*, *On the Nature of Gods* and *On Duties*. Cicero is not our only source for the Hellenistic schools, but deserves special attention as the principal conduit for Greek philosophy into the Roman and Western European worlds. Diogenes Laertius's *Lives of Eminent Philosophers* records much incidental information, uncritically. Diodorus Siculus relays something of the work of Hecataeus and Manetho, especially on the Classical perception of Egyptian thought. Such Christian writers as Clement of Alexandria are also a valuable route into the classical mind (see especially his *Exhortation to the Greeks (Protrepticus)*), as are Sextus Empiricus's *Outlines of Pyrrhonism*, and *Against the Mathematicians*. There are many modern anthologies collecting together excerpts and fragments of the philosophers: most Anglophone scholars will now use Graham 2010 (though his assumptions are more Whiggish than I would wish), LS 1987, Dillon and Gerson 2004, and Sharples 2010.

There are very many medieval and both early and late modern works about the philosophers themselves, their arguments and their historical and geographical context. A complete bibliography, even of merely introductory or elementary studies, would require a second volume. Among many valuable works in addition to those cited above, I would recommend the following:

Annas, Julia (1995) *The Morality of Happiness*. New York: Oxford University Press.

Hussey, Edward (1998) *The Presocratics*. Bristol: Bristol Classical Press (2nd edition).

Irwin, Terry (1989) *Classical Thought*. Oxford: Oxford University Press.

Smith, Andrew (2004) *Philosophy in Late Antiquity*. London: Routledge.

The geographical context is well addressed by Braudel 2001 and at much greater length by Peregrine Horden & Nicholas Purcell *The Corrupting Sea: a study of Mediterranean History* (Oxford: Blackwell 2000). Abulafia (2003) is a splendidly illustrated collection of essays on different aspects of the Mediterranean from prehistoric times till modern: the essays by Oliver Rackham, Marlene Suano, Mario Torelli and Geoffrey Rickman have a particular relevance. Strabo 1929 shows how the area was conceived in the first century AD. Additional insights into the cultural context can be obtained from the following:

Bernal, Martin (1991) *Black Athena: the Afroasiatic roots of classical civilization: Vol.2, The archaeological and documentary evidence*. New Brunswick: Rutgers University Press.

Bremmer, Jan N. (2008) *Greek Religion and Culture, the Bible and the Ancient Near East*. Boston, MA: Brill.

Brown, Peter. (1971) *The World of Late Antiquity: AD 150–750*. London: Thames and Hudson.

Buxton, Richard. (1994) *Imaginary Greece: The Contexts of Mythology*. Cambridge: Cambridge University Press.

Cameron, Averil. (2011) *The Mediterranean World in Late Antiquity 395–700*. London: Routledge (2nd edition).

Cornford, Francis M. (1957) *From Religion to Philosophy*. New York: Harper (1st published 1912).

Dodds, Eric R. (1951) *The Greeks and the Irrational*. Berkeley, CA: University of California Press.

Hengel, Martin. (1974) *Judaism and Hellenism*, tr. J. Bowden. London: SCM Press.

Rajak, Tessa. (2002) *The Jewish Dialogue with Greece and Rome: Studies in Cultural and Social Interaction*. Leiden: Brill.

Trzaskoma, Stephen M., Smith, R. Scott, Brunet, Stephen. (2004) *Anthology of Classical Myth: Primary Sources in Translation*. Indianapolis, IN: Hackett.

Vernant, Jean Pierre. (1983) *Myth and Thought among the Greeks*. London: Routledge & Kegan Paul.

The proper uses of philosophy, at least as they were understood through much of the Mediterranean, have been given greater attention in recent years. On this theme see especially the writings of Peter Kingsley, and also – with several different slants – the following:

Hadot, Pierre. (1995) *Philosophy as a Way of Life*, ed., Arnold I. Davidson, tr. Michael Chase. Oxford: Blackwell.

Nussbaum, Martha. (1996) *The Therapy of Desire: Theory and Practice in Hellenistic Ethics*. Princeton, NJ: Princeton University Press.

Sorabji, Richard. (2002) *Emotion and Peace of Mind: From Stoic Agitation to Christian Temptation*. Oxford: Oxford University Press.

Uzdavinys, Algis. (2008) *Philosophy as a Rite of Rebirth: From Ancient Egypt to Neoplatonism*. Westbury, Wiltshire: Prometheus Trust.

WORKS CITED

Ancient sources

Alexander of Aphrodisias. (1983) *On Fate*, ed., R. W. Sharples. London: Duckworth.

Apollodorus' Library & Hyginus' Fabulae. (2007) tr. R. Scott Smuth and Stephen M. Trzaskoma. Indianapolis, IN: Hackett.

Apuleius of Madaura. (1998) *The Golden Ass*, tr. E. J. Kenney. Harmondsworth: Penguin.

Aristotle of Stageira. (1984) *Complete Works*, tr. Jonathan Barnes. Princeton, NJ: Princeton University Press.

Armstrong, Arthur H. (1966–88) *Plotinus*. London: Heinemann.

Augustine. (1950) *Against the Academics*, tr. John J. O'Meara. Westminster, MD: Newman Press.

— (1998) *City of God*, tr. R. W. Dyson. Cambridge: Cambridge University Press.

Baumgarten, Alexander I. (1981) *The Phoenician History of Philo of Byblus*. Leiden: Brill.

Bede. (1990) *Ecclesiastical History of the English People*, tr. Leo Shirley-Price and D. H. Farmer. London: Penguin.

Betegh, Gábor. (2004) *The Derveni Papyrus: Cosmology, Theology and Interpretation*. Cambridge: Cambridge University Press.

Boethius. (1969) *The Consolation of Philosophy*, tr. V. E. Watts. Harmondsworth: Penguin.

Chan, Wing-tsit. (1963) ed., *Sourcebook in Chinese Philosophy*. Princeton, NJ: Princeton University Press.

Cicero, Marcus T. (1877) *Tusculan Disputations; On the Nature of the Gods; On the Commonwealth*, tr. C. D. Yonge. New York: Harper.

—(1971) *On the Good Life*, tr. Michael Grant. Harmondsworth: Penguin.

—(2006) *On Divination*, tr. David Wardle. Oxford: Clarendon Press.

Clement of Alexandria. (1919) *Works*, G. W. Butterworth. London: Heinemann.

Copenhaver, Brian. (1992) *Hermetica: The Greek Corpus Hermeticum and the Latin Asclepius*. Cambridge: Cambridge University Press.

Damascius. (1999) *The Philosophical* History, tr. Polymnia Athanassiadi. Athens: Apamea Cultural Association.

Darmesteter, James. (1880) tr. *The Vendidad: Zend Avesta, Part 1*. Oxford: Oxford University Press.

Dillon, John and Gerson, Lloyd P. (2004) eds, *Neoplatonic Philosophy: Introductory Readings*. Indianapolis, IN: Hackett.

Diodorus Siculus. (1933) *Library of History* vol. 1, tr. C. H. Oldfather. Cambridge: Harvard University Press.

Diogenes Laertius. (1989) *Lives of Eminent Philosophers*, tr. R. D. Hicks. London: Heinemann.

Eusebius of Caesarea. (1903) *Praeparatio Evangelica*, tr. E. H. Gifford. Oxford: Clarendon Press.

Gaskin, John C. A. (1995) ed., *The Epicurean Philosophers*. London: Dent.

Gerber, Douglas E. (1999) ed., *Greek Elegiac Poetry*. London: Heinemann.

Graham, Daniel W. (2010) ed., *The Texts of Early Greek Philosophy: The Complete Fragments and Selected Testimonies of the Major Presocratics*. Cambridge: Cambridge University Press.

Guthrie, Kenneth S. (1987) *The Pythagorean Sourcebook and Library*, ed., David Fideler. Grand Rapids, Michigan: Phanes Press.

Harrison, Tony. (1992) *Palladas: Poems*. London: Anvil Press Poetry.

Herodotus. (1949) *History*, tr. George Rawlinson. London: Everyman.

Huffman, Carl A. (1993) *Philolaus of Croton: Pythagorean and Presocratic: A Commentary on the Fragments and Testimonia with Interpretive Essays*. Cambridge: Cambridge University Press.

Kidd, Ian G. (1999) *Poseidonius Volume 3: The Translation of the Fragments*. Cambridge: Cambridge University Press.

Kirk, Geoffrey S., Raven, J., Schofield, M. (1983) eds, *The Presocratic Philosophers*. Cambridge: Cambridge University Press.

Long, Anthony A. and Sedley, D. (1987) eds, *The Hellenistic Philosophers*. Cambridge: Cambridge University Press.

Lucian of Samosata. (2006) *Selected Dialogues*, tr. C. D. N. Costa. New York: Oxford University Press.

Macrobius, Ambrosius T. (1952) *Commentary on the Dream of Scipio*, tr. William Harris Stahl. New York: Columbia University Press.

Maimonides, Moses. (1995) *The Guide of the Perplexed*, tr. Chaim Rabin, ed. Julius Guttman. Indianapolis, IN: Hackett (original 1190 AD).

Numenius of Apamea. (1973) *Fragmenta*, ed., Edouard des Places. Paris: Les Belles Lettres.

Philo of Alexandria. (1929–62) *Collected Works*, tr. F. H. Colson, G. H. Whitaker et al. London: Loeb Classical Library, Heinemann.

—(2005) *The Contemplative, The Giants and Selections*, tr. David Winston. Mahwah, NJ: Paulist Press.

Plant, Ian M. (2004) ed., *Women Writers of Ancient Greece and Rome: An Anthology*. London: Equinox Publishing.

Plato. (2010) *Complete Works*, tr. Benjamin Jowett. Houston, TX: Halcyon Press.

Plutarch of Chaeronea. (1936–9) *Moralia*, tr. Frank Cole Babbitt. London: Heinemann.

Porphyry. (2000) *On Abstinence from Killing Animals*, ed., Gillian Clark. London: Duckworth.

Ps-Dionysius. (1987) *The Complete Works,* tr. Colm Luibheid. London: SPCK.

Ptolemy. (1998) *Almagest*, tr. G. J. Toomer. Princeton, NJ: Princeton University Press (2nd edition).

Radhakrishan, S. and Moore, C. (1957) eds, *Sourcebook of Indian Philosophy*. Princeton, NJ: Princeton University Press.

Ross, William D. (1952) *Works of Aristotle vol 12: Select Fragments*. London: Oxford University Press.

Sextus Empiricus. (1994) *Outlines of Scepticism,* tr. Julia Annas and Jonathan Barnes. Cambridge. Cambridge University Press.

Sharples, Robert W. (2010) ed., *Peripatetic Philosophy: 200 BC to AD 200*. Cambridge: Cambridge University Press.

Sherwood, Polycarp. (1955) *The Earlier Ambigua of Saint Maximus the Confessor and his Refutation of Origenism*. Rome: Herder.

Solomon, Norman. (2009) *The Talmud: A Selection*. London: Penguin.

Sturluson, Snorri. (1916) *The Prose Edda*, tr. A. G. Brodeur. New York: American Scandinavian Foundation.

Thucydides. (2004) *The Peloponnesian War*, tr. Richard Crawley. New York: Dover.

Valerius Maximus. (2004) *Memorable Deeds and Sayings: One Thousand Tales from Ancient Rome*, tr. H. J. Walker. Indianapolis, IN: Hackett.

Vitruvius Pollio, Marcus. (2009) *On Architecture*, eds, Robert Tavernor and Richard Schofield. London: Penguin.

Waterfield, Robin. (2000) ed., *The First Philosophers: The Presocratics and Sophists*. New York: Oxford University Press.

Xenophon. (1990) *Conversations of Socrates*, tr. Hugh Tredennik. Harmondsworth: Penguin.

—(2004) *The Persian Expedition*, tr. Rex Warner. Harmondsworth: Penguin.

Modern literature

Abulafia, David. (2003) ed., *The Mediterranean in History*. London: Thames & Hudson.

Ackrill, John L. (1965) 'Aristotle's Distinction between Energeia and Kinesis,' In: Renford Bambrough, ed., *New Essays on Plato and Aristotle*. London: Routledge, pp. 121–41.

Adams, Will W. (2010) 'Bashō's Therapy for Narcissus: Nature as Intimate Other and Transpersonal Self', *Journal of Humanistic Psychology* 50, 38–64.

Adamson, Peter. (2002) *The Arabic Plotinus: A Philosophical Study of the 'Theology of Aristotle'*. London: Duckworth.

Altman, William H. F. (2009) 'Womanly Humanism in Cicero's Tusculan Disputations', *Transactions of the American Philological Association* 139, 407–41.

Amzallag, Nissim. (2011) 'Was Yahweh Worshiped in the Aegean?', *Journal for the Study of the Old Testament* 35, 387–415.

Arjava, Antti. (2005) 'The Mystery Cloud of 536 CE in the Mediterranean Sources', *Dumbarton Oaks Papers* 59, 73–94.

Armstrong, Arthur H. (1936) 'Plotinus and India', *Classical Quarterly* 30, 22–8.

—(1967) 'Plotinus', In: A. H. Armstrong, ed., *Cambridge History of Later Greek and Early Mediaeval Philosophy*. Cambridge: Cambridge University Press, pp. 195–271.

Auden, Wystan H. (1976) *Collected Poems*, ed. Edward Mendelson. London: Faber.

Baillie, Mike G. L. (1999) *Exodus to Arthur: Catastrophic Encounters with Comets*. London: Batsford.

Balme, David M. (1980) 'Aristotle's Biology was not Essentialist', *Archiv für Geschichte der Philosophie* 62, 1–12.

Barr, James. (1961) *The Semantics of Biblical Language*. Oxford: Clarendon Press.

Berkovits, Eliezer. (1969) *Man and God: Studies in Biblical Theology*. Detroit, MI: Wayne State University Press.

Blake, William. (1966) *Complete Writings*, ed. Geoffrey Keynes. London: Oxford University Press.

Bloch, Ernst. (1986) *The Principle of Hope*, tr. N. Plaice, S. Plaice and P. Knight. Oxford: Blackwell.

Bolton, John D. P. (1962) *Aristeas of Proconnesus*. Oxford: Clarendon Press.

Bowra, Cecil M. (1960) 'Palladas on Tyche', *Classical Quarterly* 10, 118–28.

Boyle, Marjorie O'Rourke (2002) 'Pure of Heart: From Ancient Rites to Renaissance Plato', *Journal of the History of Ideas* 63, 41–62.

Boys-Stones, George. (2001) *Post-Hellenistic Philosophy: A Study of its Development from the Stoics to Origen.* Oxford: Oxford University Press.

Braudel, Fernand. (2001) *The Mediterranean in the Ancient World,* tr. Sian Reynolds. London: Penguin.

Bridgman, Timothy P. (2005) *Hyperboreans: Myth and History in Celtic-HellenicContacts.* London: Routledge.

Broadie, Alexander. (1981) *A Samaritan Philosophy: A Study of the Hellenistic Cultural Ethos of the Memar Marqah.* Leiden: Brill.

Burkert, Walter. (1992) *The Orientalizing Revolution: Near Eastern Influence on Greek Culture in the Early Archaic Age,* tr. Margaret E. Pinder and Walter Burkert. Cambridge, MA: Harvard University Press.

—(1997) 'From epiphany to cult statue: Early Greek *Theos*', Lloyd 1997, pp. 15–34.

—(1999) 'The Logic of Cosmogony', Buxton 1999, pp. 87–106.

—(2004) *Babylon Memphis Persepolis: Eastern Contexts of Greek Culture.* Cambridge, MA: Harvard University Press.

Buxton, Richard. (1999) ed., *From Myth to Reason? Studies in the Development of Greek Thought.* Oxford: Oxford University Press.

Cameron, Alan. (2011) *The Last Pagans of Rome.* New York: Oxford University Press.

Cameron, Averil. (2010) *The Byzantines.* Oxford: Wiley-Blackwell.

Campbell, Gordon. (2008) '"And Bright was the Flame of their Friendship" (Empedocles B130): Humans, Animals, Justice, and Friendship, in Lucretius and Empedocles', *Leeds International Classical Studies* 7.4, 1–23.

Chancey, Mark A. (2002) *The Myth of a Gentile Galilee.* Cambridge: Cambridge University Press.

Chesterton, Gilbert K. (1960) *The Club of Queer Trades.* London: Darwen Finlayson Ltd (1st published 1905).

—(1961) *Orthodoxy.* London: Fontana (1st published 1908).

Chittick, William C. (1994) *Imaginal Worlds: Ibn al-'Arabi and the Problem of Religious Diversity.* New York: SUNY Press.

Clark, Stephen R. L. (1975) *Aristotle's Man: speculations upon Aristotelian anthropology.* Oxford: Clarendon Press.

—(1991) *God's World and the Great Awakening.* Oxford: Clarendon Press.

—(2008) 'Going Naked into the Shrine: Herbert, Plotinus and the Constructive Metaphor', In: D. Hedley and S. Hutton, eds, *Platonism at the Origins of Modernity.* Dordrectht: Springer, pp. 45–61.

Collins, John D. (2003) 'The Zeal of Phinehas: the Bible and the Legitimation of Violence', *Journal of Biblical Literature* 122, 3–21.

Copenhaver, Brian (1992) *Hermetica: The Greek Corpus Hermeticum and the Latin Asclepius.* Cambridge: Cambridge University Press.

Couliano, Ioan P. (1991) *Out of this World: Otherworldly Journeys from Gilgamesh to Albert Einstein.* Boston, MA: Shambhala.

Crombie, Ian M. (1963) *An Examination of Plato's Doctrines.* London: Routledge & Kegan Paul.

Cumont, Franz. (1960) *Astrology and Religion among the Greeks and Romans.* New York: Dover (1st published 1912).

D'Arcy, Martin C. (1946) *The Mind and Heart of Love.* London: Faber.

Davis, D. B. (1984) *Slavery and Human Progress.* New York: Oxford University Press.

De Tocqueville, Alexis. (2003) *Democracy in America*, tr., Gerald E. Bevan. London: Penguin.

Delcor, Mathias. (1989) 'The Apocrypha and Pseudepigrapha of the Hellenistic Period', In: W. D. Davies and Louis Finkelstein, eds, *Cambridge History of Judaism, vol. 2: the Hellenistic Age.* Cambridge: Cambridge University Press, pp. 409–503.

Dillon, John. (1986) 'Plotinus and the Transcendental Imagination', In: J. P. Mackey, ed., *Religious Imagination.* Edinburgh: Edinburgh University Press, pp. 55–64.

Downing, Gerald. (1987) *Jesus and the Idea of Freedom.* London: SCM Press.

Dumézil, Georges. (1988) *Mitra-Varuna*, tr. David Coleman. New York: Urzone (1st published 1948).

—(1996) *Archaic Roman Religion*, tr. Philip Krapp. Baltimore, MD: Johns Hopkins University Press (1st published 1966).

Feldman, Louis H. (2002) 'The Portrayal of Phinehas by Philo, Pseudo-Philo, and Josephus', *Jewish Quarterly Review* 92, 315–45.

Ferguson, Kitty. (2010) *Pythagoras: His Lives and the Legacy of a Rational Universe: The Biography of Our Mathematical Universe.* London: Icon Books.

Fowden, Garth. (1986) *The Egyptian Hermes: A Historical Approach to the Late Pagan mind.* Cambridge: Cambridge University Press.

Frankfurt, H. and H. A., Wilson, J. A. and Jacobsen, T. (1949) *Before Philosophy.* Harmondsworth: Penguin.

Galinsky, G. Karl. (1972) *The Herakles Theme: The Adaptations of the Hero in Literature from Homer to the Twentieth Century.* Oxford: Blackwell.

Geach, Peter. (1966) 'Plato's Euthyphro: An Analysis and Commentary', *Monist* 30, 369–82.

Gerson, Lloyd P. (2005) *Aristotle and Other Platonists.* New York: Cornell University Press.

Gilhus, Ingvild Saelid. (2006) *Animals, Gods and Humans: Changing Attitudes to Animals in Greek, Roman and Early Christian Ideas.* London: Routledge.

Glatzer, Nahum N. (1969) ed., *The Dimensions of Job.* New York: Schocken Books.

Gödel, Kurt. (1995) 'Some Basic Theorems on the Foundations of Mathematics and their Philosophical Implications' 1951, In: S. Feferman, J. Dawson, W. Goldfarb, C. Parsons, R, Solovay, and J. van Heijenoort, eds, *Collected Works, vol. 3*. Oxford: Oxford University Press, pp. 304–23.

Grainger, John D. (1991) *Hellenistic Phoenicia*. Oxford: Clarendon Press.

Grant, Edward. (1962) 'Late Medieval Thought, Copernicus, and the Scientific Revolution', *Journal of the History of Ideas* 23, 197–220.

Greene, Brian. (1999) *The Elegant Universe: Superstrings, Hidden Dimensions, and the Quest for the Ultimate Theory*. London: Jonathan Cape.

Greene, Mott T. (1992) *Natural Knowledge in Preclassical Antiquity*. Baltimore, MD: Johns Hopkins University Press.

Griffin, Jasper. (1980) *Homer on Life and Death*. Oxford: Clarendon Press.

Grimm, Jacob. (1882) *Teutonic Mythology*, tr. J. S. Stallybrass. London: George Bell & Sons.

Gruen, Erich S. (1998) *Heritage and Hellenism: The Reinvention of Jewish Tradition*. Berkeley, CA: University of California Press.

— (2002) *Diaspora: Jews Amidst Greeks and Romans*. Cambridge, MA: Harvard University Press.

— (2011) *Rethinking the Other in Antiquity*. Princeton, NJ: Princeton University Press.

Guthrie, William Keith Chambers. (1950) *The Greeks and their Gods*. London: Methuen.

Haigh, Arthur. E. (1896) *The Tragic Drama of the Greeks*. Oxford: Clarendon Press.

Harrington, Hannah K. (2001) *Holiness: Rabbinic Judaism and the Graeco-Roman World*. London: Routledge.

Hawking, Stephen. (1988) *A Brief History of Time*. London: Bantam.

Heidegger, Martin. (1949) *Existence and Being*, tr. W. Brock. London: Vision Press.

Hengel, Martin. (1974) *Judaism and Hellenism*, tr. John Bowden. London: SCM Press.

Hornung, Erik. (1982) *Conceptions of God in Ancient Egypt*, tr. John Baines. Ithaca NY: Cornell University Press.

Howland, Jacob. (2011) *Plato and the Talmud*. New York: Cambridge University Press.

Huffman, Carl A. (2012) 'Aristoxenus's Life of Socrates', In: Carl A. Huffman ed., *Aristoxenus of Tarentum: Texts and Discussions*. New Brunswick: Transaction Publishers, pp. 251–82.

Humphreys, Colin J. (1991) 'The Star of Bethlehem – a comet in 5 BC – and the date of the birth of Christ', *Quarterly Journal of the Royal Astronomical Society* 32, 389–407.

James, William. (1890) *The Principles of Psychology*. New York: Macmillan.

—(1919) *The Will to Believe*. New York: Longmans, Green.

Johnson, Aaron P. (2006) *Ethnicity and Argument in Eusebius' Praeparatio Evangelica*. New York: Oxford University Press.

Keys, David. (1999) *Catastrophe: An Investigation into the Origins of the Modern World*. London: Century.

Kingsley, Peter. (1995) *Ancient Philosophy, Mystery and Magic: Empedocles and the Pythagorean Tradition*. Oxford: Clarendon.

—(1999) *In the Dark Places of Wisdom*. Salisbury: Golden Sufi Center.

—(2003) *Reality*. Inverness, CA: Golden Sufi Centre.

— (2010) *Story Waiting to Pierce You: Mongolia, Tibet and the Destiny of the Western World*. Salisbury: Golden Sufi Centre.

Kneale, William C. and Kneale, Martha. (1962) *The Development of Logic*. Oxford: Clarendon Press.

Levenson, Carl. (1997) *Socrates among the Corybantes: Being, Reality and the Gods*. Woodstock, CT: Spring Publications.

Lewis, Clive S. (1947) *The Abolition of Man*. London: Bles.

Liebeschuetz, J. W. W. G. (1979) *Continuity and Change in Roman Religion*. Oxford: Clarendon Press.

Lloyd, Alan B. (1997) ed., *What is a God? Studies in the Nature of Greek Divinity*. London: Duckworth.

Lloyd, Geoffrey E. R. (1990) *Demystifying Mentalities*. Cambridge: Cambridge University Press.

Lopez-Ruiz, Carolina. (2010) *When the Gods Were Born: Greek Cosmogonies and the Near East*. Cambridge, MA: Harvard University Press.

Maccoby, Hyam. (2002) *The Philosophy of the Talmud*. London: Routledge.

Marchant, Jo. (2009) *Decoding the Heavens: Solving the Mystery of the World's First Computer*. London: Windmill Books.

—(2010) 'Ancient Astronomy: Mechanical Inspiration', *Nature* 468, 496–8. doi:10.1038/468496a.

Margulis, Lynn and Sagan, Dorion. (1997) *Microcosmos: four billion years of evolution from our microbial ancestors*. Berkeley, MA: University of California Press.

Mayor, Adrienne and Heaney, Michael. (1993) 'Griffins and Arimaspeans', *Folklore* 104, 40–66.

McCarthy, P. (1982) *Olaf Stapledon*. Boston, MA: Twayne.

McEvilley, Thomas. (2006) *The Shape of Ancient Thought*. New York: Allworth Press.

Miles, Richard. (2010) *Carthage Must Be Destroyed: The Rise and Fall of an Ancient Civilization*. London: Allen Lane.

Millar, Fergus. (1997) 'Porphyry: Ethnicity, Language and Alien Wisdom', In: Miriam Griffin and Jonathan Barnes, eds, *Philosophia Togata II: Plato and Aristotle at Rome*. Oxford: Clarendon Press, pp. 241–62.

Miskotte, Kornelis H. (1967) *When the Gods are Silent*, tr. J. W. Doberstein. London: Collins.

Moffat, James. (1916) 'Aristotle and Tertullian', *Journal of Theological Studies* 17, 170–1.

Momigliano, Arnaldo. (1975) *Alien Wisdom: The Limits of Hellenization*. Cambridge: Cambridge University Press.

Montaigne, Michel de. (2003) *Apology for Raymond Sebond*, tr. Roger Ariew and Marjorie Grene. Indianapolis, IN: Hackett.

Murray, Gilbert. (1934) *The Rise of Greek Epic*. London: Oxford University Press.

Navia, Luis E. (1996) *Classical Cynicism: A Critical Study*. Westwood, CT: Greenwood Press.

Nigosian, Solomon. (1993) *Zoroastrian Faith: Tradition and Modern Research*. Montreal: McGill-Queen's University Press.

O'Flaherty, Wendy. (1984) *Dreams, Illusions and Other Realities*. Chicago, IL: University of Chicago Press.

Osborne, Catherine. (1997) 'Heraclitus and the Rites of Established Religion', In: Lloyd ed., *What is a God? Studies in the nature of Greek divinity*. London: Duckworth: The Classical Press of Wales, pp. 35–42.

—(2005) 'Sin and moral responsibility in Empedocles's cosmic cycle', In: Apostolos L. Pierris ed., *The Empedoclean Κόσμος: Structure, Process and the Question of Cyclicity*. Patras: Institute for Philosophical Research Patras, pp. 283–308.

Ostwald, Martin (1969) *Nomos and the Beginnings of the Athenian Democracy*, Oxford: Oxford University Press.

Otto, Walter F. (1954) *The Homeric Gods*, tr. M. Hadas. London: Thames & Hudson.

Parke, Herbert W. (1985) 'The Massacre of the Branchidae', *Journal of Hellenic Studies* 105, 59–68.

Patterson, Orlando. (1982) *Slavery and Social Death*. Princeton, NJ: Harvard University Press.

Pickstock, Catherine. (1998) *After Writing: On the Liturgical Consummation of Philosophy*. Oxford: Blackwell.

Rosen, Frederick. (1968) 'Piety and Justice: Plato's Euthyphro', *Philosophy* 43, 105–16.

Rubenstein, Richard E. (2003) *Aristotle's Children: How Christians, Muslims and Jews Rediscovered Ancient Wisdom and Illuminated the Middle Ages*. Orlando, FL: Harcourt.

Russell, Jeffrey Burton. (1977) *The Devil: Perceptions of Evil from Antiquity to Primitive Christianity*. Ithaca, NY: Cornell University Press.

Scott, Alan. (1991) *Origen and the Life of the Stars*. Oxford: Clarendon Press.

Sedley, David N. (1998) *Lucretius and the Transformation of Greek Wisdom*. Cambridge: Cambridge University Press.

—(2007) *Creationism and its Critics in Antiquity*. Berkeley, CA: University of California Press.

Segal, Alan F. (1977) *Two Powers in Heaven: Early Rabbinic Reports about Christianity and Gnosticism*. Leiden: Brill.

Sharples, Robert W. (1996) *Stoics, Epicureans and Sceptics: An Introduction to Hellenistic Philosophy*. London: Routledge.

Sider, Robert D. (1980) 'Credo Quia Absurdum?', *Classical World* 73, 417–9.

Small, Robin. (1983) 'Nietzsche and a Platonist Tradition of the Cosmos: Center Everywhere and Circumference Nowhere', *Journal of the History of Ideas* 44, 89–104.

Smith, Nicholas D. (1991) 'Aristotle's Theory of Natural Slavery', In: D. Keyt and F. D. Miller, eds, *Companion to Aristotle's Politics*. Oxford: Blackwell, pp. 142–55.

Sorabji, Richard. (2010) *Philoponus and the Rejection of Aristotelian Science*. London: Institute of Classical Studies (2nd edition).

Spengler, Oswald. (1926) *The Decline of the West*, tr. C. F. Atkinson. New York: Knopf.

Spinoza, Benedict. (1982) *Ethics and Selected Letters*, tr. S. Shirley. Indianapolis, IN: Hackett.

Stafford, Emma. (2000) *Worshipping Virtues: Personification and the Divine in Ancient Greece*. London: Duckworth.

Stapledon, Olaf. (1937) *Star Maker*. London: Methuen.

—(1972) *Last and First Men* (1930); *Last Men in London* (1932). Harmondsworth: Penguin.

Stern, Philip D. (1991) *The Biblical Herem: A Window on Israel's Religious Experience*. Atlanta, GA: Scholars Press.

Strabo of Amaseia. (1929) *Geography*, tr. H. L. Jones, London: Heinemann.

Suano, Marlene. (2003) 'The First Trading Empires: Prehistory to c1000 BC': Abulafia (2003), pp. 67–98.

Suzuki, S. (1970) *Zen Mind, Beginner's Mind*. New York: Weatherhill.

Swinburne, Algernon Charles. (1924) *Collected Poetical Works*, London: Heinemann.

Teixidor, Javier. (1977) *The pagan god: Popular religion in the Greco-Roman Near East*. Princeton, NJ: Princeton University Press.

Ulansey, David (1989) *The origins of the Mithraic mysteries: cosmology and salvation in the ancient world*. New York: Oxford University Press.

Urbach, Ephraim E. (1979) *The Sages: Their Concepts and Beliefs*, tr. Israel Abrahams. Cambridge, MA: Harvard University Press.

Van De Mieroop, Marc. (2004) *A History of the Ancient Near East, ca. 3000–323 B.C.* Oxford: Blackwell.

Vassilopoulou, Panayiota. (2006) 'Plotinus and Individuals', *Ancient Philosophy* 26, 371–83.

Vermes, Geza. (2001) *Jesus the Jew: A Historian's Reading of the Gospels.* London: SCM (2nd edition).

Vernant, Jean Pierre. (1983) *Myth and Thought among the Greeks.* London: Routledge & Kegan Paul.

Wade, Nicholas. (2007) *Before the Dawn: Recovering the Lost History of Our Ancestors.* London: Penguin.

Walsh, John. (1984) 'The Dramatic Dates of Plato's Protagoras and the Lesson of Arete', *Classical Quarterly* 34, 101–6.

Walzer, Richard. (1949) *Galen on Jews and Christians.* London: Oxford University Press.

Weil, Simone. (1957) *Intimations of Christianity*, tr. E. C. Geissbuhler. London: Routledge & Kegan Paul.

West, Martin. (1971) *Early Greek Philosophy and the Orient.* Oxford: Clarendon Press.

—(1997) *The East Face of Helicon: West Asiatic Elements in Greek Poetry and Myth.* Oxford: Clarendon Press.

West, Stephanie. (2004) 'Herodotus on Aristeas', In: C. J. Bolton, ed., *Pontus and the Outside World: studies in Black Sea history, historiography, and archaeology.* Leiden: Brill, pp. 43–68.

Whitlock, Greg. (1994) 'Concealing the Misconduct of One's Own Father: Confucius and Plato on a Question of Filial Piety', *Journal of Chinese Philosophy* 21, 113–37.

Wiedemann, Thomas. (1988) *Greek and Roman Slavery.* London: Routledge (1st published 1981).

Wigner, Eugen. (1960) 'The Unreasonable Effectiveness of Mathematics in the Natural Sciences', *Communications on Pure and Applied Mathematics* 13(1), 1–14.

Wiley, Basil. (1934) *The Seventeenth Century Background.* London: Chatto & Windus.

Wootton, David. (2006) *Bad Medicine: Doctors Doing Harm Since Hippocrates.* Oxford: Oxford University Press.

Zhu, Rui. (2002) 'What if the Father Commits a Crime?', *Journal of the History of Ideas* 63, 1–17.

Zuckert, Caroline. (2009) *Plato's Philosophers: The Coherence of the Dialogues.* Chicago, IL: University of Chicago Press.

Zuntz, Günter. (1971) *Persephone: Three Essays on Religion and Thought in Magna Graecia.* Oxford: Clarendon Press.

INDEX